War and Peace in World Religions

War and Peace in World Religions

The Gerald Weisfeld Lectures 2003

Edited by
Perry Schmidt-Leukel

scm press

© Perry Schmidt-Leukel

British Library Cataloguing in Publication data

A catalogue record for this book is available from the British Library

0 334 02938 4

First published in 2004 by SCM Press
9–17 St Albans Place, London N1 0NX

www.scm-canterburypress.co.uk

SCM Press is a division of
SCM-Canterbury Press Ltd

Typeset by Regent Typesetting, London
Printed and bound in Great Britain by
Biddles Ltd, www.biddles.co.uk

Contents

Acknowledgements

With one exception, the chapters of this book are based on the 'Gerald Weisfeld Lectures' which were held at the University of Glasgow in Spring 2003. Hans Küng's lecture was originally delivered in Glasgow in autumn 2001 on the occasion of the Glasgow Global Ethic Conference, but revised for integration into this book. I am deeply grateful to all the lecturers and authors – good friends and great colleagues – for their contributions. Further, I would like to express my gratitude to Revd David MacKenzie Mills and to Dr Lloyd Ridgeon for looking through parts of the manuscript. Professor John Barclay and Professor John Riches have contributed in many ways to the organization of the lectures, and Anna Hardman and Barbara Laing from SCM Press enthusiastically supported the plans for publication. Hearty thanks to all of you!

In particular I am grateful to Gerald Weisfeld whose generosity and firm dedication to the issue of peace have not only led to the initiation of inter-religious peace studies at the University of Glasgow, but also to the realization of this project.

Perry Schmidt-Leukel

Notes on Contributors

Michael von Brück is Professor of Religious Studies in the Faculty of Protestant Theology of the University of Munich. After studying theology and religion at Rostock University, he taught at Gurukul Lutheran Theological College in Madras and at the Universities of Tübingen and Regensburg. His numerous publications in the field of religions and interfaith studies include *Emerging Consciousness for a New Humankind* (Goldmann, 1985), *The Unity of Reality: God, God-Experience and Meditation in the Hindu–Christian Dialogue* (Paulist Press, 1991) and *Christianity and Buddhism: A Multi-Cultural History of Their Dialogue* (Orbis, 2001, together with Whalen Lai).

Dan Cohn-Sherbok is Professor of Judaism and Director of the Centre for the Study of the World's Religions at the University of Wales, Lampeter. He is an ordained Reform Rabbi from the Hebrew Union, Jewish Institute of Religion, and holds doctorates in divinity and philosophy from Cambridge University. He taught Jewish Theology at the University of Kent and has been Visiting Professor at the Universities of Essex, Middlesex, St Andrews and Vilnius. He is the author and editor of over 60 books including *World Religions and Human Liberation* (ed., Orbis, 1992), *The Future of Judaism* (T&T Clark, 1994), *Holocaust Theology* (Lamp, 1991), *The Jewish Faith* (SPCK, 1993), *Modern Judaism* (Macmillan, 1996), and *A Vision of Judaism* (Paragon House, 2004).

Ian Hazlett, is Reader in Ecclesiastical History in the School of Divinity of the University of Glasgow, deputy editor of

Renaissance and Reformation Review and a member of the International Committee for the edition of the *Latin Works of Martin Bucer*. His research focuses on the history of Christian doctrine and Reformation Studies. Among his publications are: *Early Christianity: Origins and Evolution to AD 600* (ed., SPCK and Abingdon, 1991), *Martin Bucer. Defensio contra Axioma catholicum (1534)* (Brill, 2000), and *The Reformation in Britain and Ireland* (T&T Clark, 2003).

Norbert Klaes is Professor for the History of Religions at the University of Würzburg and since 1999 Co-President and member of the Executive Committee of the World Conference of Religions for Peace (WCRP). He studied philosophy and theology in Bonn and Innsbruck, and comparative religion and oriental studies in Louvain and Oxford. He taught theology, comparative religion and mission studies at the Universities of Bombay, Bochum, Paderborn and Würzburg. From 1982 to 1983 he was Associate Secretary General of WCRP and from 1983 to 1999 President of WCRP/Europe. Among his publications are *Stellvertretung und Mission* (Ludgerus Verlag, 1968), *Conscience and Consciousness: Ethical Problems of the Mahabharata* (Dharmaram College, 1975), and *Theologiegeschichte der Dritten Welt* (co-ed. with Th. Sundermeier, Kaiser Verlag, 1991–93).

Hans Küng is President of the Global Ethic Foundation, Tübingen, Germany. He studied philosophy and theology in Rome and Paris and was Professor of Ecumenical Theology at Tübingen University, Germany, from 1960 to 1996. He was invited professor at New York, Basel, Chicago, Ann Arbor, and Houston. Since 1995 he has been President of the Global Ethic Foundation. He has received numerous awards and honorary degrees. Among his numerous books are *Global Responsibility: In Search of a New World Ethic* (SCM, 1991) and *A Global Ethic for Global Politics and Economics* (SCM, 1997).

Gregor Paul is Professor of Philosophy at Karlsruhe University in Germany. He is the president of the German China Association and Academic Adviser of the Japanese Culture Centre in Düsseldorf, Germany. For about ten years he worked as lecturer, associate professor, and guest professor in Japan and China. His main interests are in philosophical aesthetics, philosophy of logic, philosophy of human rights, and so-called comparative philosophy, particularly with regard to Chinese and Japanese philosophy. His publications include *Aspects of Confucianism* (Lang, 1990), *Philosophie in Japan* (iudicium, 1993), *Epistemological Issues in Classical Chinese Philosophy* (co-ed. with H. Lenk, SUNY, 1993) and *Konfuzius* (Herder, 2001).

Lloyd Ridgeon was educated at the University of Durham before spending three years in Japan where he received a Masters degree in International Relations. He completed his PhD on medieval Persian Sufism at the University of Leeds in 1996; since then he has taught Islamic Studies at the University of Glasgow. His main interests include Sufism and modern interpretations of Islam and Persian culture. Among his publications are *Aziz Nasafi* (Curzon Press, 1998), *Crescents on the Cross* (Oxford University Press, 2001), *Islamic Interpretations of Christianity* (ed., Curzon Press, 2001), *Persian Metaphysics and Mysticism* (Curzon Press, 2002) and *Major World Religions* (ed., RoutledgeCurzon, 2003).

Perry Schmidt-Leukel, Professor of Systematic Theology and Religious Studies, holds the Chair of World Religions for Peace and is Director of the Centre for Inter-Faith Studies at the University of Glasgow. He studied theology, philosophy of religion, pedagogics and science of religion at Munich University. His main areas of research are Buddhist–Christian Dialogue and Theology of Religions. Among his publications are *'Den Löwen brüllen hören.' Zur Hermeneutik eines christlichen Verständnisses der buddhistischen Heilsbotschaft* (Schöningh, 1992), *Theologie der Religionen. Probleme, Optionen, Argumente* (Ars Una, 1997) and *Buddhist Perceptions of Jesus* (ed., EOS, 2001).

1. 'Part of the Problem, Part of the Solution':

An Introduction

PERRY SCHMIDT-LEUKEL

Humankind has never existed without wars and therefore never without the desire for peace. Probably history can be more easily written as an endless series of wars with some peaceful intervals than as a time of peace with a few interruptions of violent conflicts. To be sure, the development of human culture has always required peaceful periods, but on the other hand the building up of power, the striving for military strength and the development of ever new and better means of attack and defence have been a persistent motor of civilizational development. War and peace have accompanied human cultures permanently and everywhere.

Today the issue of war and peace has acquired a new dimension. The twentieth century had to endure the first wars with an almost global involvement, the so-called 'world wars' which could no longer be confined to a particular region. Moreover, the last century saw the development of a new generation of weapons, with a destructive potential that had never existed before: nuclear, chemical and biological weapons, being not only capable of devastating large areas within a couple of hours, but – if used in a comprehensive global confrontation – could terminate all human life on earth, if not all life indeed. Some authors have started to speculate about a new symbolic meaning of the moon – as a symbol for the future outlook of our planet earth, brought about by humankind.[1] It would still be a 'peaceful' symbol, symbolic of the final end to all wars, but for the price of the extinction of all life. The threat of this horrible vision as an inherent possibility of our advanced weapons' technology may indeed serve in itself as a means to prevent a global nuclear war. It may be a strong factor in stabilizing world peace, as we all have told ourselves again and again since World War Two and as we all want to believe. But it has not prevented numerous local conflicts and wars, each marked by a historically unparalleled quality of destruction, and many of them with a hard-to-calculate risk of escalation which one day might indeed transform the face of our planet into that of the moon. In the midst of this situation humankind is now becoming acquainted with a new form of war and a new threat emanating from it: relatively small groups, operating world wide and being hard to control, clearly involved in one or the other of the existent conflicts and tensions of our world, but nevertheless fighting their own private wars. And no one can presently tell what the wider consequences might be if these groups got access to weapons of mass destruction and would employ them precisely as that.

The fact that the problem of war and its immanent threats have acquired such a new dimension in the present age has an immediate impact on the desire for peace. Today, peace is not a luxury but has become an essential requirement for the survival of humankind. If human culture is to persist, the global motor of our civilizational development must be an effort to secure peace and prevent war. Of course the realities of politics are not as simple as that, and there is still the need for rational debates about whether the prevention of war will sometimes make preventive wars unavoidable. The question whether there are cases in which the limited use of force and violence is unavoidable in order to prevent far more extensive and dangerous manifestations of it, cannot be simply ruled out as illegitimate. But the horizon of these debates must now be marked unambiguously

---

[1] Cf. Horstmann, U., *Das Untier. Konturen einer Philosophie der Menschenflucht*, Wien, Berlin: Medusa Verlag, 1983.

by the awareness that there is absolutely no alternative to the global securing of peace and that all our joint efforts must be directed towards that aim.

Religion is as old as humankind. The first signs of human culture also testify to the fact that humans have been religious beings right from the start. And when the early human civilizations reached a complexity which allowed them to express their values and their taboos, their hopes and their fears, and their codes of right and wrong, in more explicit and reflective forms, the medium of that expression was religion. The issue of war and peace is therefore deeply embedded in the teachings and doctrines of the major religious traditions of the world. Building on their specific sources of religious insight – wisdom, enlightenment, revelation – they have provided basic explanations of the existential, cosmic, and at times even metacosmic roots of violence and war. And drawing on the same sources, each of them has proclaimed peace – *shanti, an, shalom, eirene, pax, salam* – as an ultimate value, not only as a hallmark of the final eschatological goal that humans could and were destined to reach, but also as an individual mental and a collective social state that is always worthy to pursue.

Throughout the centuries ideas on war and peace as we find them in the world religions have further developed and at times they have taken the shape of detailed, differentiated and sophisticated religio-political theories. But what is more important, when it comes to the more concrete and specific questions of war and peace, none of the major religions has something like an unambiguous, commonly shared view on that matter. None of them speaks with a single homogeneous voice, but they all have developed different, sometimes even contradictory, theories and attitudes. One of the objectives of this book – particularly in Parts I and II – is to provide the reader with reliable information on the more basic and characteristic views of the world religions on war and peace, but at the same time to give a glimpse at the variety of different opinions that can be found within any one of them.

Reviewing the various teachings on war and peace in the

world religions is an urgent necessity for the religions themselves. Like anyone else, members of the religious communities have to ask themselves about the particular contributions that they can make towards achieving and sustaining global peace in our times. This is not only a task for the continuous self-reflection as it is progressing within each of the world religions, but it is also a paramount issue of the dialogue between them which has begun in the last century and will surely develop into a major resource of theological/religious reflection in the twenty-first century.

Whenever religions nowadays, individually or jointly, assess their own views on war and peace, inquiring how these can still be helpful within the contemporary situation of humankind, they cannot avoid asking themselves painful questions about their own specific role in the history of human conflicts and wars, and of course within the actual tensions and outbreaks of violence. For religions have never been only the medium of social discourse on war and peace: they have rather actively participated in those processes which either led to war or to peace. This has by no means ceased to be the case. Religions have always made their active contributions to war *and* to peace. In this regard the world religions are quite ambivalent – all of them. There is none among the world religions which does not proclaim and foster peace. But equally so, there is none among them which has not also justified and fostered war.

While as a matter of historical fact the last statement will go unquestioned, there is at the same time a chorus of voices coming from the religions themselves and asserting that whenever and wherever their own religion was or is involved in wars or violent conflicts, the reason is always a form of political misuse of religion. Religion, in its true or pure form and at least their own one, is claimed to be good through and through, lofty above all human quarrels and low instincts, entirely and solely oriented towards peace. But what renders this view immediately doubtful is the simple question of why religions could be misused so well and so often for instigating violent conflicts and wars, if they were so good, so pure, so peaceful? If it were only peace that flows from the religious spirit, then it would be a crazy idea to misuse them for promoting hatred and tensions. Whoever wants to burn down a house will use petrol, not water. And this is no less true in the field of political incendiarism. I do not want to deny that there are and were cases of hijacking religions for malicious intentions of a non-religious nature, but there must exist a genuine religious potential for conflict, otherwise religions could not be misused. The question that needs to be addressed seriously by the religions is precisely the question of what it is that makes them so suitable and susceptible for such misuse. What are the genuinely religious roots of violence? If religions are not prepared to uncover and alleviate their own potential for conflict, this potential will remain effective, inhibiting and even counteracting the religious resources for peace.

When a religion consciously enters the field of social/political responsibility, absolute non-violence is not a realistic option. This does not entail that there cannot be important and some-times efficient forms of strictly non-violent political struggle. One only has to recall the names of Mahatma Gandhi, Martin Luther King, the fourteenth Dalai Lama, or Aung San Suu Kyi, to make this sufficiently evident. However, when it comes to the question of how to establish and guarantee social order and public security, no state can do without suitable means of enforc-ing the law, including police and various forms of sanctions or punishments. All these include the regular use of force and vio-lence. But if the use of violence is unavoidable in order to protect the citizens within a state against crime and chaos – and there-fore justified – is then the use of violence not equally justified when the criminal threat comes from outside the state or from its own leaders? The classical religious debates on the justifica-tion of violence have therefore usually been focused on the legiti-macy of defensive wars and tyrannicide. And these questions are far from being outdated. Could anyone condemn the states who tried to protect themselves against the attacks by Nazi Germany? Or could one condemn the decision of Christians like Dietrich Bonhoeffer to support the preparations for the assassination of Adolf Hitler? Whoever claims that religions should never and under no circumstances justify the use of violence will have to answer exactly such questions. A rigid condemnation of violence without exception may very well render religion irrelevant in the sphere of political life.

The justification of specific forms of violence is thus based on the idea of protecting or defending certain values, for example safety (individually and collectively), stability, justice and peace. Apart from a few exceptions, this view has usually been explicitly supported by the world religions whenever they addressed with a sense of political responsibility the questions of social and political life. But it is exactly this sense of responsibility, coupled with the insight that the defence of specific values may require and justify the limited use of violence, which opens the door for genuine religious forms of violence including so-called 'holy wars'. If it is, from a religious point of view, justified to use violence in order to protect worldly values like safety, stability, justice, etc., is it then not equally justified – if not even more so – to use violence for the defence of the eternal, ultimate, *religious* values? Aquinas justified the persecution and execution of heretics by the argument that this is unavoidable in order to protect the eternal life of all those faithful Christians who might become victims of the heresy and thereby end up in eternal damnation. It is the commandment to love our neighbour that forces us to destroy the heretics, says Aquinas, and he compares this with the necessity to protect the people against a deadly pestilence.[2] Or, to mention just one more example: it is the defence of the Dharma – the defence of the Buddha's teachings which guide people to final liberation – that in the eyes of some Theravāda-Buddhist monks requires and justifies violent means against Hindu Tamils on Sri Lanka.[3] A number of further examples could be added, many of which will be found in subsequent chapters of this book.

But what are the threats against which religions felt and sometimes still feel it necessary to defend – even violently – the values and insights embedded in their own traditions? Among the

---

[2] Cf. *Summa Theologica* II/II, qq. 10, 11.
[3] Cf. Bartholomeusz, T. J., *In Defense of Dharma. Just-war Ideology in Buddhist Sri Lanka*, London and New York: RoutledgeCurzon, 2002.

various possible answers to that question one obviously stands out: the threat is usually associated with the presence and activities of another religious group, either a different branch, sect, version of one's own religious tradition (the so-called 'heretics', 'heterodox', etc.) or the representatives of a different religion (the 'blind', 'infidels', 'idolators', etc.). Two things are particularly noteworthy in this regard: First, the threat being associated with different religious groups is not necessarily imaginary, but almost as a rule quite realistic, for usually a religious community believes that its own religion is in an objective sense superior to all others. This implies that ideally all the other religions should be replaced by one's own. For why should there be wrong or at least deficient religions, if the true and uniquely superior religion is available? If such ideas are only too well known within one's own religious community, one will be even more cautious against supposedly similar inclinations on the side of others, against which consequently one will have to defend oneself. So if – as an implication of their mutual superiority claims – religions harbour the tendency of mutual supersession, it is not surprising that their encounter is normally accompanied by a strong potential for conflict – a genuine religious potential, but just of the kind that can also and easily be misused for non-religious purposes.

Second, the motivation to use violence for the defence of one's religion or religious values can be subjectively entirely honest and integral. Such sentiments have nothing to do with any misuse of religions for evil and non-religious intentions. Religious people who justify religious violence can very well be motivated by selflessness, by the belief to be in accordance with whatever they regard as ultimate reality, and by the conviction of doing their fellow humans a painful but in the end wholesome service – like a physician carrying out an agonizing but healing operation, a metaphor employed so often that it almost seems to be an intercultural universal. It is precisely this conviction of doing a right and holy thing that makes religious violence so specific, so difficult, so dangerous: the total absence of any sense of guilt or moral indifference.

However, the case is by no means hopeless. There is, after all, the ideal of peace, harboured and cherished in all the world religions. Thus for the sake of peace they may at least accept the virtue of tolerating one another. But there is hope for much more.[4] The age of global inter-religious dialogue has already led significant numbers of faithful members of all the major religions to the discovery that they have much more in common than they once believed: existential values, guiding moral principles, spiritual insights. Moreover, there is a growing awareness that the differences between the religions cannot only be understood as irreconcilable antagonisms, but could also be regarded as a reservoir of diversity enabling and inspiring mutual learning and enrichment. The more that religions start not only to tolerate but to appreciate one another – intellectually, morally and spiritually – the less they will perceive each other as mutual threats, and the potential for religious violence will be healed at its roots. Through the example of two major inter-religious movements of our time – the global ethic project, closely associated with the 'Parliament of the World's Religions', and the 'World Conference of Religions for Peace' – Part III of this book demonstrates how this process materializes in our days.

Jonathan Sacks has made the remarkable statement: 'If religion is not part of the solution, it will certainly be part of the problem.'[5] The aim of this book is to show that religions have always been part of the problem, but that they have the resources to be and can indeed be part of the solution. Their most important contribution to the latter may be their overcoming of the tensions between them. Peace among the religions will surely be a significant and indispensible step towards peace on earth.[6]

---

[4] Cf. Schmidt-Leukel, P., 'Beyond Tolerance: Towards a New Step in Inter-religious Relationships', *Scottish Journal of Theology* 55, 2002, pp. 379–91.

[5] Sacks, J., *The Dignity of Difference: How to Avoid the Clash of Civilizations*, London and New York: Continuum, 2003, p. 9.

[6] Cf. Hans Küng's famous dictum: 'No peace among the nations without peace among the religions. No peace among the religions without dialogue.'

Part I

War and Peace in the Eastern Religions

2. War and Peace in Hinduism

MICHAEL VON BRÜCK

A mob of violent intruders storms an ancient mosque and destroys it within about five hours. Thousands of people get injured; later on violence sweeps the country and hundreds of people die. All for the glory of Lord Rama whose alleged birthplace needed to be liberated from Muslim desecration. Two of the most powerful Hindu organizations – the Vishva Hindu Pradishad (VHP) and the Rasthriya Svayamsevak Sangh (RSS), supported by the ruling political party, the Bharatiya Janata Party (BJP) – had called for a resurgence of Hindu ideals. 'Hindutva' ('Hindu-ness') was the political slogan which united millions of people to establish a new political Hindu identity to fight secularism which only had weakened the Hindu majority and had given the minorities of Muslims, Christians and others too much recognition and power. The events happened on 6 December 1992, when a politically orchestrated campaign led to the destruction of the Babri Masjid in Ayodhya which had been built in 1528. It is a property taken over by the modern Indian state and it has been under dispute since 1885. Countless courts have tried to solve the problem, but to no avail. Hinduism was and is on the warpath. According to tradition, the mosque had been erected on the site of the birthplace of Rāma, the righteous king of the glorious past and an incarnation (*avatāra*) of God Viṣṇu who came to bring peace on earth. The myth which connects the site of the mosque with Rāma's birthplace is an ideological construction made up for political reasons and the creation of a Hindu identity against the threat of Islam, as militant Hindus would see it. Is this an aberration from a predominantly peaceful religion,

or do we see here structures of behaviour which are deeply en-
graved in the Hindu way of life?

Harmony and Unity

What we call Hinduism is a plurality of different traditions. It
has evolved from at least three different cultures which need
to be recognized and analysed in order to understand the synthesis which is in the making even today. These three cultures
are, first, the Dravidian background which is the dominant culture in South India leaving important traces also in the North;
second, the Indus culture, so called because the first important
excavations were the cities of Mohenjo Daro and Harappa at the
River Indus, which however was spread all over Northern India
until about 1500 BCE; and third, the Indo-Germanic culture of
the migrating tribes who crossed the Hindukush and invaded the
North Indian Plains in the middle of the second millennium BCE.
They carried with them the oral tradition of the Vedas which later
became the holy scripture of India; they subsisted on the cow and
had elaborated the complex ritual of sacrifice and offering which
would become the centre of ancient Brahmanical religion until
the time of the Buddha in the middle of the first millennium BCE.
Different tribes, peoples, cultures and religions were involved in
this process of a highly complex cultural encounter. The most
important and stable cultural construct which developed as the
organizing matrix of this process was the caste system. This is a
kind of apartheid structure that saved the relatively small Indo-
Germanic tribes from becoming engulfed by the inhabitants who
had already established cultural systems. However, not only
the caste system but also the different hierarchies of gods, the
various myths and models of reality, the bewildering diversity of
philosophical systems and patterns of values are a result of these
cultural amalgamations.

What is so characteristic for the Indian cultural processes is a
constant assimilation and dissimilation of different ways of perceiving and constructing models of reality. What can be called
the mode of identification, that is, identifying one aspect of real-

ity with another, one god with another, one cultural value with another, the most stunning Hindu way of identifying everything with anything, has its root in this process. It seems to me that there are two outstanding forms of thought that are a typical result of this, and they are most relevant until today in terms of socio-psychological analysis.

The first one is a certain trend towards other-worldliness, a withdrawal from the world, because what humans can touch, see and hear such as trees, animals, other humans, inanimate matter, etc. is understood as only the external side of reality which represents (in various ways) a deeper and hidden aspect of the real reality. That is to say, what is graspable by the senses and the intellect is only the superficial construct of '*māyā*' ('supernatural power' or 'illusory appearance'), an external representation or expression, only derived reality, not reality as such (*satyasya satya*).

The second one has just the opposite tendency which I like to call the sacramental perception and understanding of reality. This is most prominently documented in the literature of the Tantras, and nearly all religious and philosophical systems are penetrated by Tantrism, including, of course, Buddhism. Accordingly, any piece of matter, any phenomenon and form of reality – an atom, a piece of dust, a tree, humans, the whole universe of hierarchies of gods and reality as such – are nothing other than a condensation of one spiritual energy. Everything, precisely that which we would consider to be unclean or dirty or less real or the dark side of reality, is an expression of the divine oneness. This divine nature of reality can be experienced, grasped and understood due to a transformation of our perception and insight. According to this basic attitude towards reality, it is not proper to devalue the world or aspects of it but to engage with it in all possible ways because everything is expression of the divine.

It is this tension between other-worldliness or asceticism and the perception of the whole of reality as divine, that marks the special flavour of Hinduism and a number of other Asian cultures. What Hinduism derives from it is its synthetic power to integrate and transform all cultural differences and place them into this cultural construct.

I want to refer to two different myths of creation which express a basic polarity that is relevant to our topic here because the tension expressed is somewhat reflected in these myths. Only together these myths represent what we can call a basic understanding of reality in Hinduism. They do appear as two different psycho-social structures which in their polarity shape the Indian cultural consciousness until today, and this holds true for the basic question of war and peace in Hinduism as well.

Two of the great gods of Hinduism who represent the ultimate standard of Indian experience of reality are Viṣṇu and Śiva. They are prototypes for a possible appearance of reality, both of them synthetic gods due to their cumulative histories. I do not need to go here into their respective histories but want to trace only some of their phenomenological traits which are relevant in our context.

Viṣṇu rests dormant down at the bottom of the ocean of the world, resting on the primordial snake Śeṣa. His rhythmical breath creates time and makes the navel move upwards and downwards. From the navel a marvellous and mysterious lotus flower grows slowly upwards, and, as in all Indian symbolism and iconography, this lotus is a representation of the power of transformation – unclean reality is transformed into the beauty of the spiritual attainment, because it is in the smelly and dirty waters that the lotus grows and extends itself above the water level in order to raise above and display a most beautiful and spotless flower of perfection. So Viṣṇu sleeps and dreams, and he manifests this lotus flower from his navel above sea level. Right in the midst of the flower sits a figure in lotus posture and this is Brahmā, the God of creation who contains everything in himself. In this miraculous manifestation the whole world of all potential and actual phenomena is contained and mirrored. That is to say, in the dream sleep of Viṣṇu the whole reality grows in the rhythm of breathing which is the unconscious aspect of reality, the preconscious movement as creative process, the systole and diastole, the exhalation and inhalation. From the pre-conscious dream of unity (Viṣṇu) emerges the all-conscious reality in differentiation (Brahmā). All contradiction of reality – creation and withdrawal, coming forth and going back – is contained in this 'coincidentia oppositorum' ('coincidence of opposites').

Śiva is a totally different character. His name means literally 'the benevolent one'. He does not dream at the bottom of the sea, but dances ecstatically on the summit of Mount Kailaśa. He is the supra-conscious counterpart to the pre-conscious God on the snake. Dance is the creative power, the unity of rhythm in a temporal sequence, the unity of the temporal movement in different special dimensions. This dance creates the order which is its matrix right in the moment of the process of dancing itself; it is not a pre-given idea, but creative presence. Time is not the frame in which the dance would occur but time is constituted by the dancing energy itself. However, Śiva bears also a second significant trait; that is to say, he is in constant sexual embrace with his spouse Parvatī, the great Goddess. From this conjunction the world is born. But at the same time he is the unmovable meditator who sits for ages deeply absorbed in contemplative union. His meditation generates creative energies. In Sanskrit this is expressed by the word *tapas* signifying heat and energy which can be experienced during meditative practice. This heat can be used to create, to destroy and to create again; in other words, the energetic process is a process of constant transformation of reality. Therefore Śiva represents three aspects of reality which are usually experienced in contradiction to each other: sexual union (his symbol is the erect phallus), meditative absorption and the ecstatic dance which creates time and differentiation and at the same time subdues the negative and evil forces of demonic ('asuric') nature.

It is in this polarity that according to Indian understanding reality is explicated. Śiva generates creative energy by his dance, and this creation process has two sides: emergence of forms and destruction of forms. Creation means both sides of the coin: there is no creation without destruction, for reality is called into being, transformed and destroyed in order to re-emerge in different forms. Life and death are not two opposites which would follow each other in temporal sequence but they are two aspects of the same process activated at the same time. This polarity of

birth and death is being represented in the myth of Śiva, for explication and implication are the two sides of the one rhythmical
dancing movement. The movement is the unity of creation and
destruction and Śiva himself as the graceful and benevolent one
keeps the process going. Better still, he is the process himself, as
the myth shows in a number of highly interesting variations. The
dark side – suffering, violence, the sublime, the terrible and so
on – is not excluded but is one moment in the process, made an
experience in the story of Śiva.

A similar intuition lies behind the Vedāntic parlance of the
ātman ('self'). In all Vedānta it is the *ātman* which is conceived to
be the final reality, which on the cosmic level is called *brahman*.
Those who attain to the *ātman* by analysis or meditative intuition experience the unity of reality. The *ātman* is also called the
inner steering force (*antaryāmin*). Expressed in theistic terms
this is to say that the one God is the inner steering force in all
cosmic and human procedures; he is the hidden subject in all
possible activities, the subject of knowing, hearing, smelling,
etc. It is not the graspable 'I' or I-consciousness that is the actor
but this unmoved mover, the 'thinker in thinking', the 'hearer in
hearing' as it is expressed in the Upaniṣads. He is all in all. The
eternal is not apart from the temporal, but right in the midst of
the seeming temporal contradictions. Therefore, the temporal is
nothing in itself. Not to know this is ignorance (*avidyā*). Being
is not a quality of individual forms, but being (*sat*) is the reality
of the One that expresses itself in ever-changing forms without
being touched or changed by this process. This is quite clearly
expressed in the *Bhagavadgītā* (13, 27 f.):

> Who sees the Highest Lord as existing in all beings,
> who does not perish when they perish, sees right.
> For who sees the same Lord, who dwells in everything,
> Hurts himself not by himself[1]
> And thus attains to the highest goal.

---

[1] *Na histaty ātmanā `tmānaṁ* ('he does not hurt the self by the self'),
i.e. the self of all beings is the same, so that each act of violence would be an
act of autoaggression. This is the strong argument for non-violence according

In their original nature all beings are explications of the One, and this is why one should recognize in them the *ātman*. What follows is that one should behave toward all beings as one would behave towards God. The Indian greeting *añjali mudrā* is a greeting of God who is present in all beings. Because this *ātman* is the real nature of all, there cannot be hatred. For the other one is the same in different form. Whoever encounters the difference in its real nature experiences always the One. The transcendent is totally present in the immanent, and the immanent cannot be without and apart from the transcendent. There is no abyss of the strange, and the otherness of the other (which might be dangerous and could require annihilation of the other in order to stay alive) fades away. The other is different only under certain aspects, but in reality it essentially has the same nature as everything else. Therefore all beings should be without fear – they encounter only themselves. When fear fades away there is no place for violence and annihilation of other beings.

Peace by Violence?

In Vedic times the cosmic order (*ṛta*) was secured by the brahmanical sacrifice. The social *dharma* ('law') however, which is derived from this cosmic order already in late-Vedic time, extends to all aspects of human life. The *dharma* structures society, establishes a system of values and provides everybody with a given place and status in society. Inasmuch as the *dharma* is practised and cherished, peace and harmony are guaranteed. Violation of the *dharma* means violence and war. *Dharma* is the source for harmony in terms of cultic as well as psychological, social and political balance. Hinduism is marked precisely by the fact that these realms and levels are distinguished but not separated.

The social and political aspect of *dharma* has produced a social order that was already established in principle in the first millennium BCE but was changed and newly regulated over the

---

to the Gītā but it does not exclude the idea of a just war, i.e. if war is necessary to keep up the 'dharma'.

succeeding centuries. However, we need to be aware that it is a brahmanical system which has had enormous influence on the upper and middle classes but less so on the lower classes and the outcastes. This order has expressed itself in two basic hierarchical value systems, i.e. the caste system (*varṇa* and *jāti*) and the system of life cycles (*āśrama*).

The caste system is, as shown above, the result of historical processes on the subcontinent; it has evolved over three millennia. Its basis seems to be the overlapping of different peoples which got mixed during the processes of invasions from the West, especially by the Indo-Germanic tribes. It has given India a stratified social order which has determined peace and war until today. Tribal cultures, Dravidian cultures and the urban civilizations extending all over the northern plains, known as the Indus culture, had existed already during the second millennium BCE before the Indo-Germanic newcomers from the West crossed the Khyber Pass and settled all over the plains. Demographically they were not strong enough to use their military advantage to assimilate the conquered populations, and this is why they invented a system of apartheid in order to avoid being assimilated by the conquered ones. This system is an exogamic caste system which was differentiated enough to evolve later into a system that also structured society according to labour and professional characteristics, much like the medieval system of guilds in Europe. The caste system made it possible that very different cultures could co-exist, though at the expense of lower castes and the excluded ones. This enormous cultural and economic gap within the system became aggravated during the British period due to the collaboration of the upper classes and castes with the British. Thus the matter of war and peace in Hinduism is not a political question alone which would require an analysis of foreign policies by the different Hindu states until independence and secularization; it is rather a topic which is intrinsically connected with the specific social structure of Indian societies, and this structure is ultimately defined by the Hindu *dharma*. Therefore we need to investigate some of the most prominent reflections of the *dharma* in normative Hindu scriptures, notably the *Epics*, the *Dharmaśāstras* and *Arthaśāstras* and especially the influential *Bhagavadgītā*. This is a selective approach which does not cover the whole range of Hindu value systems at all, but it is hoped that the selection is convincing, based on the influence that these scriptures have had on centuries of formation of Hindu societies.

Narratives

The *Mahābhārata* reports extensive wars. Most of these wars are conflicts of succession of established dynasties. Later on these wars are interpreted religiously, not only in terms of the philosophical teaching of *svadharma* (i.e. one's own duty or nature in the social and cosmic order) as it is the case in the *Bhagavadgītā*, but also in terms of mythological patterns such as fights between good and evil, the realm of *devas* ('gods') against the *asuras* ('titans' or 'demons') etc. But quite surprisingly the horror and terror of war is a topic in the *Mahābhārata* which is clearly addressed and the killing and bloodshed is not taken for granted. Thus messengers are exchanged between the enemies in an attempt to avoid the need for war. Yet the author comments, with some resignation, that humans are slaves of their lust and greed and this might never change.[2] An interesting story depicts the creator Brahmā as he realizes that there might be an unwholesome overpopulation on earth. So he sends a female being in order to destroy as many beings as possible. With tears in her eyes she refuses to perform her duty and asks that humans at least might mutually destroy themselves by their own vices.[3]

Indra is the Lord and Master of the universe. His weapons are the cosmic powers, notably thunder, and his chariot is the world. People at war call on him for help in their military undertakings so that they can conquer enemies, obtain victory and get as many material goods as possible.[4] However, it needs to be noted that Indra is not only in charge of war but also presides

---

[2] MB 6, 4, 41.   [3] MB 12, 248–50.   [4] RV 1, 7, 4.

over peace after he has helped to destroy the evil forces.[5] He is called upon in fervent prayers to support his friends and nobody else.[6] This henotheistic and exclusivistic trend in the *Ṛgveda* is already overcome by a different mentality which asks universal and metaphysically inclusive questions so that the unity of the cosmos and the unity of history is an idea on the horizon at a very early stage in history.[7] It is not only the very abstract and impersonal One (*ekam*) but also this powerful warrior god Indra who contains all the worlds and events of this world in himself like seeds or growing potentials. The explication into the variety of forms and contradicting experiences, such as violent and non-violent events, is his self-manifestation.[8]

Dharmaśāstras and Arthaśāstras

As already mentioned in the beginning of this chapter, Hinduism is not a clearly defined religion but a whole cluster of ways of life in India which encompasses all peoples there, apart from those who explicitely do not want to be part of the Hindu fold (such as Buddhists, Jains, Muslims, Sikhs and Christians and a bunch of outspoken atheists). To classify Hinduism as 'religion' is not unproblematic because the term *dharma* means something else. Dharma is the cosmic law with which society as a whole, as well as each individual, has to live its life in accordance. The *dharma* is known through divine revelation of the Vedic scriptures (*śruti*) which has been interpreted through the brahmanical literature in the Śāstras. The interpretation, however, is not confined to written sources but is also codified in oral tradition, i.e. in rules and patterns of behaviour by those who claim to live in accordance with tradition. In terms of this source of values and laws there is an enormous flexibility and potential for adaptation within the Hindu culture.

---

[5] RV 3, 46, 2; 8, 1, 2; 1, 7, 5.   [6] RV 1, 7, 10.
[7] This, of course, refers to RV 10, 129, but it is also present in RV 3, 51, 4 where Indra is praised for being the only ruler of the world and thus in RV 6, 36, 4 is worshipped as the single king of the whole universe (*viśva bhuvana*).   [8] AV 10, 7, 30.

In this context it is important to mention the most significant classifications because they determine what society, or different groups or subcultures, call peace and war. The caste system, historically conditioned and endowed with religious legitimacy, provides the 'warrior caste' (*kṣatriya*) with the duty to uphold the *dharma* also by the means of *daṇḍa*, i.e. the 'stick' or sanctioned violence. This includes war. Violence and war may be used either as punishment or as a threat to ensure that the violator will not disturb the *dharma* again. According to the 'Laws of Manu' (*Manusmṛti*) and especially to Kauṭilya's *Arthaśāstra*, war is unavoidable.

According to the classification of the stratified Hindu society, the *dharma* does not remain on an abstract level but needs to be implemented in different ways according to the *svadharma* ('duty' or 'nature') of the respective caste, i.e. the individual duty is determined by belonging to a specific caste. There is not much of individual choice. It is only when the different castes perform according to the predestined duties and each fulfils their *svadharma* that peace and order in the universe (*śānti*) are guaranteed. Thus the Brahmin has the duty to observe non-violence (*ahiṃsā*), an idea that originates in Jainism and was not yet binding for the Brahmins in Vedic and post-Vedic times. The *kṣatriya*, i.e. the king, all nobles and the upper classes, execute the punishing force (*daṇḍa*) according to the law in order to maintain harmony. It is said that a king who does not *daṇḍa* according to his *svadharma* brings evil upon the country like a Brahmin who would neglect the study of the Vedas.[9] According to the caste system not everybody has the same status and dignity in legal terms though, in abstract terms, the 'Laws of Manu' agree that all humans are metaphysically equal but not so in social terms. An example is Kauṭiliya's rule concerning adultery. If higher males molest a women of lower status they have to pay a financial compensation according to the status of the respective woman. If, however, males of a lower caste get too close

---

[9] Quoted by Walker 1983, p. 267.

to a high-caste woman, they will get most severe punishment, possibly the death penalty.[10] The modern secular Indian constitution has done away with those discriminations but they are still values in the society and shape moral consciousness. This is a cause for conflicts which instigate aggression and violence, as can be observed in the daily clashes based on caste conflicts throughout the country. In any case the 'Laws of Manu' and Kauṭilya's *Arthaśāstra* (which was rediscovered only in 1908) are certainly the most influential sources which described, systematized and at the same time shaped the cosmo-social norms of Hinduism at their time (about first or second century CE, but in their basic assumptions much older); and their influence reaches down to the present generations in India. All social rules are interpreted in the context of cosmic order, and the cultic and ethical aspect of life cannot be separated at all. The social order (of castes) is an aspect of the Indian theogony, or the self-explication of the one Brahman, and so implies an absolute authority.

Manu teaches a distinction of two powers: teaching and education which is the business of the Brahmins; and military force to protect the people from internal and external enemies, which is the business of the Kṣatriyas. It is to be noted that teaching and education is a specific power regarded as being on the same level of importance and functional validity as military power. Why? Because both, education and *daṇḍa* (controlled violent force), link and re-link a society and her individual members with the *dharma*. War is necessary to protect and enact the *dharma* against evil forces, education is necessary to link up with the contents of the *dharma* and apply it to present questions. But the main focus of using force is to strengthen and defend the caste order.[11] The key term used here is *daṇḍa*. As J. J. Meyer has shown convincingly, this term implies not only the punishing power of the king in a juridical sense, but also the use of power and force in general.[12] The *Mahābhārata* states that *daṇḍa* makes possible the

---

[10] Kauṭilya, *Arthaśāstra* 2, 36, 56.
[11] Manu 7, 24 and 35.
[12] Cf. Meyer 1926, p. LVIII.

preservation of creation, otherwise 'the strong ones would eat up the weaker ones like fish in the water'.[13] Without *daṇḍa* the girls would not live in virginity, the boys would not learn the Vedas, nobody would milk the cows and acknowledge the property rights of others, there would be uncontrolled fighting and killing, and even the animals could not be brought under the yoke in order to carry the cart.[14] The authors of the *Mahābhārata* are quite realistic; their arguments take into account the selfishness and craving of human nature for lust and wealth, the 'tamasic' aspect of laziness as well, and that it requires force to create and maintain a workable social order.

However, there is a distinction of different forms of *daṇḍa*, and this again depends on the specific stratifications of caste:

> The daṇḍa of the Brahmin (priest) is executed through the power of the word, the danda of the Kṣatriya (warrior, ruler) through the physical strength of his arm, the danda of the Vaiṣya (artisans, merchants, farmers) through the giving of material goods. The Śudra (serving class) does not have any daṇḍa.[15]

Concerning the mentioning of the Vaiṣya, whose *daṇḍa* is regarded as the giving (*dāna*) of material goods, we have to be aware that what is meant here could be called 'bribing'. This, according to the *Mahābhārata*, is also a form of force to keep society going; and if it is used in accordance with the cosmic laws (again, this is basically the reflection of these laws in the eternal caste system), bribery is a legitimate means to maintain harmony in a given society. Thus the execution of power by humans is restricted by the cosmic laws and insofar it is always bound to be used to maintain harmony. However, the masses of low caste people and much more so the no caste people are excluded from the responsible use of *daṇḍa*; this implies that they do not have any legitimate means to fight for their rights, for they just do

---

[13] MB 12, 67, 12.
[14] MB 12, 14ff.
[15] MB 12, 25, 9.

not have specific rights. This is certainly one of the reasons why violence within Hindu history has on occasion swept uncontrollably, as it continues to do in present communal clashes.

In any case, for Manu who sings the praise of *daṇḍa*, this *daṇḍa* is certainly a divine gift.[16] He legitimizes a war of aggression but calls for appropriate means. A war which is directed at gaining territory and material goods is like a purification, and this is necessary especially in times of the *Kali yuga*, the evil age, when lawlessness prevails everywhere.

I will now discuss some arguments as they are presented in Kauṭilya's *Arthaśāstra*. Here the theory of politics is rooted in the harmonious interplay of the four castes which are supposed to function like an orchestra in a concerto, with the difference that the lower castes have hardly any rights and the outcastes may be regarded as existing on a subhuman level. The legitimacy of power of the higher castes is grounded in the myth as related and quoted by Manu. However, this does not legitimate individual misuse of power, as for example by a mad ruler. This is documented by the law that a king, however powerful he may be, cannot confiscate land once it has been leased. Brahmins, however, enjoy special privileges. Two interesting areas of their special or even exempted status is the lower taxation and milder form of punishment in case of offences.

The sixth book of the *Arthaśāstra* discusses foreign policy and especially the theory of the circle of states. Here Kauṭilya refers to the idea of the *cakravartin*, i.e. the ruler of the world, which the Maurya dynasty already understood to be the founding ideology of their kingship. The most famous king of that dynasty was Aśoka (*c.*250 BCE) who is said to have converted to Buddhism and is celebrated as one of the first emperors of peace in world history after he had conquered a huge territory in extremely bloody military actions. After uniting his kingdom, however, he was disgusted by the bloodshed of his conquest and tried to rule not by violence and harsh punishments but by educating his subjects in the *dharma*. He sent messengers all over the

---

[16] Manu 7, 14–25.

country to erect pillars with his inscriptions of the common law and to teach the people righteousness. But Aśoka was a Buddhist and certainly an exception to the rule of Hindu kingship. What is obvious from his story is that his conquering of a territory was seen to be completely legitimate. Conquering other peoples was to gain wealth, to stabilize the kingdom and so on, but it had always the more or less open connotation of civilizing other people as well in the name of the real and universal *dharma*, in other words it had a missionary impulse. In Kauṭilya, however, this concept is used and 'secularized' in order to formulate a strategy of pure power politics. Here the ancient *cakravartin* has changed into the *vijigīṣu* who is a power politician with all ambitions to increase his kingdom by any means. He is seen as being surrounded by several concentric circles of states. The states bordering his kingdom form the first circle around him, and they are his natural enemies. The next ring of states surrounds them and, conversely, they are supposed to be potential friends of the *vijigīṣu* in the centre, and so on. Power politics plays on this scheme, and a good king should know and exercise all possible means to make gains. Everything which may lead to success is not only allowed but commanded by the law, including lies, bribery, espionage, etc. A treaty of peace might be useful in case the two opposing powers are equally strong, but it is not an end in itself. As soon as the king can get an advantage to break the peace treaty he may do so.[17] Against other authorities, Kauṭilya argues that the fortune of a king would not so much depend on his own intelligence and vigour (*vīrya*) but on his financial strength which would allow him to buy allies and perhaps employ people who could provide better advice. On the other hand, on that basis, it would also be useful to use reason and treason in order to gain the maximum result with a minimum of financial expenses.[18] Kauṭilya advises the king to use treason, bribery, mimicry of the military forces, special forms of battle arrangement such as circular battle orders, etc.[19]

---

[17] *Arthaśāstra* 6, 1   [18] *Arthaśāstra* 9, 1.   [19] *Arthaśāstra* 10, 3.

The Bhagavadgītā

Hardly any other text has shaped the values of educated Hindus of different *sampradāyas* (cultic forms and religious persuasions) as much as the *Gītā*, so that one can regard this poem of 700 verses (*ślokas*), which is part of the *Mahābhārata*, as a universal Hindu scripture. It has influenced even the illiterate Hindus and outcastes to quite some extent. It roughly originates from the same time as the *Dharmaśāstras*. Its narrative frame is a battle which is fought in the context of succession of royal power which happened historically at an early time after the Aryan invasions into the Northern Indian plains. This battle is the context for a *dharma* teaching that is given by Krishna to Prince Arjuna. Krishna appears as the charioteer of the prince and during the discourse reveals himself as the highest god beyond comprehension to normal mortals (chapter 11). The *dharma* teaching is first of all an exhortation to fight a just war, in which Arjuna hesitates to engage. But it is much more than that: it is a complex teaching on ethics and on its foundation in a comprehensive religious world-view which is explained in a highly differentiated manner. The problem is that, for Prince Arjuna, a conflict of duties has emerged, and the resolve of this conflict, by a number of arguments, does not only give an excellent insight into the problem of war and peace in Hindu thought but is also a most influential statement of the Hindu view of life in general.

Arjuna is a prince; that is to say, he belongs to the warrior caste of the Kṣatriyas. He is preparing for the final battle against his enemies, and there is no doubt that they are the ones who transgressed the *dharma*. But Arjuna hestitates; he does not want to fight the war but Krishna persuades him to do precisely that without any bad conscience.[20] Arjuna does not refuse to fight because he entertains any abstract idea of non-violence (*ahiṃsā*) or a pacifistic anti-war complex (those thoughts emerge in Hinduism not before the nineteenth century under the influence of the European Enlightenment, the British–American Transcen-

[20] BG 2.

dentalists and Tolstoy), but he sees among the hostile army all his relatives, uncles etc. His dutiful connectivity with the family and the clan, his *kula* ('family') *dharma*, obliges him to protect his relatives; but at the same time, as a warrior prince, he is obliged to fight for the universal *dharma*, i.e. to fight the battle against the unlawfulness. Thus we have a classical conflict of duties. Arjuna's *svadharma*, as a member of the Kṣatriyas, contradicts his *kuladharma*. Krishna convinces him successfully that his duty to uphold the universal *dharma* in society is a higher value than his duties towards his relatives because it is a just war which serves the reinstallation of the true and right dharmic order in society. Arjuna's war, therefore, is not a war of aggression (as in the case of Kauṭilya's *Arthaśāstra*), but a form of *daṇḍa* in a universal dharmic sense. Hence, the battlefield of historic *Kurukṣetra* (north of Delhi) is, in reality, the battlefield of trans-historic *dharmakṣetra* ('*dharma*-place') which includes the historic dimension and realization.

Krishna actually presents three arguments to Arjuna to encourage him to fight the battle.

1. The difference of spirit and body. Krishna declares that during the war only the physical body is killed which would be perishable anyway, whereas the eternal (*nitya*), unborn (*aja*) and therefore imperishable (*anāśina*) Self (*ātman*) could not be killed.[21]

2. Selfless action. Action as fulfilling duty and responsibility, with respect to the *dharma*, should not aim at any goals. There should be no intention to reap the fruits of action (*phala*) which would be to obtain wealth or power.[22] The war should be fought, not considering the question who would win it, but only on the basis of the *dharma*. As a Kṣatriya Arjuna is to defend the *dharma*, so he needs to fight.[23]

3. Participation in divine action. Salvation is not to be obtained either by asceticism or by the attempt not to act at all but by dedication of one's will and action to God who is the

---

[21] BG 2, 18. [22] BG 2, 47 *et al.* [23] BG 2, 38.

ultimate source and cause of all acting. The highest Creator God himself is present in any action for he creates, sustains and destroys the world permanently.[24] Therefore it is not Arjuna who is ultimately acting in killing, but the divine power itself.[25] This power is beyond time; therefore, due to the transtemporal nature of God, all those who are to be killed right now in battle have already been killed.[26] Again this killing is not to be misunderstood: it is part of the loving and saving action of God.

This discourse of the *Gītā* is significant for the whole of Hinduism for two reasons: first because of the combination of *dharma*, *svadharma* and *karman*; and second because of the spiritual qualification of all action, including political action. Both aspects shall be explained further.

For the issue of war and peace the concept of *karma* (*karman*) is of crucial importance. It signifies the interdependence of reality and the reciprocal causality between cause and result. This causality works not only in the physical but also in the mental and moral sphere. An old Hindu saying, quoted in the Upaniṣads, says that what one thinks, one becomes. This is to say that any action has consequences for the actor; it shapes the karmic field and forms the actor's character. And this again has consequences for the actor's further intentions and future actions. The karmic field is not interrupted or finished once a person dies but, quite to the contrary, it shapes the conditions for the person's future existence in a different physical form. Only when all karmic formations have been worked out and the potential karmic energies have been spent can an individual experience peace, that is the cessation of the results of karmic conditioning. Thus salvation or liberation (*mokṣa*) is a process that is neither a purely spiritual event, nor is it exhausted in external, that is historical material action, but it is a reality comprising both, because it is rooted in the cessation of new formations in the field of intentions and motivations which would lead to further action. Peace of

---

[24] BG 3, 15.   [25] BG 3, 24 ff.   [26] BG 11, 26 f. and 34.

mind (*śānti*), which is the central goal of Hindu life, is the end of *karman*. How this can happen is interpreted quite differently under the influence of different philosophical systems (*darśana*) in Hinduism; but that it can happen and will happen is one of the central tenets of Hinduism.

Thus any action in war or other circumstances in which a living being is killed has a result not only to the object of this action (the loss of life) but it has also immediate consequences for the acting subject. Hindu thinkers are usually much more interested in this second aspect when dealing with the consequences of violence and killing in war. Aggression is the result of an I-consciousness (*ahaṃkāra*) which is the product of an illusion anyway. The illusion consists of a wrong assumption that the actor in an action is the individual ego on the basis of its will power whereas, in reality, the acting subject is somebody else: God who works in the individual as the person's inner life-force (*prāṇa*).

All reality, including war and peace in the history of humankind, is the result of the divine energies or the divine play (*līlā*). The game follows certain rules and they are defined by the *dharma* which humankind has to acknowledge. *Dharma* is not only the law which rules the contradicting reality of the cycle of rebirth (*saṃsāra*), but *dharma* is the guideline for the kind of behaviour and action that does not cause any more karmic consequences which would bind humans again in the cycle of rebirth. Here we have to point to the four ends of human life (*puruśārtha*) according to Hinduism. They are wealth (*artha*), sensual pleasure (*kāmā*), virtue or harmonious action (*dharma*) and liberation (*mokṣa*) from the cycle of rebirths. The first three are concerned with worldly existence and they interpenetrate each other in such a way that they are to be pursued in harmony with each other. That is to say that to acquire wealth and enjoy sensual pleasure is all very well but it needs to be in accord with *dharma*, otherwise negative karma would be created. And all three are the prerequisite for the final end of karmic conditioning, that is the cycle of rebirth, in order to attain liberation (*mokṣa*). Any worldly action needs to be seen in this perspective and thus is to be qualified through such a spiritual end.

So far we have not yet mentioned Mahātma Gandhi,[27] the father of the modern Indian nation, whose name comes to mind first when war and peace in Hinduism are being discussed. His method of 'holding on to the truth' (*satyāgraha*) on the background of unconditional non-violence (*ahiṃsā*) has become standard, not only in Hindu social ethics. However, one also has to note that his concept of non-violence comes from Jainism and is not what the *Bhagavadgītā* teaches historically. He reads this concept into the *Gītā* and into much of Hindu thought. This might be one of the reasons why Gandhi's thinking and morality in present-day India are not much followed by the majority of Hindus, though he certainly has become an icon. Gandhi's non-violence is not compatible with the classical concept of *svadharma* as it is taught in the *Dharmaśāstras* and the *Gītā*; that is why both Gandhi and the one who assassinated him justified their action with reference to the teaching of the *Gītā*. This again refers to an ambiguity which is at the heart of Hinduism and probably other religions as well: an ideal of harmony and peace is preached and ritually enacted but the attempt to realize it in the historical-political sphere creates violence and disharmony.

Conclusion

Taking into account the social reality, Hinduism offers an ambiguous picture which is not only the result of the common difference between ideal and reality. There is no need to argue that the repressive caste system, and especially the justification of the repression of the outcastes (pariahs or *harijans*, children of God, as Gandhi euphemistically called them; *dalits*, the oppressed ones, as they call themselves today) is the reason for a continuous civil war within Hindu society. This problem is one of the main reasons for violence in present-day India. Tensions and violence between Muslims and Hindus are caused culturally and historically but in most cases they are the cultural expression of an eco-

---

[27] Gandhi's religious thought has been convincingly investigated by Chatterjee 1985.

nomic and political frustration, an outlet for the group solidarity which is defined by the caste. Mass conversions of Hindus towards Islam in the 1970s are an example of how social deprivation was used religiously and this led to open violence and war between different groups of Indian society.[28] On the basis of our analysis of the *Dharmaśāstras*, it is obvious that the Hindu myth as such has to do with the justification of this social and political violence which seems to be regarded as an unavoidable condition of the *saṃsāra*, the cycle of rebirth.

As an example of a classic Hindu response to the problem of peace and war I would like to recall the following experience. During the 1980s I lived in Madras and one of my obligations was to organize academic seminars on the basis of inter-religious dialogue. Thus, in 1983, I organized a seminar on 'War, Peace and Disarmament' at the Gurukul Lutheran Theological College, Madras. I also invited a Hindu speaker to represent the Hindu perspective. He was one of my Yoga teachers, a respected guru living in the outskirts of Madras, Pundit Kanniah Yogi from Ambattur. After he had entered the room to deliver his presentation on peace in Hinduism he climbed on the table, squatted in the lotus-posture (*padmāsana*) there, fell into a *samādhi* state of consciousness and remained for about 20 minutes in this position. Afterwards he bowed to the audience who remained in peaceful silence and left. He had demonstrated what it means to experience silent peace of mind in Hinduism in the midst of all turmoil on the social level of *māyā*.

SELECT BIBLIOGRAPHY

Akbar, M. J., 1991, *Riot After Riot: Reports on Caste and Communal Violence in India*, New Delhi: Penguin Books.
Berg, R. E., 1987, The Bhagavad-Gītā on War: The Argument from Literature, in: Arvind Sharma (ed.), *New Essays in the Bhagavadgītā. Philosophical, Methodological and Cultural Approaches*, New Delhi: Books & Books, pp. 25–35.

---

[28] See the excellent analysis by Khan 1983.

Bhatt, S. C., 1998, *The Great Divide: Muslim Separatism and Partition*, New Delhi: Gyan Publishing House.

Chatterjee, M., 1985, *Gandhi's Religious Thought*, London: Macmillan.

Engineer, A. A., 1989, *Communalism and Communal Violence in India: An Analytical Approach to Hindu–Muslim Conflict*, Delhi: Ajanta Publishing.

Houben, J. E. M. and K. R. van Kooij (eds.), 1999, *Violence Denied: Violence, Non-Violence and the Rationalization of Violence in South Asian Cultural History*, Leiden–Boston–Köln: Brill.

Kakar, S., 1996, *The Colors of Violence: Cultural Identities, Religion and Conflict*, Chicago: University of Chicago Press.

Kane, P. V., 1968, *History of Dharmaśāstra*, vols. I–IV, Poona: Bhandarkar Oriental Research Institute.

Khan, M. A., 1983, *Mass Conversions of Meenakshipuram, A Sociological Enquiry*, Madras: Christian Literature Society.

Krishna, D., 1996, *The Problematic and Conceptual Structure of Classical Indian Thought about Man, Society and Polity*, Delhi: OUP.

Lipner, J., 1994, *Hindus – Their Religious Beliefs and Practices*, London: Routledge.

MacGuire, J., 1996, *Politics of Violence: From Ayodhya to Behrampada*, New Delhi: Sage Publishing.

Malkani, K. R., 1993, *The Politics of Ayodhya and Hindu Muslim Relations*, New Delhi: Har-Anand Publishing.

Meyer, J. J., 1926, *Kautilya. Das altindische Buch vom Welt- und Staatsleben: das Arthacastra des Kautilya*, Leipzig: Harrassowitz.

Michaels, A., 1998, *Der Hinduismus*, München: Beck.

Varshney, A., 2002, *Ethnic Conflict and Civic Life. Hindus and Muslims in India*, New Haven: Yale University Press.

Walker, B., 1983, *Hindu World: An Encyclopedic Survey of Hinduism*, Vol. I, New Delhi: Manoharlal.

Wijesekera, O. H. De A., 1994, Kṣatra-Dharma and Rājā-Dharma, in: O. H. De A. Wijesekera, *Buddhist and Vedic Studies: A Miscellany*, Delhi: Motilal Banarsidas, pp. 339–53.

3. War and Peace in Buddhism

PERRY SCHMIDT-LEUKEL

In the Western world Buddhism presently enjoys the fame of being an extraordinarily and unusually peaceful religion. Particularly among Western followers of Buddhism you can find opinions like the following one by Walter Karwath, former president of the Austrian Buddhists, claiming that Buddhism is 'the absolutely and principally peaceful religion'[1] which historically has 'distinguished itself among all religions as essentially the most peaceful one'.[2]

A number of contemporary examples seem to confirm such a view. Thus among the Nobel Peace Prize laureates of the recent years we find two prominent Buddhists: the 14th Dalai Lama, who was awarded the prize in 1989 because of his consistent non-violent struggle for the liberation of his people from Chinese occupation; and Aung San Suu Kyi of Burma who received the prize in 1991 'for her non-violent struggle for democracy and human rights'.[3] Among the nominees for the Nobel Peace Prize we find another three Buddhists: Thich Nhat Hanh, a monk from Vietnam, Mahā-Ghosānanda, a Theravāda-monk from Cambodia, and A. T. Ariyaratne, a Buddhist layperson from Sri Lanka. While Thich Nhat Hanh and Mahā-Ghosānanda are famous for their work for reconciliation after the Vietnam War and the Khmer Rouge regime in Cambodia respectively, Ariyaratne is

---

[1] '. . . die absolut und grundätzlich friedliche Religion des Buddhismus . . .' Karwath 1984, p. 200.

[2] 'Von allen Religionen hat sich der Buddhismus als die essentiell friedlichste profiliert . . .' Karwath 1984, p. 202.

[3] From the statement of the Nobel Committee, reprinted in: Aung San Suu Kyi 1991, p. 236.

the founder of Sarvōdaya Śramadāna, a large non-governmental organization, which has not only contributed enormously to rural development in Sri Lanka, but also to the peaceful settlement of the conflict between Tamils and Sinhalese.[4]

Additional startling evidence of the strong peace potential of Buddhism which is worth mentioning is the crucial role that Japanese Nichiren Buddhists, in particular Nikkyō Niwano, have played in the formation of the largest and probably most important of all inter-religious peace initiatives, the World Conference of Religions for Peace, which officially came into existence in 1969.[5]

However, the twentieth century also provides a number of examples of a close connection between Buddhism and violence, thereby exhibiting a side of Buddhism which is usually much less present in contemporary public awareness in the West. In 1997 the Sōtō-Zen priest Brian Victoria published his important book *Zen at War*[6] which came as a shock to many Western Zen followers. Here Victoria carefully documents a broad and deep involvement of Buddhists in Japanese nationalism and imperialism during the Russo-Japanese War and World War Two. Among other things, Victoria shows that highly renowned Zen masters like, for example, Daisetz Suzuki, who played a major part in the mediation of Zen to the West, or Suzuki's master, Shaku Sōen, who represented Buddhism on the famous World Parliament of Religions in Chicago 1893, had provided religious justification for Japanese military enterprises.[7] Even the suicide attacks carried out during the final days of World War Two by the so-called *kamikaze* pilots had been praised by the Zen scholar and priest, Reihō Masunaga, as the perfection of selflessness and as such 'the achievement of complete enlightenment'.[8]

---

[4] Cf. Harvey 2000, pp. 112f., 270f., 275–84.
[5] Cf. the last chapter of this book and Jack 1993.
[6] Cf. Victoria 1997. Concerning the relationship between the 'Kyōto school' – a school or line of twentieth century Buddhist philosophy in Japan – and Japanese nationalism see the papers in: Heisig; Maraldo 1995.
[7] Cf. Victoria, pp. 21–30.
[8] Victoria 1997, p. 139.

During the Vietnam War and in subsequent years when South Vietnam, Laos and Cambodia all became Communist states, some Buddhists in Thailand vehemently justified and encouraged violent action against Communism. Kittivuḍḍho, a popular Thai-Buddhist monk, declared that the killing of Communists is not demeritorious because Communists should not be regarded as real 'persons' but as *māras*, that is manifestations of evil forces who strive to destroy nation, religion and monarchy. To kill them would therefore not be the same as killing human persons but would be ridding the world of devils and should be regarded as the 'duty of all Thai'.[9]

Another, even stronger example of the involvement of Theravāda-Buddhists in violent conflict is the so-called ethnic conflict in Sri Lanka whose nature is by no means purely ethnic but has a religious dimension as well.[10] Sri Lanka has a long tradition that 'this island . . . belongs to the Buddha himself'[11] as it is expressed in a Sinhalese work of the thirteenth century. And therefore, says the same scripture, 'the residence of wrong-believers in this Island will never be permanent' and thus 'Lanka is suitable only for Buddhist kings'. Being primarily Hindus who descended from South Indian invaders, Tamils are therefore perceived by many Sinhalese Buddhists as a constant threat to Sri Lanka's identity as Buddha's own country. This feeling has formed the attitude of those Buddhists who justified and supported the war against Tamils which has caused so much bloodshed during the last two decades.[12]

The perhaps most awful, bizarre and best-known example of a relatively recent blend of violence and Buddhism is probably provided by the Japanese Tantric Buddhist sect Aum Shinrikyō which carried out the poison-gas attack on Tokyo subway in 1995 and is also responsible for a number of other cases of murder. The leader of the sect, Shōkō Asahara, had employed

---

[9] Cf. Harvey 2000, p. 260f.
[10] Cf. Peter Harvey's assessment that the 'conflict also has a religious dimension'. Harvey 2000, p. 258.
[11] Pūjāvaliya p. 656, as quoted in: Rahula 1993, p. 63.
[12] Cf. Bartholomeusz 1999 and 2002.

traditional Mahāyāna and Vajrayāna ideas in order to justify
these killings – as for example the idea that the timely death of
the victims was in their own best interest for it prevented them
from further accumulation of bad *karma*.[13]

It would be a temptingly easy interpretation to regard my first
list of examples as good and typical manifestations of true or
genuine Buddhism and the second set of examples as various
cases of deviation, either in the sense of political abuse of religion
or as a kind of fanatical and insane perversion against which no
religion is entirely immune. While I would not deny that there
is some element of truth to this, the whole truth is nevertheless
much more complicated and far more irritating. The history of
Buddhist theory and of Buddhist practice reveals that, underlying my examples of Buddhist ambivalence, there is a profound
and unsolved tension concerning the right Buddhist attitude to
violence and war – a tension between a radical Buddhist pacifism
on the one hand and a much more flexible Buddhist *realpolitik*
on the other.[14] In four points I would like to explicate this in
more detail.

In my first point I will try to sketch briefly the doctrinal foundations of a Buddhist understanding of war and peace. My second
point will deal with what I call 'radical Buddhist pacifism', while

---

[13] Cf. Schmithausen 1999, pp. 61f. See also Repp 1996, p. 197. For the
self-understanding of Aum Shinrikyō as a Buddhist community cf. Repp
1995.

[14] Such a tension is acknowledged – under different terminology – in
several recent investigations of the issue. Michael Zimmermann (refering
to Lingat, Robert: *Royautés Bouddhiques, Asoka et la Fonction Royale
à Ceylon*, Paris: Éditions de l'École des Hautes Études en Sciences Sociale
1989) speaks of 'the two poles of "Buddhist fundamentalism" and "har-
monisation of Buddhist ethics with politics"' (Zimmermann 2000, p. 207).
Steven Collins speaks of 'Dhamma Mode 1' ('an ethics of reciprocity, in
which the assessment of violence is context-dependent and negotiable') and
'Dhamma Mode 2' ('an ethic of absolute values, in which the assessment
of violence is context-independent and non-negotiable') (Collins 1998,
pp. 419f.). Schmithausen (1999) distinguishes four different attitudes
regarding violence/non-violence which can however easily be seen as variations of the two more basic ones. For an earlier attempt by myself see:
Schmidt-Leukel 1996.

my third point is about 'Buddhist realpolitik'. In my final point I will show how Buddhist realpolitik has prepared the ground for a number of cases of religious wars and violent conflicts.

Basic Buddhist Reflections on War and Peace

It is one of the most foundational Buddhist beliefs that true and lasting peace cannot be found in this world. This world, says a famous Buddhist parable, resembles a burning house – burned by the flames of aging and dying,[15] and by the flames of greed, hatred and delusion.[16] The only safe place is the transcendent reality of Nirvāṇa, which is called 'supreme bliss'[17] and 'immortal peace'.[18,19] Nirvāṇa can be reached by following the Buddha's path but, being 'unproduced' (*akataṁ*) and 'unconditioned' (*asaṅkhataṁ*),[20] it is not the type of reality which could ever be created or produced by human efforts. The crucial choice of human existence is whether to strive after the deathless reality of Nirvāṇa or after the transitory pleasures of this burning world.[21] The things of this world, however, can never provide lasting satisfaction. The deepest longing of humans, according to Buddhism, is that of the deathless peace of Nirvāṇa. Therefore all striving for the things of this world will first result in unsatisfied greed for more and more and ultimately in dissatisfaction and frustration.[22] This 'perverted' orientation, i.e. an existential orientation turned into the wrong direction, is called *taṇhā* or *tṛṣṇā*, literally meaning 'thirst'. A telling metaphor – because, just like water, the worldly pleasures can still our thirst only temporarily but can never ever really quench it. And as a result, thirst will thus lead unfailingly to suffering (*dukkha, duḥkha*).

---

[15] Cf. Saṁyutta-Nikāya I, 31.
[16] Cf. Mahāvagga I, 21.
[17] *Nibbānaṁ paramaṁ sukhaṁ.* Dhammapada 203 and 204.
[18] . . . *amataṁ santiṁ nibbānapadaṁ accutaṁ.* Sutta Nipāta 204.
[19] Cf. Chandrkaew 1982, pp. 32ff.
[20] Cf. Udāna VIII, 1.
[21] This is the situation of human beings according to Majjhima-Nikāya 26.
[22] Cf. Majjhima-Nikāya 75 and Majjhima-Nikāya 82.

So thirst is grounded in delusion and manifests itself in greed and hatred or in their more subtle forms of attraction and aversion, while self-centredness is the central mode of both: greed is seeking one's own pleasure first, and hatred is kindled by anything which gets in greed's way as it is said in the *Dhammapada* verse 291: 'He who, by causing pain to others, wishes to obtain pleasure for himself, he, entangled in the bonds of hatred, will never be free from hatred.'[23]

'Thirst' as manifested in greed, hatred and self-centredness, is therefore not only seen as the cause of one's own frustration and suffering but also as the principal source for the affliction of suffering upon others, be this on the small level of personal quarrels or on the large level of collective conflict or war:

> kings dispute with kings, nobles dispute with nobles, brahmans dispute with brahmans, householders dispute with householders, a mother disputes with her son, a son disputes with his mother, a father disputes with his son, a son disputes with his father, a brother disputes with a brother, . . . a friend disputes with a friend. Those who enter into quarrel, contention, dispute and attack one another with their hands and with stones and with sticks and with weapons, . . . having taken sword and shield, having girded on bow and quiver, both sides mass for battle and arrows are hurled and knives are hurled and swords are flashing. These who wound with arrows and wound with knives and decapitate with their swords, these suffer dying then and pain like unto dying. This too, monks, is a peril in pleasures of the senses that is present, a stem of ill having pleasures of the senses as the cause. . . .[24]

Given this analysis of suffering and 'thirst' as its major root, the Buddhist path of salvation aims at a conversion in the sense of a complete change of our existential orientation; that means abandoning 'thirst' and turning towards Nirvāṇa. Since 'thirst' is grounded in delusion, such a u-turn becomes possible only

---

[23] Müller 2000, p. 36.
[24] Majjhima-Nikāya I, 86. Horner 1976, p. 113f.

through insight brought about by the word of the Buddha and its resonance within one's own experience. As 'thirst' is manifested in greed, hatred and self-centredness, the overcoming of 'thirst' is realized through the development of the opposite mental attitudes. Thus greed, hatred and selfishness are to be replaced by generosity, loving kindness and selflessness. Within Buddhism the so-called Golden Rule of morality is based on the insight that others are just the same as oneself – an insight which should result particularly in non-violence: 'Life is dear to all. Comparing others with oneself, one should neither kill nor cause to kill.'[25] In this context 'generosity' or 'giving' (*dāna*) can acquire a comprehensive meaning: Living a non-violent and morally good life means making one's life into a gift for others, because – as one Buddhist text says – this gives them the gift of liberation from fear.[26]

'Loving kindness' (*mettā, maitrī*) is expressed as sympathy (*muditā*) and as compassion (*karuṇā*). Buddhaghosa, the undisputed authority of classical Theravāda-Buddhism, characterizes compassion or *karuṇā* as 'evolving the mode of removing pain'.[27] But how can this be realized in a world marked by an abundance of pain resulting from violence? When it comes to this question, the Buddhist tradition gives two different answers: 'radical Buddhist pacifism' and 'Buddhist realpolitik'.

Radical Buddhist Pacifism

A basic Buddhist principle is that *within oneself* 'thirst' together with delusion as its root, and greed, hatred and selfishness as its manifestations are to be overcome through the development of their opposites, that is through striving after Nirvāṇa, by developing insight, generosity, loving kindness and selflessness. Radical Buddhist pacifists are convinced that what is true for

---

[25] Dhammapada 130 as quoted in Harvey 2000, p. 34. See also Sutta Nipāta 157.
[26] Cf. Anguttara-Nikāya IV 245f.
[27] Cf. Visuddhi Magga 318. Tin 1922, p. 366.

the spiritual struggle *within* oneself is also true for interpersonal relationships and social organisms. In that sense the *Dhammapada* (verse 223) says: 'Conquer anger by love, conquer evil by good, conquer the stingy by giving, conquer the liar by truth.'[28] In particular this implies that the appropriate reaction to violence must not be counter-violence but non-violence. Once again this is clearly expressed in the Dhammapada (197, 201, 5):

> We live happily indeed, not hating those who hate us! Among men who hate us we dwell free from hatred.
> Victory breeds hatred, for the conquered is unhappy. He who has given up both victory and defeat, he, the contented, is happy.
> For hatred does not cease by hatred at any time: hatred ceases by love – this is an old rule.[29]

The classical commentary on the last verse underlines the basic idea:

> A spot smeared with impurities like spit and nasal mucous cannot be cleaned and freed of smells (by) washing it with the same impurities; on the contrary, (thereby) that spot will be all the more unclean and foul-smelling. In the same way, one who reviles the reviler, one who strikes back at the striker, is not able to pacify hatred with hatred. On the contrary, one (thereby) creates more hatred still.[30]

It should be clear that a non-violent reaction to violence does not mean not to react at all. Non-violence does not necessarily imply to remain passive. The canonical records of the Buddha's life provide some impressive examples of how the Buddha himself confronted violence actively but strictly non-violently. When

---

[28] As quoted in Harvey 2000, p. 242.

[29] Müller 2000, pp. 24 and 1.

[30] Carter, Palihawadana 1987, p. 95f. While Nyanatiloka believed that this commentary was composed by Buddhaghosa, Buddhaghosa's authorship is denied by Carter and Palihawadana. Nevertheless it may date from the fifth century CE or shortly after. Cf. Carter, Palihawadana 1987 p. 4 and p. 418, fn 1; Nyanatiloka 1992, p. 12.

the bandit and cruel murderer Aṅgulimāla terrorized the kingdom of Kosala and King Pasenadi was unable to get hold of
him, the Buddha went there to meet Aṅgulimāla and succeeded
in converting him by enabling him to understand the existential
roots and the futility of his violent behaviour. Subsequently King
Pasenadi praised the Buddha with the words: 'Him, revered sir,
that I was unable to tame with stick and sword, the Lord has
tamed without stick or sword.'[31] On another occasion, when a
conflict between two tribes over rare water reservoirs was escalat-
ing, the Buddha succeeded in preventing an imminent war by
teaching the hostile parties the great value of human lives, the
disadvantages of war and the advantages of peace.[32]

The spiritual weight which Buddhism gives to non-violence is
expressed by the fact that not to harm or kill any sentient being
is the first and foremost of all Buddhist precepts. As such it is
also an integral part of the Buddhist path of salvation, the so-
called Noble Eightfold Path. Even an indirect involvement with
violence has to be avoided. Monks are therefore not allowed to
watch manoeuvres or military parades or to stay without need
in a military camp.[33] Similarly laypeople are not allowed to earn
their livelihood by trading in arms.[34] The ancient Vedic belief,
that a soldier who dies during the battle will go to heaven, is
explicitly rejected by the Buddha. On the contrary, the Buddha
taught that such a soldier will go to hell because at the moment
of his death his mind is governed by the intention to kill.[35] One
of the Jātakas,[36] canonical narratives about former lives of the
Buddha, tells the story of Prince Temīya who had been King of
Benares for 20 years in a former existence. Subsequently he was
reborn in hell where he had to suffer for 80,000 years because of
the violent deeds that had been unavoidably connected with his

---

[31] Majjhima-Nikāya II 102. Horner 1975, p. 288.
[32] Cf. Jātaka 536.
[33] Cf. Vināya Piṭaka IV 104ff. Cf. Schmithausen 1996, p. 64f.
[34] Cf. Anguttara-Nikāya III 208.
[35] Cf. Saṃyutta-Nikāya IV 308-3011. Cf. Schmithausen 1996, pp. 65f.
and Schmithausen 1999, pp. 48f.
[36] Jātaka 538.

former royal duties, such as carrying out the law and punishing the evil-doers. When Temīya was once more reborn as the legal successor to the throne he pretended to be lame, deaf and dumb in order to avoid becoming king again.[37]

In the eyes of radical Buddhist pacifism all this amounts to the view that there is no acceptable justification for violence under any circumstances.[38] This throws up the question whether Buddhists could participate in any form in ruling a country responsibly. Insofar as political power is intrinsically connected with the use of violence, the answer of radical Buddhist pacifism is clear: Buddhists have to abstain from this.[39] However, does that not entail a grave restriction to the realization of compassion? How can Buddhists evolve *karuṇā*, 'the mode of removing pain', if their efforts to do so cannot be transferred to the crucial realm of politics? Is it not somehow self-contradictory if Buddhist moral principles would force Buddhists to leave political responsibility in the hands of all those and only those who are not willing to accept Buddhist morality?

No doubt this is a serious problem for radical Buddhist pacifism. Its response to this is the utopic picture of the *Cakravartin*, that is a king who rules the whole earth without force but only by the power of the *Dharma*, i.e. the Buddhist teaching.[40] This idea has taken several forms. In one of its forms it is connected to the coming of the future Buddha Maitreya, whose appearance is preceded by an all-encompassing peace:

> No one will stir up quarrels because of villages, towns, wealth, crops, fields, property or soil; all human beings will be handsome, with beautiful bodies, (and will be) loving and pleasant to each other. Crows will become friendly with owls, cats with mice, deer with lions, mongooses with snakes, lions with deer . . .[41]

---

[37] Cf. Collins 1998, pp. 426ff.
[38] See for example Deegalle's view that 'as a Buddhist one cannot justify violence under any circumstance'. Deegalle 2002, p. 16.
[39] Cf. Schmithausen 1996, p. 68; Collins 1998, p. 420.
[40] Cf. Collins 1998, pp. 470–96.
[41] As quoted in: Collins 1998, p. 623.

The utopian nature of this vision gets particularly clear by the idea that even among animals enmity and violence would disappear. But what else can the function of such an utopia be than providing a permanent critical impetus to work towards it – while at the same time remaining soberly conscious that the utopian goal itself can never be achieved? In one Jātaka[42] two different ideals of kingship are contrasted. The one king is praised for his just and well-balanced rule, that is because he 'matches . . . the strong with strength . . ., the mild with mildness; he wins over the good by good, and defeats the bad with bad'. The other king is praised because of his strictly non-violent rule, that is because he conquers 'an angry man by kindness, a bad man by good, a miser with generosity and a liar by the truth'.[43] The story makes clear that the second ideal is superior, but suprisingly it does not blame the first one as false. Both are characterized as just forms of rule and as being compatible with the Buddhist Dharma.[44] This leads us to the next point.

Buddhist Realpolitik

An ancient Buddhist myth[45] explains the origin of violence as follows: in the beginning of each world period, sentient beings live as pure, etherial, shining beings. But driven by the force of subtle forms of greed they start to enjoy the taste of food. As a consequence they first develop material bodies and subsequently female and male forms. After they start cultivating and storing rice, the dynamics of greed lead to some cases of stealing. As a result of stealing, accusation, lying and violent struggle come

---

[42] Cf. Jātaka 151.

[43] Quotations from Collins 1998, p. 457. The last verse is identical to Dhammapada 223. As further evidence for a Buddhist acceptance of the first ideal see Hsüan Tsang's comments on the rule of the Buddhist king Śīlāditya (Harṣavardhana, 606–647 CE) whose rule is praised by Hsüan Tsang with an indirect reference to the above mentioned verses: 'He rewarded the good and punished the wicked, degraded the evil and promoted the men of talent.' Beal 1983, vol. I, p. 214.

[44] Cf. Collins 1998, pp. 457f.

[45] Aggañña Sutta (Dīgha-Nikāya 27).

into existence. In order to avoid anarchy the beings then decide
to elect one among them as king so that he should 'criticize whoever should be criticized, accuse whoever should be accused, and
banish whoever should be banished'.[46] Other beings react to the
upcoming violence by withdrawing from the world in order to
keep themselves away from bad and unwholesome things and
live a life of seclusion and meditation.

This mythical story provides a kind of Buddhist rationale for
two different legitimate reactions to the problem of violence: on
the one hand withdrawal from the world with the aim to erode
the root of evil within oneself, and on the other hand the institution of the ruler with a monopoly of force and the prospect of
securing peace by a limited and just exertion of force. Such a
form of violence is explicitly and deliberately legitimized in the
'Sūtra of Golden Light' (*Suvarṇabhāsottamasūtra*), an influential Mahāyāna-Buddhist scripture dating from the third or
fourth century CE. According to this text a king has to inflict
punishment on evil-doers in order to protect and enforce moral
order in his country. By punishing the evil-doers and by reward-
ing the good, the king has to demonstrate the basic karmic law
that good deeds will bear good fruits while bad deeds will have
bad consequences.[47] Through this the king establishes beings in
good activity. His own motivation has to be selfless and lawful, his judgements must be impartial and the punishment should
conform to the crime. But, says the Sūtra of Golden Light,

> when a king overlooks an evil deed in his region and does
> not inflict appropriate punishment on the evil person, in the
> neglect of evil deeds lawlessness grows greatly, wicked acts
> and quarrels arise in great number in the realm.[48]

---

[46] Quoted from Collins 1998, p. 632.

[47] This argument is by no means confined to Mahāyāna-Buddhism. It
is already used in the Milindapañha (184–186) – a work which has for
Theravāda Buddhists semi-canonical and in some branches even full canonical status – in order to harmonize the ideal of non-violence with the duties
of a king.

[48] Emmerick 1970, p. 59.

Therefore a king who would refrain from using violence in order to punish the evil-doers would himself be responsible for the bad consequences of this neglect. He would destroy his own realm and would be himself 'unlawful' because he thereby, says the Sūtra, 'supports the side of the lawless'.[49] This is perhaps one of the strongest arguments against a radical non-violent position. For this argument shows that, within the realm of political responsibility, refraining from violence may in fact mean supporting evil-doers, that is, non-violence would function as encouragement and support of violence. Consequently political responsibility does not really allow the choice between violence and non-violence. The only realistic choice is between lawful, just and well-intentioned violence on the one hand, and lawless, unjust, and evil-motivated forms of violence on the other.

Nevertheless, the utopic ideals of radical Buddhist pacifism exerted their influence on Buddhist realpolitik insofar as the maxim was always to use as little violence as possible. For example, a chapter on royal ethics in another Mahāyāna scripture[50] blames the standard Hindu codices for kings (the *Arthaśāstras*) as justifying far too much violence. In contrast, this Buddhist text admonishes kings that punishment should not only be fair and just, taking into account the intention of the accused, but should primarily seek the transgressor's return to the right path. Punishment should be understood as and used like a medicine in order to 'cure the transgressor'.[51] It should be inflicted in the mood of a father who 'wants to cure a dishonourable son'.[52] Capital punishment and bodily mutilation should therefore be entirely excluded.[53] In the Theravāda-Buddhist Pāli-Canon we find the advice that if a country is shaken by lawlessness and internal violence, the king should not introduce more severe forms of punishment but should grant grain and fodder

---

[49] Emmerick 1970, p. 59.
[50] *Bodhisattva-gocaropāya-viṣaya-vikurvaṇa-nirdeśa-sūtra.* Cf. Zimmermann 2000.
[51] Zimmermann 2000, p. 184.
[52] Zimmermann 2000, p. 195.
[53] Zimmermann 2000, pp. 183f., pp. 194f.

to the farmers, should lend capital to the traders and pay proper wages to the officials.

> Then those people, being intent on their own occupations, will not harm the kingdom. Your Majesty's revenues will be great, the land will be tranquil and not beset by thieves, and the people, with joy in their hearts, will play with their children and dwell in open houses.[54]

When it comes to the question of war, Buddhist realpolitik follows the same line. It is seen as a royal obligation to protect the people not only from criminals but also against foreign aggression. Thus, while radical Buddhist pacifism knows to tell its stories about kings who non-violently surrendered their countries to the invaders,[55] Buddhist realpolitik held that a defensive war might become inevitable and can be justified. If a country is threatened by foreign troops the aforementioned Mahāyāna scripture[56] advises the king that, in the first instance, he should see if there are still some ways left to settle the conflict peacefully, as by 'encountering the enemy with kindness', or by 'granting favours', or even 'by surrounding and frightening the enemy with the assumed superiority of his own army'.[57] If all this turns out to be futile, the king is justified in entering into war but he should do so with the motive of protecting his people and sparing the lives of hostile soldiers as far as possible. The text assures that under these conditions the behaviour of the king will not have any negative karmic consequences 'because he has thus performed . . . the tasks with a mind (full of) compassion . . .'.[58]

---

[54] Dīgha-Nikāya 5. Quotation from: Harvey 2000, p. 198.

[55] For example Jātaka 538.

[56] The limitation to a defensive war is explicitly made in the Chinese version of the text, but not in the Tibetan one. Zimmerman has therefore suggested to take this limitation 'with caution' (Zimmermann 2000, p. 199f.). However, the text itself justifies the behaviour of the king under the premise that he 'protects (his) subjects' (Zimmermann 2000, p. 204) which seems to be further evidence that the imagined situation is one of defence.

[57] Zimmermann 2000, p. 200.

[58] Zimmermann 2000, p. 204.

For a Buddhist realpolitik the crucial aspect which makes the use of violence acceptable, under certain circumstances, is the right intention.[59] The motivation for using violence must be primarily governed by compassion.[60] Under this condition legitimate violence or martial action are not confined to just punishment or defensive wars. A third important form is the effort to overthrow unjust or tyrannical rule. Several such cases are recorded throughout Buddhist history.[61] One of the most famous was the assassination of the Tibetan king, Glang Dar-ma, in 842 CE by a Buddhist monk. Glang Dar-ma had persecuted Buddhism heavily and tried to extinguish the Buddhist order. The traditional Buddhist record describes his assassination as a compassionate act because it saved the evil king from committing further evil deeds and thereby from accumulating further evil *karma*.[62]

The conviction that there are cases of compassionate violence has been illustrated again and again by the analogy of a physician who must carry out painful surgery in order to treat a serious

---

[59] Cf. also the emphasis on the right intention among contemporary Theravāda-Buddhists with regard to the justification of the war against Tamils in Bartholomeusz 2002, pp. 121–3.

[60] For the principal justification of killing if it is motivated by compassion see for example Upāyakauśalya Sūtra 132–137 (Tatz 1994, pp. 73f.). Buddhist emphasis on the right motivation was sometimes also extended to other motives than compassion. A clear historical example are the 'Five Commandments for Laymen', given by the Korean Buddhist Master Won'gwang (sixth/seventh centuries CE). 'Serve your sovereign with loyalty; tend your parents with filial piety; treat your friends with sincerity; do not retreat from a battlefield; be discriminating about the taking of life' (Lee 1969, pp. 79f.). The latter is explained as not to kill during certain periods, not to kill domestic animals and tiny creatures, and as: 'Though you may have the need, you should not kill often' (Lee 1969, p. 80). Obviously the emphasis is on 'virtues as loyalty, filial piety, sincerity, courage, and goodness (benevolence)' (Lee 1969, p. 13) and thus represents an adaptation of Buddhist values to Confucian virtues (see also Grayson 2002, pp. 38f.).

[61] For example, the coming into power of the Buddhist king Harṣavardhana (606–647) through a violent coup against the unlawful ruler Śaśāṅka (cf. the traditional record in: Beal 1983, vol. 1, pp. 209–15), or the various rebellions in China in which Buddhists had been involved (cf. Schmithausen 1996, p. 83).

[62] See the classical reccord of this instance in: Obermiller 1986, pp. 197ff.

injury or disease.[63] Someone who follows the Bodhisattva Path of
Mahāyāna-Buddhism is particularly obliged to put the development of compassion above everything else. If compassion requires a violation of the Buddhist precepts to be carried out, it
has to be done.[64] Thus it is not surprising that Buddhist kings
– and not only in Mahāyāna-Buddhist but also in Theravāda
countries – frequently regarded and designated themselves as
Bodhisattvas.[65] However, using violence must of course be the
ultimate resort. Thus the famous *Vimalakīrti-Nirdeśa Sūtra*
underlines that the Bodhisattva's foremost duty is peacemaking:

> In times of war he teaches
> Kindliness and pity
> To convert living beings
> So that they can live in peace.
> When armies line up for battle
> He gives equal strength to both.
> With his authority and power, he forces
> Them to be reconciled and live in harmony.[66]

As we have seen, usually Mahāyāna-Buddhist attempts to justify
violence are closely connected to those types of ethical dilemmas
as can arise out of a compassionate and responsible living. But
it needs to be mentionend that there are also cases of a far more
problematical reasoning. Especially in the Tantric developments
of Mahāyāna-Buddhism, the teaching that all views are at best
only relatively but never absolutely true has been occasionally
employed in order to place the enlightened Tantric master above
all ethical norms and standards.[67] Thus for example the Caṇḍamahāroṣaṇa Tantra says about the Tantric adept: 'Although he
may kill a hundred Brāhmans, he will not be stained by sin.'[68]

---

[63] So already in Milindapañha 112. For further examples see: Schmithausen 1996, p. 82; Wickremeratna 1995, p. 294.

[64] Cf. Śikṣāsamuccaya 167.

[65] Cf. Harvey 2000, p. 117, pp. 261f.

[66] Luk 1990, p. 89.

[67] See for example the Tantric interpretation of the monastic rules in
Sobisch 2002, particularly pp. 435–437.

The fact that here the victims of such an excessive killing are presented as Brāhmans leads us to the issue of religious wars.

Religious wars

In the semi-canonical Theravāda-Buddhist scripture *Milindapañha*, we find the following statement on the Buddha:

> The Tathāgata, O king, wounds people but to their good, he casts people down but to their profit, he kills people but to their advantage. Just as mothers and fathers, O king, hurt their children and even knock them down, thinking the while of their good; so by whatsoever method an increase in the virtue of living things can be brought about, by that method does he contribute to their good.[69]

In the *Milindapañha* the 'wounding' and 'killing' is clearly meant metaphorically. But the very type of reasoning – that is, using violence for the religious well-being of people – can be and was in fact employed for justifying violent religious conflicts and wars.

The relationship between *Hindus* and Buddhists has frequently been rather strained. The Buddhist canonical writings are full of polemics against the Brāhmans and their Vedic beliefs and practices. Emperor Aśoka's ban on killing animals should not only be understood as an act of Buddhist non-violence and love of animals. It was a general ban on animal sacrifices which in the time of Aśoka, i.e. third century BCE, formed a major part of Vedic ritual practice. Aśoka's order must therefore be seen as a massive blow to the Brāhmans and came close to a ban on their profession.[70] Consequently, Hindu or Brāhmanical reactions towards the rapidly growing Buddhist tradition have also been quite hostile.[71] To mention just one example: according to a

---

[68] George 1974, p. 79. See also Schmithausen 1999, pp. 60f.

[69] Miliñdapanha 109 (Rhys Davids 1963a, pp. 164f.)

[70] Cf. Schneider 1980, pp. 152ff.

[71] Thus immediately after the end of the Maurya dynasty, i.e. in the second century BCE, there was a severe persecution of Buddhism under King Puṣyamitra in the name of defending and re-establishing Brāhmanism. Cf. Hazra 1995, pp. 388ff.

traditional Hindu record the great Hindu philosopher Kumārila had persuaded King Sudhanvan so strongly of the allegedly evil nature of Buddhism, that King Sudhanvan not only ordered that all Buddhists should be expelled from his realm but that they should be eliminated, including their children and aged ones.[72] Anti-Buddhist sentiments and occasional measures from the side of the Hindus have conversely increased Buddhist fears and the feeling that they have to defend themselves. Mutual suspicion and fear have contributed enormously to the Sinhala–Tamil conflict in Sri Lanka which is, and has always been, not only an ethnic conflict but also a conflict between Buddhists and Hindus. The *Mahāvaṃsa*, the main Buddhist chronicle of Sri Lankan Buddhism, composed perhaps in the fifth century CE, reports how the Buddhist Sinhala King Duṭṭhagāmaṇī (101–77 BCE) waged a war against the Tamils in order to defend Buddhism. His army was accompanied by 500 Buddhist monks and in his spear Duṭṭhagāmaṇī carried a relic of the Buddha. After the victorious but extremely bloody battle, when he felt remorse, Duṭṭhagāmaṇī was comforted by eight enlightened monks (Arhats) who told him that he had not killed thousands of people but only one and a half (a Buddhist who had taken the triple refuge and one who had taken the five precepts as well) – while all the others had been 'unbelievers and men of evil life . . . not more to be esteemed than beasts'.[73] Today this narrative still plays a significant role in the rhetoric and arguments of those Sri Lankan Buddhists who provide religious justification for the war against Hindu Tamils.[74]

Relations between Buddhists and *Muslims* have usually also been quite tense. When Muslim troops invaded India most Muslim theologians did not regard the Buddhists as people of the book; that is, they did not acknowledge a genuine prophetic quality of or within the Buddhist scriptures. This gave them reason to fight against Buddhism and to remove it from the conquered areas.[75] While there are some records of non-violent

---

[72] Cf. Halbfass 1988, p. 176; Hazra 1995, p. 387.
[73] Mahāvaṃsa 25, 110. Geiger 1912, 178.
[74] Cf. Bartholomeusz 2002.
[75] Cf. Scott 1995.

reactions from the side of the Buddhists[76], the *Kālacakratantra*, an influential Buddhist scripture, dating perhaps from the tenth century, fantasizes about a 'kind of eschatological war in which the army of the Bodhisattva king of Śambhala . . . finally conquers and annihilates the Muslim forces . . . in order to destroy their barbarian religion . . . and to re-establish Buddhism'.[77]

Christianity appeared at the beginning of modern times in Asian Buddhist countries in the form of martial colonialists accompanied by militant missionaries, but has, as far as I can see, not provoked very much of *violent* Buddhist reactions,[78] with the great exception of Japan. As a reaction to the rapid spread of Christianity during the second half of the sixteenth century and due to well-grounded fears of Western colonialist interests, seventeenth-century Japanese rulers have carried out one of the most fierceful persecutions of Christianity ever seen. The sentiment of a potential threat coming from Christianity was reactivated in the beginning of the twentieth century when the Russo-Japanese war was imminent. At that time the Buddhist priest and scholar Enryō Inoue wrote:

> In Russia state and religion are one . . . religion is used as a chain in order to unify the (Russian) people. Therefore, when they (the Russian people) see Orientals, they are told that the latter are the bitter enemies of their religion. It is for this reason that on the one hand it is a war of politics and on the other hand it is a war of religion . . . If theirs is the army of God, then ours is the army of the Buddha. It is in this way that Russia is not only the enemy of our country but of the Buddha as well.[79]

Several Buddhist countries have also seen violent conflicts and wars between *different Buddhist denominations*. Tibet has

---

[76] Cf. Conze 1980, p. 99.

[77] Schmithausen 1999, p. 58.

[78] Buddhist authors have inspired and demanded several persecutions of Christians at the beginning of the seventeenth century in China, but compared to Japan these persecutions were relatively mild. Cf. Kern 1992, pp. 8–38.   [79] Victoria 1997, p. 30.

experienced quite a number of wars between its different Buddhist orders, particularly between the twelfth and sixteenth
centuries and once again during the eighteenth century.[80] Violent hostilities between different Buddhist monasteries which
at the same time represented different forms of Buddhism are
also documented in the history of Sri Lanka.[81] The most severe
and longest struggles between different Buddhist denominations
have taken place in Japan, where between the twelfth and sixteenth centuries all the major monasteries maintained their own
armies and were almost constantly involved in violent conflicts.[82]
The justification of these conflicts has frequently taken a religious shape, as for example in the case of Nichiren who quoted
from a number of authoritative Mahāyāna Sūtras in order to substantiate 'the aggressive way of eliminating the destroyers of the
Dharma'.[83] From the influential Mahāyānist *Mahāparinirvāṇa
Sūtra* Nichiren quoted the lines:

> suppose a good bhikṣu (Buddhist monk), upon seeing people
> who destroy the Dharma, does not reproach them, drive them
> away, or punish them. Know this! He is an enemy of the teach-
> ings of the Buddha. If he drives them away, reproaches, or
> punishes them, he is my disciple, my hearer in the true sense of
> the word. . . .
>   Those who protect the right teaching of the Buddha do not
> have to keep the five precepts, . . . but have to carry swords,
> bows, arrows, and halberd . . .[84]

In the eyes of Nichiren, the other Japanese Buddhist schools of
his time, Tendai, Shingon, Zen, or Jōdo, were all slanderers of the

---

[80] Cf. Schmithausen 1996, pp. 80–2; Brück 1999, pp. 59–64.

[81] Particularly during the fourth century CE. Cf. Rahula 1993, pp. 90–4.

[82] Cf. Harvey 2000, pp. 264ff. The phenomenon of armed Buddhist
monasteries and even special 'warrior monks' did not only exist in Japan
but also in China (cf. Zürcher 1989, p. 245f.) and Korea (cf. Grayson 2002,
p. 89f.). In Korea the warrior monks contributed significantly to the
country's defence against the Japanese invasion in the sixteenth century
(cf. Grayson 2002, p. 123).

[83] Cf. Nichiren 2000, pp. 121 and 123.

[84] Nichiren 2000, p. 124.

true *dharma* because they did not share his interpretation of the *Lotos-Sūtra*. But since they were so strong and influential they were a danger to the spiritual and social well-being of the people of Japan. Therefore Nichiren was convinced that compassion for the people of Japan required protecting the true *dharma* against its distortion and therefore fighting – even violently – against the other Buddhist schools.

So while it is true that there have hardly been any 'religious wars for the sake of spreading the Buddhist religion by force to non-Buddhist regions'[85] it would be wrong to assume that there have been *no* religious wars in Buddhism at all. The basic arguments and principles of Buddhist realpolitik were extended to the religious realm and thereby led to the idea of a violent defence of Buddhism, or particular forms of it, against other religions and other Buddhist denominations. The practical realization of this idea has a widespread, and by no means insignificant, tradition in Buddhism.

Conclusion

All Buddhists believe that ultimate and lasting peace can only be found in Nirvāṇa. However, it is seen as a genuine implication of religious life to overcome the roots of violence, to be peaceful and to remove as far as possible the pain of others. According to radical Buddhist pacifism this excludes the use of violence under any circumstances and for any reason. Only non-violent means are seen as justifiable reactions to violence. Buddhist realpolitik holds that one should exert as little violence as possible and should basically prefer non-violent means. However, it accepts that, under certain circumstances, violence is inevitable and is justified as the lesser evil or as the only means to bring about some higher good. But it should be used only out of truly compassionate intentions. This refers primarily to that kind of violence which is needed to uphold and protect a just order by responsible rulers. However, in several cases this principle was

---

[85] Schmithausen 1999, p. 63.

also extended to the protection of the *dharma*, in the specific sense of Buddhist religious norms and values. In combination with the conviction that one's own denominational form of Buddhism is the true or superior one, this principle has served to legitimate violent religious conflicts of an inter-religious and of an inner-Buddhist kind as well.

SELECT BIBLIOGRAPHY

Aung S. S. K., 1991, *Freedom from Fear and Other Writings*, ed. with an introduction by Michael Aris, London: Penguin Books.

Bartholomeusz, T. J., 1999, In Defense of Dharma: Just-War Ideology in Buddhist Sri Lanka, in: *Journal of Buddhist Ethics* 6, pp. 1–11.

Bartholomeusz, T. J., 2002, *In Defense of Dharma: Just-War Ideology in Buddhist Sri Lanka*, London and New York: RoutledgeCurzon.

Beal, S. (trans.), 1983, *Si-Yu-Ki: Buddhist Records of the Western World. Translated from the Chinese of Hiuen Tsiang AD 629*, 2 vols (1st edn 1884), 2nd edn, New Delhi: Oriental Book Reprint Corporation.

Bendall, Cecil, Rouse, W. H. D. (trans.), 1971, *Sikshā-Samuccaya: A Compendium of Buddhist Doctrine. Compiled by Śāntideva*, Delhi: Motilal Banarsidass.

Brück, M. von, 1999, *Religion und Politik im Tibetischen Buddhismus*, München: Kösel.

Carter, R., Palihawadana, M. (trans.), 1987, *The Dhammapada: A New English Translation with the Pāli text and the First English Translation of the Commentary's Explanation of the Verses*, With Notes Translated from Sinhala Sources and Critical Textual Comments, New York and Oxford: Oxford University Press.

Chandrkaew, C., 1982, *Nibbāna: The Ultimate Truth of Buddhism*, Bangkok: Mahachula Buddhist University.

Collins, S., 1998, *Nirvāna and Other Buddhist Felicities: Utopias of the Pali Imaginaire*, Cambridge: Cambridge University Press.

Conze, E., 1980, *A Short History of Buddhism*, London: Allen & Unwin.

Deegalle, M., Is Violence Justified in Theravāda Buddhism?, in: *Current Dialogue* 39, pp. 4–16.

Emmerick, R. E. (trans.), 1970, *The Sūtra of the Golden Light: Being a Translation of the Suvarṇabhāsattamasūtra*, London: Luzac & Company.

Geiger, W. (trans.), 1912, *The Mahāvaṃsa or The Great Chronicle of Ceylon*, London: Pali Texts Society through Oxford University Press.

George, C. S. (ed. and trans.), 1974, *The Caṇḍamahāroṣaṇa Tantra: A Critical Edition and English Translations, Chapters I–VIII*, New Haven, Conn.: American Oriental Society.

Grayson, J. H., 2002, *Korea – A Religious History*, revised edn, London: RoutledgeCurzon.

Halbfass, W., 1998, Der Buddha und seine Lehre im Urteil des Hinduismus, in: P. Schmidt-Leukel (ed.), *Wer ist Buddha? Eine Gestalt und ihre Bedeutung für die Menschheit*, Diederichs: München, pp. 176–94, 260–2.

Harris, E., 1990, Violence and Disruption in Society: A Study of the Early Buddhist Texts, in: *Dialogue* (N.S.) 17, pp. 29–81.

Harvey, P., 2000, *An Introduction to Buddhist Ethics: Foundations, Values and Issues*, Cambridge: Cambridge University Press.

Hazra, K. L., 1995, *The Rise and Decline of Buddhism in India*, New Delhi: Munshiram Manoharlal Publishers.

Heisig, J. W. and Maraldo, J. C. (eds), 1995, *Rude Awakenings: Zen, the Kyoto School, and the Question of Nationalism*, Honolulu: University of Hawaii Press.

Horner, I. B. (trans.), 1975, *The Collection of the Middle Length Sayings (Majjhima-Nikāya)*, Vol. II, London: Pali Text Society.

Horner, I. B. (trans.), 1976, *The Collection of the Middle Length Sayings (Majjhima-Nikāya)*, Vol. I, London: Pali Text Society.

Jack, H. A., 1993, *WCRP: A History of the World Conference on Religion and Peace*, New York: World Conference on Religion and Peace.

Karwath, W., 1984, Buddhismus und Krieg, in: *Bodhi Baum. Zeitschrift für Buddhismus und meditatives Leben* 9, no. 4, pp. 188–202.

Kern, I., 1998, *Buddhistische Kritik am Christentum im China des 17. Jahrhunderts*, Peter Lang Verlag.

Lee, P. H., 1969, *Lives of Eminent Korean Monks: The Haedong Kosung Chon*, trans. with an Introduction by P. H. Lee, Cambridge, Mass.: Harvard University Press.

Luk, C. (ed. and trans.), 1990, *The Vimalakīrti Nirdeśa Sūtra*, Boston and Shaftesbury: Shambhala.

Müller, F. M. (ed. and trans.), 2000, *Wisdom of the Buddha. The Unabridged Dhammapada*, New York: Dover.

Nichiren, 2000, *Kaimokushō or Liberation from Blindness*, trans. from the Japanese (Taishō Vol. 84, No. 2689) by Murano Senchū (BDK English Tripitaka 104–IV), Berkeley: Numata Center for Buddhist Translation and Research.

Nyanatiloka, 1992, *Dhammapada und Kommentar*, Uttenbühl: Jhana Verlag.

Obermiller, E. (trans.), 1986, *The History of Buddhism in India and Tibet by Bu-ston. Translated from Tibetan (Bibliotheca Indo-Buddhica No. 26)*. 2nd edn, Delhi: Sri Satguru Publications.

Rahula, W., 1993, *History of Buddhism in Ceylon*, 3rd edn, Nedimala: The Buddhist Cultural Centre.

Repp, M., 1995, Who's the First to Cast the Stone? Aum Shinrikyō, Religions and Society in Japan, in: *The Mission Journal* 49, pp. 225–55.

Repp, M., 1996, Religion und Gewalt im gegenwärtigen Japan – Der Fall Aum Shinrikyō, in: *Dialog der Religionen* 6, pp. 190–202.

Rhys Davids, T. W. (trans.), 1963a, *The Questions of King Milinda. Translated from the Pali. Part I* (SBE 35) (1st edn 1890), New York: Dover Publications.

Rhys Davids, T. W. (trans.), 1963b, *The Questions of King Milinda. Translated from the Pali. Part II* (SBE 36) (1st edn 1894), New York: Dover Publications.

Schmidt-Leukel, P., 1996, Das Problem von Gewalt und Krieg in der buddhistischen Ethik, in: *Dialog der Religionen* 6, pp. 122–40.

Schmithausen, L., 1996, Buddhismus und Glaubenskriege, in: *Glaubenskriege in Vergangenheit und Gegenwart. Referate gehalten auf dem Symposium der Joachim Jungius-Gesellschaft der Wissenschaften*, Hamburg am 28 und 29 Oktober 1994, herausgegeben von Herrmann, Peter, Göttingen: Vandenhoeck & Ruprecht, pp. 63–92.

Schmithausen, L., 1999, Aspects of the Buddhist Attitude Towards War, in: Jan E. M. Houben and Karel R. Van Kooij (eds), *Violence Denied. Violence, Non-Violence and the Rationalization of Violence in South Asian Cultural History*, Leiden: Brill, pp. 45–67.

Schneider, U., 1980, *Einführung in den Buddhismus.* Darmstadt: Wissenschaftliche Buchgesellschaft.

Scott, D., 1995, Buddhism and Islam: Past to Present Encounters and Interfaith Lessons, in: *Numen* 42, pp. 141–51.

Sobisch, J. U., 2002, *The Three-Vow Theories in Tibetan Buddhism: A Comparative Study of Major Traditions from the Twelfth through Nineteenth Centuries*, Wiesbaden: Ludwig Reichert Verlag.

Tatz, M. (trans.), 1994, *The Skill in Means (Upāyakauśalya) Sūtra*, Delhi: Motilal Banarsidass.

Tin, P. M. (trans.), 1922, *The Path of Purity. Being a Translation of Buddhaghosa's Visuddhimagga*, Part II, London: Pali Text Society by Oxford University Press.

Victoria, B. A., 1997, *Zen at War*, New York: Waterhill.

Wickremeratna, A., 1995, *Buddhism and Ethnicity in Sri Lanka. A Historical Analysis.* Delhi: Vikas Publishing House.

Zimmermann, Michael, 2000, A Mahāyānist Criticism of *Arthaśāstra*: The Chapter on Royal Ethics in the *Bodhisattva-gocaropāya-viṣaya-vikurvaṇa-nirdeśa-sūtra'*, in: *Annual Report of The International Research Institue for Advanced Buddhology at Soka University of the Academic Year 1999 (ARIRIAB 3)*, Tokyo: The International Research Institute for Advanced Buddhology, Soka University, pp. 177–211.

Zürcher, E., 1989, Buddhismus in China, Korea und Vietnam, in: H. Bechert, and R. Gombrich. (eds), *Der Buddhismus. Geschichte und Gegenwart*, München: C. H. Beck, pp. 215–51.

4. War and Peace in Classical Chinese Thought,

with Particular Regard to Chinese Religion

GREGOR PAUL

War and Peace in Classical Chinese Thought: A General Overview

'War and peace' is a very broad topic, and designations like 'classical China', 'Chinese thought' and 'Chinese religion(s)' refer to more than 1,500 years of history (from about 1100 BCE through 900 CE) in areas that sometimes even exceeded the extension of the Chinese People's Republic. Also, such designations refer to large numbers of different philosophies and religions. This even applies, if one restricts – as I do – the reference of the term 'classical thought' to ideas generated between 1100 and 221 BCE, and to the history of these ideas. Accordingly, I cannot but limit my discussion to those classic theories and practices which I regard as particularly relevant or significant for the history of war and peace in China. By 'particularly relevant or significant' I mean theories and practices that, first, exemplify more or less general features of Chinese approaches to questions of war and peace, and second, were of great historical influence.

As to the first point, I hold that most theories and practices, especially most arguments and decisions in favour of peace, were determined by the following convictions:

1. war is utterly evil and ought only be resorted to if indeed unavoidable;

2. peace – and also order and welfare – is more important than realization of truth; and
3. (thisworldly) governmental power is the highest power that exists. In other words, there exists no power superior to governmental power, especially no transcendent power like a god.

I further hold that most arguments and decisions in favour of war were determined:

1. by the wish to gain, strengthen or defend (political) power;
2. by other personal motives as for instance feelings of revenge;
3. by the wish to topple an inhumane, or cruel, government;
4. by the wish to free oneself from an unbearable situation, as for instance the threat of starvation.

As to the second point, the question of historical impact, I hold that the theories and historical developments characterized by the listed features also proved most influential in Chinese history. What I have said so far could be considered the guiding hypotheses of my following deliberations. In providing examples and explanations, in discussing some possible counter-arguments to my views, and in speculating about possible consequences of the addressed Chinese theories and practices of war and peace, I try to substantiate these hypotheses, and – finally – to suggest some solutions to the problem of religious war.

Arguments and Decisions in Favour of Peace

The argument that war is utterly evil and ought only be resorted to if indeed unavoidable

Let me begin with the beginning, or at least with what was the beginning of explicit theory of war and peace. This was the attempt to justify the wars of the Zhou against the Shang which took place in the eleventh century BCE. The *Shijing*, 'The Classic of Songs', and the *Shujing*, 'The Classic of Documents', explain and justify these wars as the only means to do away with the cruel and despotic reign of the Shang, and they point out that such inhumane rule ought to be removed. On a general level, they argue that it is only humane government that receives, possesses, or can claim, *tianming*, the 'mandate of heaven'. In other words, this means that a government is legitimate then and only then when it is humane government. Of course, the word 'humane' needs qualification. I shall come back to this later on. People subjected to inhumane rule have the right, and are ultmately even obliged, to go against it. In the first instance, however, they ought to use peaceful means, especially criticism, to achieve a change. Only after having exhausted all peaceful means, are they allowed to resort to force. This notion of justified tyrannicide and revolution is also alluded to in the *Lunyu*, the 'Analects [of Confucius]'. It is then expressly formulated, and emphasized, in the other two Confucian classics *Mencius* and *Xunzi* which go back to the fourth and third centuries BCE respectively, and in many other so-called Confucian writings.[1]

However, what might be called the *tianming* theory of legitimate rule and revolution does not deal extensively, or in detail, with the horrors of war, though it leaves us in no doubt that war *must only be the last resort*. The *tianming* theory rather focuses on the question whether, and for which reasons, it is justified to use force against one's own ruler. I shall refer back to this topic later.

After the Zhou had toppled the Shang, they nominally reigned until 221 BCE, having already lost power in the eighth century BCE. Sovereign local states emerged that fought for supremacy. Eventually war became so ubiquitous, continuous and intense that the era from 475 to 221 BCE received the name *zhangguo*, 'Epoch of the Warring States'. It was scholars of this era who developed elaborate and detailed theories of war and peace. A certain group even became known as *bingjia*, 'School of War'. Its most famous representative, often mistakenly called its founder, was Sunzi (fifth century BCE), 'Master Sun'. Attributed to him is what is probably the most renowned and most influential treatise on war ever written, namely the *Sunzi bingfa*, 'Sunzi's Art of

---

[1] Cf. Paul 2001.

War'. This treatise influenced numerous Chinese scholars, politicians and military leaders, including Mao Zedong.[2]

What impresses me most with this treatise is, however, not its uncompromising advice regarding the question of how to wage and win a war, but its disgust for war. In other words, the *Sunzi bingfa* makes it very clear that war is utterly evil and should be avoided. But if a war must be waged, and if one wants to win the war, then one must not shrink from resorting to immoral means to succeed. To quote some crucial passages:

> If one is not fully cognizant of the evils of waging war, he cannot be fully cognizant either of how to turn it to best account.[3]

> To win a hundred victories in a hundred battles is not the highest excellence; the highest exellence is to subdue the enemy's army without fighting at all.[4]

> [But also:] Warfare is a way (*dao*) of deceit.[5]

Another Chinese treatise about war that also dates back to the Epoch of the Warring States, the *Sun Bin bingfa*, 'Sun Bin's Art of War', even states:

> Abhorrence of war is the highest military principle.[6]

> A distaste for war is the most basic principle of the True King.[7]

> Between heaven and earth there is nothing more valuable than man.[8]

> [This being the case:] You must go to war only if there is no alternative.[9]

---

[2] Cf. Griffith 1963a.
[3] Ames 1993, pp. 107–8.
[4] Ames 1993, p. 111.
[5] Ames 1993, p. 104.
[6] Following the translation in Yingjie 1994, p. 94.
[7] Ames 1993, p. 85.
[8] Following the translation in Yingjie 1994, p. 95.
[9] Ames 1993, p. 85.

These two treatises, and other writings of the *bingjia*,[10] indicate what might have been the basic Chinese attitude towards war until the beginnings of the twentieth century. Confronted with the situation of the Warring States, and realizing that it was probably impossible to completely do without war as a means of gaining and securing power, the *bingjia* in a certain sense were resigned to it. In order to minimize evils the *bingjia* developed theories that could at least reduce the interest in waging war as much as possible. Their views prevailed. Mohists and so-called Confucians put more emphasis on questions of morality, and argued that at least aggressive, offensive and invasive wars are unacceptable and must be avoided at all costs; unfortunately their arguments almost never played a *dominant* role in Chinese political history. Nevertheless, these arguments were much admired and perhaps best testify to the fact that traditional Chinese culture neither celebrated nor glorified war, and that in it, 'military heroism [was] a rather undeveloped idea'.[11]

In my view, greatest importance lies in the originality, rationality and validity of the Mohist and Confucian arguments. Mozi (468?–376? BCE) is credited with the following famous statement:

If a man kills an innocent man, steals his clothing and his spear and sword, his offence is graver than breaking into a stable and stealing an ox or a horse. The injury is greater, the offence is graver, and the crime of a higher degree. Any man of sense knows that it is wrong, knows that it is unrighteous. But when murder is committed in attacking a country it is not considered wrong; it is applauded and called righteous. Can this be considered as knowing what is righteous and what is unrighteous? When one man kills another man it is considered unrighteous and he is punished by death. Then by the same sign when a man kills ten others, his crime will be ten times greater, and should be punished by death ten times. . . . If a

---

[10] For respective lists and translations see Cleary 1989; Griffith 1963a, pp. 150–68, 184–6; Strätz 1979.

[11] Ames 1993, p. 40.

man calls black black if it is seen on a small scale, but calls
black white when it is seen on a large scale, then he is one who
cannot tell black from white . . . Similarly if a small crime is
considered crime, but a big crime such as attacking another
country is applauded as a righteous act, can this be said to be
knowing the difference between righteous and unrighteous?[12]

In this argument against war, Mozi appeals to logic, to common sense, general human experience, the general moral law
to respect human life, and he points to the unacceptability of
double standards. He also implicitly questions the idea of 'might
makes right'. This, and the honesty and verve of his views, make
his argument a very impressive plea for peace.

The *Xunzi*, attributed to the Confucian philosopher Xunzi
(313?–238? BCE), includes a chapter entitled 'Debate on the
Principles of Warfare'. Concurring with the *Mozi*, its main
point is that there must not be aggressive and invasive wars. 'In
the rule of a True King there are punitive expeditions but no
warfare.'[13] Arguing against the pragmatism of the *bingjia*, the
Xunzi tries to show that this pragmatism is not only inhumane
but also short-sighted. Even while at war or preparing for war,
in the long run, following principles of humaneness (*ren*) and
honesty (*xin*), would prove more efficient than trying to succeed
by means of deception, terror and fright, and paying soldiers the
highest prices.[14]

The argument that peace – and also order and welfare – is more important than realization of truth

The conviction that peace is more important than realization
of truth further strengthened the traditional Chinese aversion
to war. This conviction lies at the bottom of the philosophical
classics, and pervades most, if not all, of them, particularly the
so-called Confucian writings *Lunyu*, *Mencius* and *Xunzi*, the

---

[12] Griffith 1963a, p. 22.
[13] Knoblock 1988ff., vol. 2, p. 227.
[14] Cf. Knoblock 1988ff, vol. 2, pp. 211–34.

Mohist writings, the Daoist *Daode jing* and *Zhuangzi*, and the Legalist *Shangjun shu* and *Han Feizi*, the books of Lord Shang (390–338 BCE) and of Master Han Fei (280–233 BCE) respectively. While Pope Pius XII maintained that what is not true in religion has no objective right to exist,[15] I do not know of any similar statement from a Chinese scholar or religious leader. This is not to say that Chinese philosophers did not value, or that they even discarded, truth; however, their highest goal was not realization of truth but (except for the Legalists) realization of humaneness and welfare; and as everybody knows, humaneness and welfare are often more efficiently realized by, for example, telling or promoting lies than by conveying, insisting on or even enforcing, truth. Since Chinese philosophers regarded peace as an almost indispensable condition of humaneness and welfare, due to the experience of the Epoch of the Warring States, they had also to consider it more important than truth.

The Legalists followed the different aim of realizing ideas of centralized, absolute and totalitarian power. However, precisely because of this goal, they too regarded peace as top priority. The lesson the Legalists learned, or drew, from the Epoch of the Warring States was that a ruler or government must not permit of any contending opinions. According to their judgement, contending opinions lead to socio-political disunity and ultimately to war, and thus endanger the position of the ruler. Hence they argued for the enforcement of peace, though it might be the kind of peace called in German *Friedhofsruhe*, i.e., the peace of a graveyard.

Evidently, the classic Chinese views on peace and truth also worked against the force of religious truth.

The argument that governmental power is the highest power that exists

The argument that governmental power is the highest power that exists is closely related to the traditional Chinese interest in peace

---

[15] Cf. Lübbe 1986, p. 90.

(rather than truth). First of all, Chinese élites almost never believed in transcendent entities. In particular, they did not believe in mighty gods, or in an afterlife. Of course, there were exceptions, especially with regard to some followers of popular Daoist and Huang-Lao[16] religions, and certain Buddhist religions. I shall discuss them when I turn to the arguments and decisions in favour of war. The *Lunyu* takes an agnostic stand. It further demythologizes the concept of *tian* ('heaven'), which in some passages of the *Shijing* and *Shujing* is still used for referring to a kind of god. In the *Mencius*, the notion of *tian* still carries numinous connotations, but its numinosity does not indicate a transcendent entity, and in this sense remains unimportant. The *Xunzi* is expressly atheistic,[17] as are the Legalist *Shangjun shu* and *Han Feizi*. The Mohists maintained that there exist gods and ghosts, but they did this perhaps because of pragmatic considerations. In their view, morality ought to be based on, or at least supported by, a belief in a god, i.e., *tian*. However, it was the agnostic and atheistic line of thought that prevailed among the élites from Qin times (221–207 BCE) up to the twenty-first century of Communist China. Neither the average scholar-bureaucrat nor the average Communist cader believed, or believe, in a god who should or could be relied on, or in an afterlife. This might explain why the idea that in order to rule correctly, or to lead one's life correctly, one could, or even ought to, refer to an otherworldly instance, was at best regarded as awkward, and at worst as dangerous. For how could one refer to something that probably did not exist, or that if it existed could not be known, in order to decide what one ought do here and now? How could one refer to such a thing in order to go against one's own government or fellow beings and cause and justify strife and uprisings? The underlying argument was that reliance on transcendent entities would permit, and even promote, moral and political wantonness and wilfulness. Accordingly, from Qin times up to the present Communist China, with only few exceptions, Chinese government

---

[16] For information about the Huang-Lao religions, see Yates 1997.
[17] Cf. Paul 2001.

was secular; and whenever this secularity was seriously threatened by a religious movement, the state reacted by forcibly suppressing or at least containing this movement.

For example, it was mainly because the then rulers were afraid that Buddhism could become a state within the state that Buddhism was persecuted in 446, 557 and 845, though such fear was of course only one motive among others. The persecution of 446 (which took place in the empire of the Northern Wei, 386–534) was also caused by a Daoist official's ambition 'to make Daoism the supreme faith of the land', i.e., by what could be called a religious interest, and by the Confucian chancellor's xenophobia against the foreign Indian teaching.[18] But to realize their goals, these two officials had to convince their emperor that Buddhism posed a threat to (his) state power. The persecution of 574 occurred during the reign of the Northern Zhou (557–581), and besides the question of political power, controversies between Daoism and Buddhism, and a certain xenophobia, were again instrumental in bringing it about. The emperor's respective decree, however, did not only proscribe Buddhism, but also Daoism.[19] While the persecutions of 446 and 557 were limited to the northern parts of the Chinese world, the third persecution affected the whole Chinese realm, and marked the 'beginning of the decline' of Buddhist influence on state power. For the Tang dynasty (618–907), the persecution was also a means to improve its desperate economic situation.[20]

Arguments and Decisions in Favour of War

War as a means to gain, strengthen or defend (political) power, especially state power

This leads me to the arguments and decisions in favour of war. In China, as probably always and everywhere, each war was

---

[18] Cf. Ch'en 1972, pp. 147–51.
[19] Cf. Ch'en 1972, pp. 184–94.
[20] Cf. Ch'en 1972, pp. 226–33, and *The Cambridge History of China*, vol. 3, pp. 666–9.

a struggle for power, notwithstanding other reasons and aims.
The most significant examples of wars mainly fought because of
what could aptly be called a 'lust for power' were: the wars of
the Warring States, particularly the wars led by the state of Qin
and the unifier and First Emperor of China, Qin Shihuang Di
(?–210 BCE); the aggressive and expansive wars led by Han Wu Di
(157–87 BCE), the 'martial emperor' of the Han; the wars at the
end of the Han dynasty (206 BCE–220 CE); and finally the civil
wars in the twentieth century. As indicated, a number of wars
were also motivated by the aim to strengthen, or defend, state
power, particularly the campaigns against religious movements.

I have already mentioned the forcible suppression of Buddhism. The state had indeed reason to fear the Buddhist order. Its
members owned huge territories, had accumulated much wealth,
and did not pay taxes. Hence, the Buddhist order continuously
attracted more and more people. Contrary to the 'Confucian'
minded scholar-officials, many Buddhists believed in its religious
rather than its philosophical traditions and teachings – in gods,
in simple notions of *karma* and rebirth, in an afterlife in Buddhist
paradises, and so on. Accordingly, some Buddhists were indeed
inclined to give priority to Buddhist norms, and reliance on
Buddhist supernatural beings, over earthly (thisworldly) government. Some of the most illustrative examples of state campaigns
against religious movements, motivated by the fear that its
power was threatened by anti-secular interests and tendencies,
are provided by the history of so-called Daoist or, perhaps more
precisely, Huang-Dao sects, especially the Yellow Turban, the
Five Pecks of Grain, and the Tai Ping movements.

The Yellow Turbans and the Five Pecks of Grain sects developed during the turmoils of the last decades of the Han dynasty
(206 BCE–220 CE). The two sects' rebellions, and the civil wars
they caused, were among the forces that led to the dynasty's
final downfall. Both religious movements shared similar beliefs,
but probably developed independently from each other. Both
believed in a deified Laozi[21] and both were convinced that illness

---

[21] For the deification of Laozi cf. Seidel 1969, and Yates 1997, p. 11.

resulted from sins. To secure or regain one's health, one had to publicly confess one's evil doings and do good deeds. Also, the leading figures were thought to possess magical powers. Among other things, both teachings relied on respective scriptures which were regarded as heavenly revelations. The Yellow Turbans further believed that with the start of the new calendaric cycle of 60 years in the year 184, the Han dynasty would come to an end. According to the Yellow Turbans' understanding of the traditional 'five elements' theory the rule of the wood element and of 'green heaven' (which they associated with the Han) would be overcome by the power of the earth element and 'yellow heaven'. Hence the adherents of the sect wore yellow turbans. The generally influential notion of the 'mandate of heaven' (*tianming*), a notion of legitimate government and its due changes, also contributed to the conviction that the Han government should be ousted; for it was – rightly – blamed for the political turmoils, the unsecurity, and the dire needs of large portions of the people, especially the peasants. The highest leader of the Yellow Turbans, Zhang Jie (second half of the second century), styled himself 'General of Heaven'. In sum, it was belief in otherwordly, or supernatural, beings and powers; numerology; the doctrines of the Five Elements (*wuxing*); the notion of *tianming*; and dissatisfaction with, and suffering from, the sociopolitical situation that led the Yellow Turbans into rebellion and civil war. Calling their teaching *taiping dao*, the 'Way of Great Peace', their leaders promised to bring peace and welfare back to the people. However, by about 205, the Yellow Turbans were defeated in brutal warfare. Nevertheless, it testifies to the enduring influence of the Yellow Turbans' aims that, in the nineteenth century, the *taiping* revolutionaries adopted the name and goal of 'Great Peace'.[22]

While the Yellow Turbans were active in eastern China, particularly the area that finally became Shandong, the Five Pecks

---

[22] For more information about the Yellow Turbans cf. *The Cambridge History of China*, vol. 1, pp. 338–9, 366–9, 801f., 814–20, and 874–6. For the Five Pecks of Grain sect, see Bokenkamp 1997.

of Grain sect (*wudou midao*) was active in western China, particularly the area of Sichuan. Its popular name is derived from the sect's prescription that its members had to donate a certain amount of grain to the community each year. The sect had named itself *Tianshi Dao*, 'Way of the Master of Heaven', and its leader was called 'Master of Heaven'. The general reasons for the development of the movement and for its rebellion against the Han were the same as in the case of the Yellow Turbans. The movement succeeded in establishing its own state (within the state), though in 215 it surrendered to the warlord Cao Cao (died 220), the actual founder of the Wei dynasty (220–265) and the man who wrote the most famous commentary of the *Sunzi bingfa*. The 'Way of the Master of Heaven' still exists, with its present 'Master' residing in Taiwan.

War as a means to realize personal interests such as feelings of revenge

As commonly known, and once more confirmed from what I have said thus far about war in Chinese civilization, reasons for initiating and waging war are numerous and complex. In some cases, even thirst for personal revenge plays a role. Accordingly, theories on war also have to account for this possibility. Even *bingjia* treatises advise military leaders to treat their enemies and prisoners as humanely as possible, rather than harbouring hate and plans of revenge, so as to win them over. The Confucian *Xunzi* emphasizes this approach. However, there is also what could be called a classic theorem that warns against showing too much humaneness and leniency towards a defeated enemy. As I see it, this theorem goes back to Wu Zixu (–485 BCE), an adviser of Fu Chai, the king of the state of Wu. After Fu Chai had defeated and taken the king of the neighbouring state Yue prisoner, Wu Zixu warned his king against treating his enemy too friendly. However, his warning was dismissed, Wu Zixu rebuked and finally forced to commit suicide. The defeated king feigned thankfulness and even devotion to his successful rival, while harbouring ideas of revenge. Eventually, on his release, he returned to his own country, and later used the first opportunity to take revenge, completely destroying the state of Wu, and driving Fu Chai into committing suicide.[23]

War as a means, and just instrument, to topple an inhumane, or cruel, government

As indicated, until today there has existed only one Chinese theory justifying war that was rarely disputed, namely the *tianming* theory of justified tyrannicide, revolution and civil war.[24] To be sure, some emperors, officials and scholars argued in favour of absolute, totalitarian power and absolute, blind loyalty. In their view, people should serve their superiors by what in German is called *Kadavergehorsam*, i.e., 'obedience of a corpse', unconditional and slavish obedience, but this was certainly not the classic position. Even the Legalists argued against such kind of total submission, pointing out that, in some circumstances, a ruler ought to permit honest criticism.

In its very early stages the *tianming* doctrine implied reference to 'Heaven' (*tian*) as a personal deity, but by about 500 BCE at the latest, *tianming* had become a designation for something like universally valid moral rules.[25] To be granted, and be in possession of, the 'mandate of heaven' (*tianming*), meant to rule humanely and justly, and thus legitimately. This applied independently from whether *tian* was understood as referring to a (personal) deity, or whether it was taken as a metaphorical reference to universally valid moral norms. In the first case, to be in possession of the heavenly mandate implied acceptance and execution of a divine decree. In the second case, it meant that a sovereign or government possessed the superior moral integrity and political capability that was regarded as necessary and sufficient for humane and just rulership. The *Xunzi* sums this up by stating: 'Whether a man is a son of heaven (*tianzi*) solely depends

---

[23] Cf. Paul 1990, pp. 67–8.
[24] Cf. Paul 2001.
[25] Cf. Paul 1990, Paul 2001 and Pines 2002.

on what kind of man he is (i.e., depends on his character and abilities).'[26]

By 'humane and just government', the *Lunyu*, *Mencius* and *Xunzi* implied a government that cared for its people, e.g. protecting their lives, providing them with sufficient food and water, and protecting them from humiliation, cruelty and other kinds of suffering. To achieve this, peace was considered a necessary condition. To realize peace, in turn, stable hierarchical social order was regarded as a necessary prerequisite. The *Xunzi* puts forward an eleborate theory of such an order. It says that each person's place in society and state should be determined by his or her integrity and ability, thus arguing for a strict and just application of principles of merit. To prevent or minimize dissatisfaction and resulting unrest, the *Xunzi* demands that the privileged, especially the sovereign and the officials, live exemplary lifes. Also, to further secure stable hierarchical order, the *Xunzi* advocates education, self-cultivation and – perhaps most importantly – an aesthetics of morality, that is a transformation of morality from pure duty into a personal preference.

Summing up, according to *Lunyu*, *Mencius* and *Xunzi*, humane and just government presuppose peace, which in turn requires stable hierarchical order. Thus, the *Lunyu*, *Mencius* and *Xunzi* include a theory of peace which amounts to a theory of hierarchical social order. Except for Daoism, all classical Chinese schools of thought shared the conviction that peace presupposed stable hierarchical order. One should be aware of this, if one tries to understand Chinese rulers' and governments' abhorrence of socio-political disorder, their respective mistrust, and their often harsh suppression of those movements which in their view are potential sources of unrest. As indicated, the Legalists went much further than the so-called Confucians, advocating a kind of order that could be compared to the peace of graveyards. More recent events like the Tiananmen massacre in June 1989, and the ban on the Falun Gong sect, must also be judged in the context of the classic Chinese theories of peace and social order.

---

[26] *Xunzi* 18, Zhenglun, 'Rectifications'.

As stated above, the *tianming* doctrine not only justified, but even demanded tyrannicide, rebellion and civil war, if there were no other means for changing cruel, inhumane politics. By logical inversion, this implied that such violence must not be used against a sovereign or government who defended hierarchical order. Thus, in Chinese thought, an egalitarian society was almost never honestly regarded as a legitimate political goal. It was rather viewed as a notion, and source, of possible sociopolitical instability and, ultimately, civil war. It is not easy to criticize this position, for the utopia of an egalitarian and stateless society cannot be realized. Societies need organization, and organization implies an unequal distribution of power.

War as a means, and just instrument, to free oneself from an unbearable situation, as for instance the threat of starvation

Perhaps the classical Chinese doctrines of order as a necessary prerequisite for peace contributed to the longer phases of relative domestic peace that the Chinese enjoyed during the first halves of the Han, Tang (618–709), Song (960–1279) and Qing (1644–1911) dynasties. But doubtlessly these phases were also times of rather strict social order, and like other epochs in Chinese history not completely free from social upheavals, especially peasant uprisings. As indicated, the Yellow Turbans and Five Pecks of Grain sect rebellions were, among other things, also peasant uprisings. Among the Chinese people, the peasants suffered most in Chinese history. Often, they had to pay enormous taxes, and were repeatedly recruited into forced labour and military service. On the brink of starvation, they had to sell themselves or their children to great landowners or rich nobles. As a matter of consequence, intelligent rebels found in the peasants willing instruments to realize their schemes of civil war. To justify their goal to topple a ruler or government, they, too, could conveniently resort to the *tianming* doctrine, and often did, though sometimes overstreching it.[27]

---

[27] For a history of peasant uprisings in China, see Franke 2001.

Classical Chinese Summaries of Theories on War and Peace

Chinese thinkers were well aware that one should distinguish between different kinds of war and peace. As indicated, the widely acknowledged and most fundamental distinction was that between unrighteous and righteous war (*yibing*), although opinions differed as to what ought be regarded as 'righteous'. Also, except for the Daoists, Chinese thinkers were convinced that to avoid war, hierarchical socio-political order must be upheld, though how such an order was understood differed too. Most important perhaps were disagreements regarding the acceptability of aggressive war and totalitarian order. Whereas the so-called Confucians and the Mohists rejected aggressive war, the *bingjia* and the Legalists, but also some syncretist schools, approved of certain kinds of it. While the Confucians advocated an *aesthetical and harmonious* order, the Legalists especially favoured strict, if not totalitarian, order.

To quote two systematic summaries, I cite from the *Wuzi bingfa*, 'Wuzi's' (430?–381 BCE) 'Art of War', another outstanding *bingjia* treatise, and from a Huang Lao text (from the third or fourth century BCE?).

> There are five matters which give rise to military operations. First, the struggle for fame; second, the struggle for advantage; third, the accumulation of animosity; fourth, internal disorder; and fifth, famine.
>
> There are also five categories of war. First, righteous war (yibing); second, aggressive war; third, enraged war; fourth, wanton war; and fifth, insurgent war. Wars to suppress violence and quell disorder are righteous. Those which depend on force are aggressive. When troops are raised because rulers are actuated by anger, this is enraged war. Those in which all propriety is discarded because of greed are wanton wars. Those who, when the state is in disorder and the people exhausted, stir up trouble and agitate the multitude, cause insurgent wars.
>
> There is a suitable method for dealing with each: a righteous

war must be forestalled by proper government; an aggressive war by humbling one's self; an enraged war by reason; a wanton war by deception and treachery; and an insurgent war by authority.[28]

The Dao of warfare [*bingdao*] of the present generation are three: there are those who act for profit; those who act out of righteousness [*yi*]; and those who act out of anger.[29]

Some *bingjia* thinkers also provided an anthropological explanation for war. They pointed out that war is but a particular kind of *natural* aggression, contest, strife and struggle, and thus inevitable. In other words, they considered war *a function of human nature*, and they regarded it as justified, or even righteous (*yibing*), if it, generally speaking, increased humaneness, did away with socio-political disorder, or punished evil-doers, thus at least implicitly justifying aggressive war too. The *Sun Bin bingfa*, for example, voiced these convictions.[30] Other classics, especially the *Lüshi chunqiu*, 'The Spring and Autumn [Annals] of Lü Buwei [third century BCE]', and the *Huai Nan Zi*, '[The Book] of the Lord of Huai Nan [second century BCE]', reiterated and stressed such views.[31] Their statements, made from a mainly *bingjia*, Legalist and perhaps Huang Lao perspective, but not completely neglecting the Mohist and Confucian positions, also constitute a kind of historical sum total of the classical discourses, and hence deserve extensive quotation.

The sage kings of old used their warriors for righteous purposes, but did not abolish the warrior class. The origins of the warrior class are deeply rooted in the nature of man. There have been warriors since there have been men . . . The art of war cannot be abolished, and armament cannot be terminated . . .

---

[28] Griffith 1963a, p. 153.
[29] *Jing*, 'The Canon'. Yates 1997, 141.
[30] Cf. Gawlikowski, p. 451.
[31] *Lüshi chunqiu*, e.g., 7:2, and 8:4. See also Wilhelm 1979, pp. 82–100. *Huai Nan Zi*, chapters 15 and 19. See Morgan 1966.

Gregor Paul

The beginnings of fight date far back. Fight cannot be forbidden nor (can it be) precluded. Hence, the sage kings of old used their warriors for righteous purposes, but did not abolish the warrior class . . .

When, in a state, there is neither punishment nor penance, it becomes clear right away that the people oppress and cheat each other. When, in the world, there is neither war nor punitive expeditions, it becomes clear right away that the feudal lords (the rulers of the different states in the world) threaten each other. . . .

(Sometimes) it happens that people are suffocated by eating. But, because of this, to forbid eating, would be foolish . . . (Sometimes) it happens that rulers lose their states because of their use of warriors. But, because of this, to abolish the warrior class, would be foolish . . .

It is similar to the use of medicine. Good medicine saves human life. Bad medicine kills human life. Also, the military, when used for righteous purposes, is good medicine . . .

There is no single moment in which man is free from thinking about war . . . Those persons who nowadays noisily speak of abolishing the military use their whole life to fight the military, without being aware of their self-contradiction . . . Hence, about a truly righteous war that destroys the oppressors and frees the oppressed peoples, man are happy . . .[32]

For everybody who wants to become the leader of men, the most important task is to honour those who keep order, to eliminate (or deprive of their power?) those who create disorder, to reward those who fulfil their obligations, and to punish those who do not fulfil their obligations.

Among the scholars of today, disapproval of aggressive war is widespread. Whereas they disapprove of aggressive war, they approve of defensive war. However, were one to restrict oneself to defensive war, it would be impossible to consistently honour those who keep order, to eliminate (or deprive of

---

[32] *Lüshi chunqiu* 7:2. Following the German translation in Wilhelm 1979, pp. 82–4.

their power?) those who create disorder, to reward those who fulfil their obligations, and to punish those who do not fulfil their obligations. . . .

The weal and woe of the rulers and peoples on earth depends on understanding these words.[33]

Weapons are the instruments of unhappiness . . . , braveness is the disastrous virtue . . . To use the instruments of unhappiness and to execute the disastrous virtue, (this) needs a reason which excludes that one can act differently. When using the instruments of unhappiness, one must kill. But one ought to kill (only) to save the lives of many men . . .[34]

Concluding Thoughts on War, Peace and Religion

As I have tried to show, in China, religious beliefs or religious zeal were never, or almost never, decisive, when it came to the question of war and peace. In more than 3,000 years of Chinese history, there have been no religious wars comparable to those that have occurred in Jewish, Muslim, Christian and Hindu history. In particular, there were no aggressive, or missionary, religious wars. Of course, since reasons for wars are numerous and complex, religious motives sometimes played a role in Chinese civil wars, in uprisings and persecutions. In particular, they were among the causes that led to the rebellions of the so-called Daoist and Huang Lao sects, though dissatisfaction with socio-political conditions for example was certainly a more important cause. The main reasons for the insignificance of religious thought in classical Chinese attitudes to war and peace are the convictions that, first, peace is more important than realizing truth, and that, second, the state, or government, power must be supreme, and, as matter of consequence, it must also rule over religious interest and influence. In other words, according to classic Chinese

---

[33] *Lüshi chunqiu* 7:3. Following the German translation in Wilhelm 1979, pp. 85.

[34] *Lüshi chunqiu* 8:2. Following the German translation in Wilhelm 1979, pp. 95.

thought, supreme power must be secular. The basic conviction that men should resort to war only if, third, they ought to
do away with a cruel, inhumane rule, and if, fourth, they had
already exhausted all possible peaceful means for achieving this
goal, further reduced the possibility for religious war. In Chinese
history, religious freedom has always been restricted – as it is
actually also the case in the so-called Western democracies of the
twenty-first century.[35] One could even say, that not later than
from Tang times onwards, religious communities were subjected
to an institutionalized legal code, contrary to the 'Confucian'
suspicion against the notion of a rule by law.

SELECT BIBLIOGRAPHY

Ames, R. T., 1983, *The Art of Rulership: A Study in Ancient Chinese Politi-
cal Thought*, Honolulu: University of Hawaii Press.
Ames, R. T. (trans.), 1993, *Sun-Tzu: The Art of Warfare*, New York: Ballan-
tine Books.
Blakney, R. B. and Lin, Yu-tang, 1971, *The Sayings of Lao Tzu*, Taipei:
Confucius Publishing Co.
Bokenkamp, S. R., 1997, *Early Daoist Scriptures*, Berkeley: University of
California Press.
Brooks, E. B. and Brooks, A. T., 1998, *The Original Analects: Sayings of
Confucius and his Successors*, New York: Columbia University Press.
Ch'en, K., 1972, *Buddhism in China: A Historical Survey*, Princeton: Prince-
ton University Press.
Cleary, T. (ed. and trans.), 1989, *Mastering the Art of War: Zhuge Liang's
and Liu Ji's commentaries on the classic by Sun Tzu*, Boston and London:
Shambala, .
Crump, J. I. (trans.), 1996, *'Intrigues of the Warring States.' Chan-kuo
Ts'e*, trans. and annotated and with an Introduction by J. I. Crump,
revised edn, Ann Arbor: The University of Michigan.
Dubs, H., 1973, *The Works of Hsuntze*, Taipei: Confucius Publishing Co.
Duyvendak, J. J. L., 1974, *The Book of Lord Shang*, San Francisco: Chinese
Materials Center.
Franke, O., 2001, *Geschichte des chinesischen Reiches*, 5 vols., 2nd edn,
Berlin and New York: De Gruyter.

---

[35] For example, no democracy permits believers who are convinced that
they must spread their religion by force to do this.

Gawlikowski, K., 1990, Drei Ansätze des klassischen chinesischen Denkens zu den Themen Krieg und Kampf, in: Silke Krieger and Rolf Trauzettel (eds), *Konfuzianismus und die Modernisierung Chinas*, Mainz: Hase & Koehler, pp. 451–8.

Graham, A. C., 1981, *Chuang Tzu: The Inner Chapters*, London: George Allen.

Graham, A. C., 1978, *Later Mohist Logic, Ethics and Science*, Hong Kong: The Chinese University Press.

Griffith, S. B. (trans. and comm.), 1963a, *Sun Tzu: The Art of War*, Oxford: Oxford University Press.

Griffith, S. B. (trans. and comm.), 1963b, Wuzi's 'Art of War', in: Samuel B. Griffith (trans. and comm.), *Sun Tzu: The Art of War*, Oxford: Oxford University Press, pp. 150–68.

Kaltenmark, M., 1979, The Ideology of the T'ai-p'ing ching, in: Holmes Welch and Anna Seidel (eds), *Facets of Taoism: Essays in Chinese Religion*, New Haven: Yale University Press, pp. 19–52.

Knoblock, John, 1988, *Xunzi. A Translation and Study of the Complete Works*, 3 vols. Stanford: Stanford University Press.

Lau, D. C., 1970, *Mencius*, Harmondsworth: Penguin Classics.

Lau, D. C., 1992, *Confucius: The Analects*, Hong Kong: The Chinese University Press.

Lau, D. C. and Ames, Roger T., 1996, *Sun Pin: The Art of Warfare. A Recently Discovered Classic*, trans, with an Introduction and Commentary by D. C. Lau and Roger T. Ames, New York: Ballantine Books.

Le Blanc, Charles, 1985, *Huai Nan Tzu [Zi]: Philosophical Synthesis in Early Han Thought*, Hong Kong: Hong Kong University Press.

Leary, T. (trans.), 1992, *The Book of Leadership and Strategy: Lessons of the Chinese Masters from Huai-Nan*, Shambala Publications.

Legge, J., 1983a, *Confucian Analects: The Chinese Classics, Vol. I*, Taipei: SMC Reprint.

Legge, J. 1983b, *The Works of Mencius. The Chinese Classics, Vol. II*, Taipei: SMC Reprint.

Legge, J., 1983c, *The Shoo King. The Chinese Classics. Vol. III*, Taipei: SMC Reprint.

Legge, J., 1983d, *The She King or The Book of Poetry: The Chinese Classics, Vol. IV*, Taipei: SMC Reprint.

Liao, K., 1959, *Han Fei-tzu*, 2 vols, London: Arthur Probsthain.

Lübbe, H., 1986, *Religion nach der Aufklärung*, Graz, Wien: Köln.

Mei, Yi-pao, 1977, *The Works of Motze*, Taipei: Confucius Publishing Co.

Morgan, Evan, 1966, *Tao, the Great Luminant: Essays from the Huai-nantzu*, Shanghai: Kelly and Walsh, 1933. Taipei reprint: Ch'eng-wen Publishing Co. (with translations of Huai Nan Zi 1, 2, 7, 8, 12, 13, 15 and 19).

Paul, G., 1990, *Aspects of Confucianism*, Frankfurt am Main and New York: Lang.

Paul, G., 2001, *Konfuzius*, Freiburg: Herder.

Pines, Yuri, 2002, *Foundations of Confucian Thought: Intellectual Life in the Chunqiu Period, 722–453* BCE, Honolulu: University of Hawaii Press.

Roberts, M. (trans.), 1994, *'Three Kingdoms.' A Historical Novel. Attributed to Luo Guangzhong*, trans. from the Chinese with Afterword and Notes by Moss Roberts, 3 vols, Beijing: Foreign Languages Press.

Seidel, A. K., 1969, *La Divinisation de Lao Tseu dans le Taoisme de Han*, Publications de l' École Française d'Extrême-Orient, vol. 71, Paris: École Française d'Extrême-Orient.

Shapiro, S. (trans.), 1980, *'Outlaws of the Marsh' by Shi Nai'an and Luo Guanzhong*, 3 vols, Beijing: Foreign Languages Press.

Strätz, V., 1979, *Luh-T'ao: Ein spätantiker Text zur Kriegskunst*, Bad Honnef: Bock + Herchen.

The Cambridge History of China, Vol. 1, 1987, Cambridge University Press.

The Cambridge History of China, Vol. 3, 1989, Cambridge University Press.

Waley, A., 1938, *The Analects of Confucius*, New York: Random House.

Ware, J. R., 1971, *The Sayings of Chuang Tzu*, Taipei: Confucius Publishing Co.

Wilhelm, R., 1979, *Frühling und Herbst des Lü Bu Wei*, Aus dem Chinesischen übertragen und herausgegeben von Richard Wilhelm, Düsseldorf, Köln: Diederichs.

Yates, R. D. S. (trans.), 1997, *Five Lost Classics: Tao, Huang-Lao, and Yin-Yang in Han-China*, trans., with an Introduction and Commentary by Robin D. S. Yates, New York: Ballentine Books.

Yingjie, Zhong (trans.), 1994, *Sun Zi über die Kriegskunst*, trans. into German by Zhong Yingjie, Beijing: Verlag Volkschina.

Zhizhong Gu (trans.), 1992, *Feng shen yan yi. 'Creations of the Gods'*, 2 vols, Beijing: New World Press.

Part II

War and Peace in the Abrahamic Religions

5. War and Peace in Judaism

DAN COHN-SHERBOK

A Challenging Interview

When I was a rabbinical student at the Hebrew Union College in Cincinnati, Ohio – the main seminary of the Reform movement – I had a perplexing interview with the Dean and others concerning war and peace in Judaism. During my second year all students in my class were required to register with the military chaplaincy. This was in preparation for graduation when those of us who had not married would be required to enter one of the branches of the armed services. The Vietnam War was in progress and there was thus a constant need for chaplains.

Those who had families were exempt – this was a major inducement to find a wife. I refused to go along with this scheme. I had no intention of serving in the army, and I also had deep reservations about the efficacy of armed conflict. I wanted no part of it. To the astonishment of the seminary authorities, I declared that I wished to be registered as a conscientious objector.

In the history of the seminary, no one had made such a protest. I was summoned to see the Dean. When I entered his office, I discovered that he had assembled there an array of professors from the seminary as well as rabbis affiliated with the military. This panel was seated in comfortable armchairs in a semi-circle. I was told to sit on a stiff chair in front of them.

'We've had your request,' the Dean began. 'And quite frankly, we are puzzled. You say that you wish to have conscientious objector status. And you state that you want to have nothing to do with the armed services.'

'Yes,' I said meekly.

'We are interested in your reasons.'

I swallowed. This, I perceived, was not going to be a pleasant interview. My interrogators stared at me. 'You see,' I stammered, 'I am against war.'

'So are we,' the Dean sneered.

'Yes, but Judaism says that peace is all-important. That's what the prophets declared. The Bible prophesies peace for all nations. You know, "the lion will lie down with the lamb", and all that.'

'I don't think you need to fill us in on the Bible,' Dr Smirnoff said. He was my Bible teacher. 'Dare I say all of us know the Bible a bit better than you. What we are curious to learn is why you, as a rabbinic student, think you can stand out against everyone else.'

'I'm a pacifist!' I blurted out.

'Ah a pacifist,' Dr Roth, the Jewish philosophy professor announced. 'I am pleased to make the acquaintance of a real-life pacifist. It isn't often that we have one of these exotic creatures here in the college. So, permit me to ask you, just why you are a pacifist?'

'Because I don't think war ever solves any problems.'

'You think it just makes things worse?' he asked.

'Yeah, I do.'

'Force is always wrong, then? Never right.'

'Well, yes, I suppose so. Certainly military force is.'

'Let's take a little example, then.' Stroking his moustache, he grinned. 'Let's imagine that you were at home with your mother. And you heard a terrible noise. And there was the sound of breaking glass. There in front of you stood a known murderer, holding a large axe. He then grabbed your mother and threatened to rape her. Would you stand by and let him get on with it?'

'I can't imagine there would be much else I could do', I said.

'But let's say you had a little revolver in your pocket. Would you use it?' he persisted.

'I'd try and reason with him.'

'Good. Good. Reason with a mad, axe-wielding rapist! What if he refused to listen?'

'I'd reason more loudly,' I objected.

I shifted uneasily. Things were not going well. And it was not surprising that this was so. I had not seriously considered the place of warfare in scripture, nor was I aware of the rabbinic tradition concerning war and peace. Judaism is not a pacifist tradition. As I will illustrate in this chapter, Judaism contains a moral licence which permits war despite the recognition that peace is the ethical ideal.

The Biblical and Rabbinic Tradition on War

Unfortunately I had not prepared sufficiently for my interview with the Dean – I had failed to reflect critically on the role of warfare in the history of the ancient Israelites. If I had, I would have observed that the Bible is full of gory detail about battles between the Israelites and their neighbours. War, however, was not perceived as the ideal solution to political conflict: steps were frequently taken to avoid military engagement. It was a common practice for negotiations to be carried out by messengers or ambassadors in order to avert conflict.[1] In addition, the ancient Israelites were forbidden to make an attack without first demanding the surrender of the enemy. This stipulation was stated explicitly in the Book of Deuteronomy (Deut. 20.10–14):

> When you draw near to a city to fight against it, offer terms of peace to it. And if its answer to you is peace and it opens to you, then all the people who are found in it shall do forced labour for you and shall serve you. But if it makes no peace with you, but makes war against you, then you shall besiege it; and when the LORD your God gives it into your hand you shall put all its males to the sword, but the women and the little ones, the cattle and everything else in the city, all its spoil, you shall take as booty for yourselves.

When war did take place, divine assistance was sought. In the

---

[1] Judg. 11.12–28; 1 Sam. 11.1–10; 1 Kings 20.2–11.

Book of Judges, for example, the Israelites turned to God before engaging in battle:

> The people of Israel arose and went up to Bethel, and inquired of God 'Which of us shall go up first to battle against the Benjaminites?' And the LORD said, 'Judah shall go up first.' . . . and the people of Israel went up and wept before the Lord until the evening; and they inquired of the LORD, 'Shall we again draw near to battle against our brethren the Benjaminites?' And the LORD said, 'Go up against them.'[2]

In these passages the manner of such consultation is not clarified, yet from other texts it appears that the priest put on the ephod and stood before the Ark to consult the Urim and Thummim.[3] In some cases consultation took place through dreams or prophets, or even through spirits evoked by a witch.[4] Of course, it is difficult today to envisage Jewish leaders participating in such activities. Imagine the Chief Rabbi or Rabbi Lionel Blue using the Urim and Thummim to determine whether American and British troops should be sent into battle against Iraq. Or Rabbi Julia Neuberger consulting witches to ascertain God's will. Nonetheless, these practices appear to have been common in ancient Israel.

Scripture relates that troops were usually summoned by blowing the shofar – this was a signal that also warned the people of an enemy's approach.[5] At times banners were placed on the tops of mountains or messengers were sent through the different tribes of Israel.[6] On some occasions extraordinary means were used to evoke hostility against enemies, such as the case of the Levite who cut the body of his concubine into 12 parts and sent them to the other tribes of Israel, thereby provoking anger between them and the Benjaminites. The resulting war led to the destruction of

---

[2] Judg. 20.18, 23.
[3] A device for telling oracles. Judg. 20.27–8; 1 Sam. 14.18; 28.6; 30.7.
[4] Judg. 7.13; 1 Sam. 28.6; 1 Kings 22.15.
[5] Judg. 3.27; 2 Sam. 20.1.
[6] Judg. 7.24; 1 Sam. 11.7; Isa. 13.2.

the Benjaminite tribe.[7] Again, it is difficult to conceive of modern Israeli leaders, such as Ariel Sharon or Shimon Peres, sending pieces of their mistresses in DHL packages to Hamas and Islamic Jihad to enrage them against Israel! But it did happen in ancient times.

It is important to note that when the Israelites went out to battle they were always accompanied by a priest; his duty was to care for the spiritual welfare of the soldiers. In addition, before the attack he encouraged them and inspired their enthusiasm, as the Book of Deuteronomy relates:

> And when you draw near to the battle, the priest shall come forward and speak to the people, and shall say to them, 'Hear, O Israel, you draw near this day to battle against your enemies: let not your heart faint; do not fear, or tremble, or be in dread of them; for the LORD your God is he that goes with you, to fight for you against your enemies, to give you the victory.'[8]

At times the High Priest went into battle accompanying the Ark which was carried into action. This practice was paralleled by the Philistines' determination to carry idols into battle.[9] Like other Semitic peoples, the Israelites commenced a war with burnt offerings and fasting.[10] In this way they sought to sanctify war.

As far as tactics were concerned, the Bible reports that the usual mode of warfare involved a raid against enemy troops. In the course of time, however, regular battles were fought involving sophisticated tactics. The first instance of such a battle took place in Gibeah between the tribes of Israel and the Benjaminites.[11] After the Israelites laid siege to the city, they pretended to flee from the Benjaminites, thereby enticing them from their fortified positions. The Israelites then surrounded them. It is also probable in the battle of Gilboa between the Philistines and Saul's

---

[7] Judg. 19.29.
[8] Deut. 20.2–4.
[9] 1 Sam. 4.3–4; 2 Sam. 5.21; 11.11.
[10] Judg. 6.20, 26; 20.26; 1 Sam. 7.9; 13.10.
[11] Judg. 20.30ff.

army, the Philistines went northwards at the plain of Esdraelon instead of attacking the Israelites by the shorter route from the south-west. In this way they lured Saul's troops from the valleys to the open plain where they were overcome by force of numbers.[12] On other occasions a strong army was sometimes divided so that the enemy might be attacked from different directions.[13] Night marches were sometimes used as well.[14] All this is reminiscent of contemporary military strategy.

To defend themselves from incursion, both the ancient Israelites and their enemies protected themselves by building fortresses. The chief method of conquering a fortified town was to throw up a bank around the walls from which archers could shoot arrows. Scripture records that the Syrians used engines in their effort to reduce Samaria, and similar machines were employed as battering-rams. Some sieges took a significant length of time, as in the case of the Babylonian conquest of Jerusalem which took two years despite Nebuchadnezzar's systematic onslaught.[15]

In their sieges the Hebrews were forbidden to fell fruit-trees for use in building bulwarks against fortified cities, as the Book of Deuteronomy relates:

> When you besiege a city for a long time, making war against it in order to take it, you shall not destroy its trees by wielding an axe against them; for you may eat of them, but you shall not cut them down. Are the trees in the field men that they should be besieged by you? Only the trees which you know are not trees for food you may destroy and cut down that you may build siegeworks against the city that makes war with you, until it falls.[16]

Such ecological considerations are of considerable significance. Clearly, the ancient Israelites were sensitive to the destructive consequences of military conflict, and took steps to protect the land.

---

[12] 1 Sam. 28.1–31.7.
[13] Gen. 14.15; 2 Sam. 18.2.
[14] Josh. 10.9; Judg. 7.19; 1 Sam. 11.11.
[15] 2 Kings 25.1–4.
[16] Deut. 20.19–20.

Regarding captives, the Bible illustrates that conquered peoples were reduced to captivity and their property taken as spoils. In the case of the Shechemites, however, all the males were massacred by the sons of Jacob, while the women and children and all their possessions were carried off.[17] In Deuteronomy 20.10–17, a distinction was drawn between the inhabitants of the land whom they were to replace and the Gentiles outside the land who were to be treated more leniently in case they were prepared to surrender without fighting and pay tribute. But if they were conquered by force of arms, every man was to be slain, while the women, children and cattle were to belong to the victors. Such treatment was far different from the inhabitants of the land who were to be slaughtered. Yet such harsh measures were not invariably followed.[18] In the later period, however, gross cruelty was practised by both the Israelites and other nations.

We can see, therefore, that warfare was a constant feature of Jewish life in ancient times. Wars of the early period were religious in nature and divinely sanctioned. Steps were frequently taken to ascertain God's will, and he was seen as actively involved in the course of military conflict. Priests and prophets involved themselves in the direction of battle, and took an active role in encouraging the people. In some cases, no mercy was shown to the vanquished. Even though peace was viewed as an ideal, the realities of political turmoil and military struggle were a constant feature of everyday life in biblical times.

However, once the Temple was destroyed by the Romans in the first century CE, Jews were compelled to live in the diaspora. For over 2,000 years they were without their own country; nonetheless, rabbinic sages engaged in torturous discussions about the nature of war and its justification. In the Talmud, a general principle is established: 'If someone intends to kill you, get in first and kill him.'[19] Although it is not possible to extrapolate from this single principle rules concerning warfare, it provides a general basis for justifying military engagement. Even if warfare

---

[17] Gen. 34.25–29.
[18] Judg. 1.28, 30, 33, 35.
[19] Sanhedrin 72a.

results in the killing of innocent individuals, the nation must defend itself from attack.

According to the *Mishnah* – a second-century compendium of Jewish law – a distinction is made between a commanded war (*milhemet mitzvah*), and an optional war (*milhemet reshut*).[20] A *milhemet reshut* (optional war) is defined as a war engaged in by the king to secure his borders or to obtain glory. According to the *Mishnah*, such a conflict can only be engaged in with the approval of the Sanhedrin which must decide whether the proposed war possesses some element of legality. However, it should be noted that such an issue was entirely academic since the Sanhedrin had ceased to function long before the *Mishnah* was completed.

Even though there is considerable discussion about the meaning of a *milhemet mitzvah* (commanded war), there was general agreement that a war in self-defence comes under this heading. It is not only permitted but advocated. Within the Jewish tradition, the prohibition against murder is understood as one of the seven Noahide laws which apply to both Jews and Gentiles. Despite this prohibition against unlawful killing, Jewish authorities agree that any nation is entitled to defend itself against attack, even if this aim can only be achieved by declaring war. Whether a *milhemet reshut* (optional war) is permitted to Gentiles is not relevant. Obviously, it was unknown for Gentiles to ask rabbinic scholars whether or not they are allowed to wage war – but even if they did, Jewish authorities are divided on whether an optional war is permitted to non-Jews. Some maintain that if Jews are not allowed to engage in such a war in the absence of the Sanhedrin, this must also apply to Gentile nations. Others, however, state that Gentiles are not bound by the decisions of the Sanhedrin; hence while murder is forbidden, it is nonetheless permitted for Gentiles to engage in warfare even where there is no question of self-defence.

The biblical and rabbinic tradition thus provide concrete cases of warfare among the Jews when they had a land of their

---

[20] Sotah 8.7; Sanhedrin 1.5.

own, as well as theoretical discussions about the legitimacy of commanded and optional warfare. Yet, it is obvious that these religious sources do not furnish a comprehensive basis for determining the legitimacy of the wars which the State of Israel has been obliged to fight. There are numerous issues which arise in modern warfare that are not envisaged in classical Jewish sources, such as the use of weapons of mass destruction. Furthermore, the political policies of the State of Israel are not determined by the rabbis who have no voice in assessing the acceptability of warfare. Instead politicians and generals formulate military policy. Nonetheless, rabbinic authorities have not been inhibited from stating what appears to them to be the acceptable Jewish view. Without exception, Jewish scholars have maintained that the wars engaged in by Israel when attacked or threatened by their neighbours have been justified on the basis of self-defence.

The Ideal of Peace

This survey of Jewish attitudes to warfare illustrates that Judaism is not in any sense a pacifist tradition. The Dean and the other teachers at the Hebrew Union College were correct in challenging my determination to be classed as a conscientious objector. As we have seen, Judaism treats warfare as a necessary evil. The ideal, of course, is peace. The Hebrew word for peace, *shalom*, carries overtones of wholeness, completeness and integrity. It is the everyday greeting, used both in the diaspora and Israel. As the biblical psalmist put it,

> Come, O sons, listen to me,
> I will teach you the fear of the LORD.
> What man is there who desires life, and covets many days,
>   that he may enjoy good?
> Keep your tongue from evil, and your lips from speaking
>   deceit.
> Depart from evil and do good; seek shalom (peace) and pur-
>   sue it.[21]

---

[21] Psalm 34.12–14.

The sages whose words are recorded in the *Mishnah* saw peace as a highly exalted ideal. In the Sayings of the Fathers, the first-century sage Hillel said: 'Be of the disciples of Aaron, loving shalom (peace) and pursuing shalom, loving thy fellow creatures and drawing him to the Torah', and according to Rabban Simeon b. Gamaliel: 'By three things the world is preserved, by truth, by judgement and by shalom.'[22] Numerous stories are told of the desirability of this state of harmony, particularly within the community itself. The following from the Talmud is one among many:

> There were two men whom the devil incited against each other. Every Friday evening they wrangled with one another. It happened that Rabbi Meir came thither and restrained them three Fridays running, till he made shalom between them. Then he heard the Devil cry, 'Woe is me! R. Meir has driven me away from my house.'[23]

Midrashic sources similarly extol peace as of paramount importance. 'So great is peace, said R. Simeon b. Lakish, that scripture speaks fictitious words in order to make peace between Joseph and his brothers:

> For it says, 'Thy father commanded before his death, saying, Forgive I pray thee, the trespass of thy brothers' (Gen. 50.16–17), and we do not find in the Scripture that Jacob had given such command, but it used fictitious words for the sake of peace.[24]

Commenting on the passage in the Sayings of the Fathers: 'Be of the disciples of Aaron loving peace', the *midrash* extols Aaron as a marriage counsellor:

> If a man quarrelled with his wife, and the husband turned the wife out of the house, then Aaron would go to the husband and say, 'My son, why did you quarrel with your wife?' The

---

[22] Pirke Avot 1.18.
[23] Gittin 52a.
[24] Deut. R. Shofetim, 5.15.

man would say, 'Because she acted shamefully towards me.' Aaron would reply, 'I will be your pledge that she will not do so again.' Then he would go to the wife, and say to her, 'My daughter, why did you quarrel with your husband?' And she would say, 'Because he beat me and cursed me.' Aaron would reply, 'I will be your pledge that he will not beat you or curse you again.' Aaron would do this day after day until the husband took her back. Then in due course the wife would have a child, and she would say, 'It is only through the merit of Aaron that this son has been given to me'.[25]

Despite such attitudes, Judaism is not uncompromisingly pacifist; as we have noted, warfare was a constant feature of Jewish life in the biblical period, and rabbinic sages debated the theoretical justification for military conflict even when Jews were dispossessed of their own land. Peace was perceived as an ideal which will be achieved only in the messianic age. In his *Code* the twelfth-century Jewish philosopher Moses Maimonides stated that in the messianic age there will be neither famine nor war, jealousy nor strife. But prior to the advent of the Messiah, war is inevitable. Only at the end of days will peace reign on earth and war shall be no more.

Pre-eminent among the prophetic books which portray the eventual triumph of God's kingdom on earth, the Book of Isaiah eloquently depicts a time when nation shall no longer make war:

> It shall come to pass in the latter days
>   that the mountain of the house of the LORD
> shall be established as the highest of the mountains,
>   and shall be raised above the hills;
> and all the nations shall flow to it,
>   and many peoples shall come, and say:
> 'Come, let us go up to the mountain of the LORD,
>   to the house of the God of Jacob;
> that he may teach us his ways
>   and that we may walk in his paths.'

---

[25] Av. R. N. 25.25b.

For out of Zion shall go forth the law,
   and the word of the LORD from Jerusalem.
He shall judge between the nations,
   and shall decide for many peoples;
and they shall beat their swords into ploughshares,
   and their spears into pruning hooks;
nation shall not lift up sword against nation,
   neither shall they learn war any more.[26]

In a later chapter, Isaiah emphasizes that only the faithful will remain, from which a redeemer will issue forth to bring about a new epoch in the nation's history when even animals will dwell together in peace:

There shall come forth a shoot from the stump of Jesse,
   and a branch shall grow out of his roots.
And the Spirit of the LORD shall rest upon him . . .
He shall not judge by what his eyes see,
   or decide by what his ears hear;
but with righteousness he shall judge the poor,
   and decide with equity for the meek of the earth; . . .
The wolf shall dwell with the lamb,
   and the leopard shall lie down with the kid,
and the calf and the lion and the fatling together.[27]

As time passed, the rabbis elaborated the themes of peace and reconciliation found in the Bible and Jewish literature of the Second Temple period. In the Midrashim and the Talmud they formulated an elaborate eschatological scheme divided into various stages. Some scholars emphasized that the prevalence of iniquity would be a prelude to the messianic age of peace. Yet despite such dire predictions, the rabbis believed that the prophet Elijah would return prior to the coming of the Messiah to resolve all earthy problems.

In their depictions of the Messiah, the rabbis formulated the doctrine of another Messiah, the son of Joseph, who would pre-

---

[26] Isa. 2.2–4.
[27] Isa. 11.1–2, 3–4, 6.

cede the king-Messiah, the Messiah ben David. According to legend this Messiah would engage in battle with Gog and Magog, the enemies of Israel, and be slain. Only after this would the Messiah ben David arrive in his glory. With the coming of the second Messiah, the dispersion of Israel will cease and all exiles will return from the four corners of the earth to the Holy Land with God at their head. Clouds of glory shall spread over them, and they will come singing with joy on their lips.

In rabbinic literature, there is frequent speculation about the Days of the Messiah. In their descriptions of the messianic age, the rabbis stressed that the Days of the Messiah will be totally unlike the present world. On the length of this epoch, the rabbis differed. Yet, despite such dispute, it was generally accepted that at the end of this era a final judgement will come upon all humankind. Those who are judged righteous will enter into heaven (*Gan Eden*) whereas the wicked will be condemned to hell (*Gehinnom*). Perfect peace will only be a reality in the Messianic Age. The Messiah will only come when God sends him, and human beings have no alternative but to wait in patience. Since full reconciliation between human beings can only be achieved in that future age, in the here-and-now people must be content to live in a state of disharmony. Hence, war is an inevitable feature of the pre-messianic age.

Thus, according to traditional Judaism, true peace is a utopian ideal which can only be achieved with the coming of the Messiah. Friction between human beings leading to military engagement is understood as an inevitable feature of earthly life. As we have seen, the Bible and rabbinic sources provide a framework for legitimizing such conflict. Yet, it should be noted that within the Jewish community there are many who have abandoned the belief in the coming of the Messiah. For these individuals, Jewish eschatological longings for the advent of the messianic age have no relevance.

There has thus been a major transformation of Jewish thought in the modern world. In the past Jews longed for the advent of a personal Messiah who would establish peace on earth. Although this doctrine continues to be upheld by devout Orthodox believers, it has been eclipsed by a more secular outlook on the part of most Jews. As a result, Jews no longer anticipate that earthly life will be superseded by the reign of peace in the final days. Given this shift in orientation, what hope can there be for a peaceful future in which human conflict will not erupt into violence and bloodshed?

A Jewish Model for Conflict Resolution

In ancient times, warfare was a constant feature of life in Israel. Besieged by their neighbours, the Jewish people continually resorted to military might to subdue their enemies. Today, however, hostilities between nations are more dangerous than ever before given the existence of weapons of mass destruction. As we noted, neither biblical nor rabbinic sources provide comprehensive guidelines for conducting war in such a context. What is needed instead is a mode of conflict resolution which will enable antagonists to live together in peace.

Arguably, the Jewish tradition itself provides a model for such conflict resolution: Jews perceive themselves to be an argumentative and quarrelsome people, and in general feel no shame about this. A well-known Yiddish story describes how a prominent Jew is shipwrecked on a desert island. He immediately sets to work building all the institutions necessary to sustain Jewish life. After living in complete solitude for 20 years, another Jew is also shipwrecked on the same island. With huge pride, the original inhabitant shows off his magnificent synagogue, his ritual bath, his house of study, his orphanage, his hospital, his old-age home, his burial society premises and his cemetery. Eventually, in the far corner of the island, the newcomer finds a small, dilapidated shack and wonders what this could possibly be. 'Oh that,' replies his guide. 'That's the synagogue I wouldn't attend at any price.'

This story illustrates the conflict that exists on every level. Today throughout the dispersion, rival Jewish organizations proliferate. The United Kingdom has fewer than 300,000 Jews, but the highest synagogue affiliation. However, the members do not all belong to one denomination. There is a whole group of independent synagogues that have nothing to do with one another. There are no fewer than four Orthodox organizations (the fairly Orthodox United Synagogue, the more Orthodox Federation of Synagogues, the even more Orthodox Union of Orthodox Hebrew Congregations, and the Sephardim). There are also three groups of non-Orthodox synagogues (the moderate Masorti, the Progressive Reform Synagogues of Great Britain, and the more radical Union of Liberal and Progressive Synagogues). Most of these organizations have their own religious courts, schools, administrators, *kashrut* (religious suitability of food) inspectors and burial grounds, and there is a constant state of tension between them.

Even at a local level, there is an ongoing atmosphere of conflict. In Denver, Colorado – my home town – for example, there is a Jewish population of perhaps 40,000. It is a highly assimilated community with an intermarriage rate of approximately 60 per cent. The city cannot even support a kosher butcher. Those who keep the laws of *kashrut* have their meat sent in frozen from Chicago. Nonetheless, there are two *kashrut* authorities. It is fairly hard for bread to be *tref* (unkosher), but when a bakery supervised by one authority sent ten dozen bagels to a wedding reception, the other authority, who was inspecting the rest of the banquet, had no hesitation in rejecting them and sending them back. The community leaders regard this dispute with wry resignation. It is the way things are in the Jewish world.

Such conflict is an intrinsic feature of the Jewish tradition. Education, for example, is to take place through conflict. Unlike the Christian community which extols harmony, Jews relish debate and disagreement. To those who are accustomed to well-disciplined, traditional Anglo-Saxon schools in which children are encouraged to be seen and not heard, a *yeshivah* (talmudic academy) is an astonishing establishment. All activity takes place in one large hall. There is no religious hush; no one pays breathless attention to the master in charge. Instead, there is constant noise, movement and hub-bub. Piles of books spill over all available surfaces. The students study in pairs. Rocking backwards and forwards, they read to each other and then argue out the meaning of the sacred text. If they cannot agree, they leaf through the available commentaries, and in well-rehearsed gestures they thump on the books, on the tables and even on each other to emphasize their points. Eventually they may go to consult their teacher, but this only provides material for further debate.

These are only a few examples of the ways in which the Jewish heritage promotes internal conflict. They illustrate the truth of the adage: where there are four Jews, there are six opinions. This is not to say that hatred and enmity are regarded as good things – quite the reverse. But there is a recognition that a state of perfect peace is unrealistic. Human conflict is inevitable. In this respect the Jewish religion has a most valuable insight which can contribute to world peace. Among themselves, Jews are content to differ.

After 40 years of experience teaching Christians and Jews together, one university teacher remarked to me: 'I think Jews tend to respond in a different way. Number one. Jews are much more comfortable with argument and enjoy arguing. Number two. Jews are comfortable with something left incomplete or un-settled. This is generalizing and allowing for many exceptions. Christians often don't like argument; they are more inclined to try to convert, to try to reach agreement; and they are often un-comfortable with things left incomplete. A Jewish man will say, 'Well it's like you say, who knows?' And he's comfortable with the 'who knows?' He's comfortable with plaster not on the walls, while the Calvinist wants to get that plaster on there!'

This is an important insight. Since rabbinic times, Jews have recorded the minority as well as the majority opinion: they have taught their children through debate and argument rather than through authoritative pronouncements and they are prepared to support a huge array of religious institutions, all in perpetual conflict with one another In other words, Jews have learnt to agree to differ. Despite the bitter altercations between the Ortho-dox and Reform, between the Israeli Likud and Labour parties, and between the religious and the secular, Jews continue to have a strong sense of being one people. For more than 3,000 years, they have maintained their identity in a hostile world, and it is through their arguments that they have formed their convictions and their ways of life.

Increasingly the Jewish people are realizing their commonality not only with other Jews, but also with the whole human family. It is a cliché to say that we live in a global village, but nonetheless, through the mass media, everyone in the developed world is aware of events on the other side of the globe. If Jews could only extend their sense of kin beyond the Jewish people, they have an important lesson to teach the world's peacemakers. For centuries they have known how to express, how to accept and how to deal with difference among themselves. With the loosening of ethnic ties, it is not too much to hope that this skill can be disseminated beyond the Jewish world and be assimilated by all peoples.

Conclusion

My teachers then were right to criticize my pacifist stance at the Hebrew Union College. As we have seen, war frequently took place in ancient Israel between the Jewish people and their neighbours. Such engagements were divinely sanctioned, and the priests encouraged the nation to stand firm against their enemies. Although Jewry did not possess their own country for nearly two millennia, rabbinic sages discussed the legitimacy of armed conflict in sacred sources, and their reflections have provided a legal framework for the religious justification for war between modern Israel and its Arab neighbours.

Nonetheless, *shalom* is viewed as a utopian ideal – the Jewish hope is for a future when nations shall turn their swords into ploughshares. In the quest to realize this prophetic vision, the Jewish people have a vitally important message for all nations. From biblical times to the present, Jews have encouraged internal dispute and conflict – disagreement has been a vital element of Jewish existence. Yet such division is contained within the framework of *klal Israel*, the community of Israel. We are a people fraught with disagreement and dissent, but united together by bonds of kinship and ethnic loyalty. This pattern of unity despite division can, I believe, serve as a model for human reconciliation among all peoples in our divided and war-torn world.

SELECT BIBLIOGRAPHY

Cohn-Sherbok, D., 2002, *Antisemitism: A History*, Stroud, Gloucestershire: Sutton.

Cohn-Sherbok, D. and El-Alami, D., 2003, *The Palestine–Israeli Conflict*, Oxford: Oneworld.

Friedlander, A., (ed.), 1968, *Out of the Whirlwind*, New York: Schocken.

Gilbert, M., 1980, *Holocaust*, Houndmills: Macmillan.

Landes, D. (ed.), 1991, *Confronting Omnicide: Jewish Reflections on Weapons of Mass Destruction*, Northvale, NJ: Jason Aronson.

Lind, M., 1980, *Yahweh is a Warrior: The Theology of Warfare in Ancient Israel*, Scottdale, PA: Herald Press.

New, D. S., 2002, *Holy War: The Rise of Militant Christian, Jewish and Islamic Fundamentalism*, Jefferson, NC: MacFarland and Co.

Randall, A., 1998, *Theologies of War and Peace Among Jews, Christians and Muslims*, Lewiston, NY: Edwin Mellen.

Rosenthal, M. (ed.), 1990, *Wars of the Jews*, New York: Hippocrene Books.

6. War and Peace in Christianity

IAN HAZLETT

I once caught sight of two graffiti messages in a lecture room that have a degree of relevance for the subject of this book. The first intimated with Damoclean menace that 'when the Revolution comes, you will be the first against the wall'. This gave rise to the thought: why is it that revolution and violence are usually paired? The other declared serenely that 'atheists are content'. The possible implication is that religious believers are discontented, maybe malcontents, and so fomenters of troubles.

A remit of the contributors has been to reflect on why, as a matter of fact, religions have traditionally been ambiguous on the issue of violence, war and peace.[1] How can it be explained that in religions there are inherent tensions between legitimizing or blessing war on the one hand, and renunciation of force and violent action on the other? The earlier chapters deal with Hinduism and Buddhism, faiths often romantically depicted as religions of peace *par excellence*. Yet it has been demonstrated that even in these, there are inbuilt and living traditions of ritual, sacred and spontaneous violence. It was also indicated that the non-violence singularly associated with Mahatma Gandhi did not in itself embody a magnificent recrudescence of Hindu political theology. In Indian Hinduism apparently, the non-violent way of Gandhi has had little significance beyond the struggle for

---

[1] On the holy and the bloody in religious phenomena see Girard 1977. For a useful basic introduction to the comparative religious context, see Ferguson 1977. Historical Christian attitudes are critically outlined by Maron 1996. On the dilemma in Christian ethics of appeals to military force and other coercive means see Aquino and Mieth (eds) 2001.

independence from the British. That way was more of an *ad hoc* strategic use of 'soul force' than a normal application of 'faith in action'. Like the 'boycott' invented in Ireland, or strikes, this phenomenon illustrated that in the moral evaluation of coercive action, it is not 'force' or 'compulsion' in itself that is primarily at issue. This can be passive, indirect and non-violent, normally adjudged as morally acceptable. Rather, the classical debate about what is normally understood as the 'use of force' revolves around the legitimacy of recourse to arms or direct physical action in making a claim or in repudiating it.

Standard Examples of Christianity's Compromised Legacy

During the Boer War (1899–1902), a letter replete with Swiftian irony appeared in the *Manchester Guardian* in 1900. It satirizes the accommodation of British Imperial Christianity to, as it were, the stoical, martial ethos of ancient Sparta. Here is an extract:

> I see that at the next Church Congress, the topic to be discussed is 'The Church's duty in regard to war'. That is right. For a year, the heads of our Church have been telling us what war is and does – that it is a school of character, that it sobers men, cleanses them, strengthens them, knits their hearts, makes them brave, patient, humble, tender, prone to self-sacrifice. Watered by 'the red rain of war', one bishop tells us, 'virtue grows'. A cannonade, he points out, is an oratorio – almost a form of worship. Consequently, the Congress should devise a new liturgy for 'war in our time', and so emend – in the spirit of the best modern thought – those passages in the Bible and Prayer-book by which even the truest of Christians have been blinded to the duty of seeking war and ensuring it.[2]

Some years later, during World War One, the Anglican Bishop

---

[2] Quoted in Martin 1997, p. 128.

of London, Arthur F. Winnington-Ingram, urged English con-scripts to do that which in war had to be done:

> Kill Germans. Kill them, not for the sake of killing, but to save the world, kill the good as well as the bad, kill the young as well as the old, kill those who have shown kindness to our wounded. As I have said a thousand times, I look upon it as a war for purity, I look upon everyone who dies in the war as a martyr.[3]

In 1915, the Revd John Adams, a United Free Church of Scot-land minister, published a book entitled *The Great Sacrifice, or the Altar-fire of War*. In this he states that the trenches are a scene of 'solemn purification by fire'. By spilling their blood, the soldiers are reaffirming the nation's 'covenant with God'.[4] Three years later, undeterred by the reality of the scale of the mutual slaughter, Adams adhered to the dubious prophecy that the war is about the 'ultimate consecration of the nation . . . it is a divine flame which is going to burn up all the dross in Church and nation, and leave the pure gold of righteousness, brother-hood, and faith'. Through their 'baptism of fire', war survivors have been chosen 'not simply to defeat the modern Huns, but to receive their anointing for the nobler service that is to be'.[5] The spectrum of contemporary American and German attitudes to World War One among Christians included predictably similar views.[6] And just over 800 years before, Odo de Chatillon, oth-erwise known as Pope Urban II (eventually beatified in 1881),

---

[3] Quoted in Bainton 1961, p. 207. The source of the quotation is in *Would I Fight?*, edited by Keith R. Briant and Lyall Wilkes, Oxford 1938. Cf. Marrin 1974; Wilkinson 1978.

[4] *The Great Sacrifice*, pp. 4–5. Cf. Brown 1994. See also n. 22 below (James Moffatt), and *Dictionary of Scottish Church History & Theology* (Edinburgh 1993), articles 'First World War', pp. 322–3, and 'Pacifism', p. 641.

[5] *The Suffering of the Best, or Service and Sacrifice* (Edinburgh 1918), pp. 14–15.

[6] For the USA, cf. Abrams 1969; Piper 1985. For Germany, cf. Pressel, 1967; Missala 1968. See also Arlie J. Hoover 1989.

declared in his famous sermon at Clermont launching the Crusades in the year 1098:[7]

> Any volunteer shall make a vow to God and shall offer himself as *a living sacrifice, holy, acceptable to God*.[8] He shall wear a cross on his brow or on his breast. And when he returns after having fulfilled his vow, he shall wear the cross on his back. In this way he will obey the instruction of the Lord:[9] *Whoever does not bear his cross and follow me is not worthy of me.*

For those viscerally inimical to Christianity, such statements provide welcome ammunition. It can, however, hardly be denied that they do represent that unacceptable face of historical Christianity. Moreover, for most Arab Muslims in the world today, such a sanguinary image of Christianity is what actually springs to mind. Their psyche is still haunted by the Crusades and later Western imperialism. This helps explain, for example, why the International Red Cross Organisation is currently under pressure to change its blood-red logo evoking the Christian religion. This then means that – as one usually hears from space flights in difficulty – 'We have a problem'.

We can hardly expect most Arab Muslims to know anything about other kinds of Christians like, for example, Francis of Assisi (1181–1226) – 'Make me an instrument of your peace'. Francis was something of a thirteenth-century Tony Benn. For during the Fifth Crusade he journeyed on a personal peace crusade to Egypt, where he had lengthy interviews with Sultan al-Kamil, and tried vainly to convert him.[10] One must hasten to add that the Sultan was not comparable to the recently deposed

---

[7] Text in *The Medieval Record. Sources of Medieval History*, edited by Alfred J. Andrea (Boston and New York 1997), p. 348, col. 2. Cf. Colin Morris, 'Propaganda for War. The Dissemination of the Crusading Ideal in the Twelfth Century', in Sheils (ed.) 1983, pp. 79–101.

[8] Cf. Romans 12.1.

[9] Conflation of Matthew 10.38 and Luke 14.27.

[10] Tony Benn is a contemporary Old Labour English MP and advocate of lost causes. He is viewed as slightly ingenuous and high-minded compared to the alleged fan of Ba'athist Iraq, Scottish MP George Galloway. On Francis' peace mission to Moslems, cf. Mastnak 2002, pp. 184–8.

leader of Iraq. It is however very poignant that other Arabs, ~~Arab~~ Christians, are aware of the alternative image of Christianity. That explains the pre-Iraq War pilgrimage of Saddam Hussein's one time deputy, Tariq Aziz, a Christian, to the shrine of Francis in Italy to make a very interesting point.

Christianity and War in Contemporary Opinion

In current mainstream Western attitudes to our topic, there are two poles that define the spectrum of opinion. One is the view that religion is a generator and fertilizer of war. Cited to justify this is the bag of old chestnuts like 'religious' belligerence, intolerance, fanaticism, persecution, censoriousness, indoctrination, dogmatism, and that bogey word of modern religious discourse, 'fundamentalism' – all nourished by combustible beliefs that cause conflagrations. The world would be a far better place without religion. Any appeal, for example, to defend 'Christian civilization' is oxymoronic, since in this view, no religion is civilized.

Such a position tends to be held by people who have either only modest knowledge of religion, or very limited experience of it. It is attributable to blinkered modern secularism. Nonetheless, as early as the century before Christ, the Roman Epicurean poet and religious sceptic, Lucretius (*c.*100–*c.*55 BCE), already articulated such a dismissive judgement with famous remarks such as: 'More often than not it is precisely religion that is the mother of malicious and outrageous deeds . . . religion has had so much power to encourage evil behaviour.'[11] For Lucretius, as among many modern people, traditional 'religion' and 'superstition' are synonyms.[12]

The other pole – just short of absolute pacifism, which is

---

[11] 'Saepius illa religio peperit scelerosa atque impia facta . . . tantum religio potuit suadere malorum', in *On the Nature of the Universe* (*De natura rerum*), Book 1, lines 82–3, 101. Cf. Penguin Classics English edn, p. 12 (*religio* rendered as 'superstition').

[12] On Lucretius' views on religion and theology, see the edition of *De natura rerum* by Cyril Bailey (Oxford 1947), vol. 1, pp. 66–72.

outside the mainstream – embodies the view that authentic religion and war are barely compatible. Since religion is ultimately about love, peace and harmony, then even allegedly just war – it is argued – is in practice grossly indecent and intrinsically immoral, an offence to God and humanity. This position has currently a high-profile status. A central component of it is a rediscovered concern about 'civilian losses', 'the lives of the innocent' and 'mass destruction'. This arises partly out of the indiscriminate killing potential of modern munitions, especially if nuclear or chemical, partly out of the recession of pre-modern military values of chivalry and etiquette, replaced by notions of total violence, 'dirty war', and 'awesome' destruction, and partly out of the emotive (and manipulative) power of front-line journalism, photography and television. If not unconditionally pacifist, many modern Christians (especially church leaders) urge that everything possible should be undertaken to inhibit war. Further, when it does break out, all energies should be devoted to stopping it. The Christian response, therefore, to even legitimate war should be more than dutiful participation tempered by stoical lamentation or resignation. It could also involve contrition and repentance over human failure, as well as 'witness' to justice and peace, and 'protest' against injustice and war – although this might be socially and politically somewhat imprudent.

To return to the first proposition, that religion breeds war: a recent way of characterizing it has been as 'the argument from Bosnia'.[13] Its most popular modern exponent in the United Kingdom is the Public Enemy Number One of theologians, the zoologist and publicist, Richard Dawkins. His thesis is simple: religion causes war by generating *certainty*. Confessionally, Dawkins is a scientific materialist, a self-styled Internet Infidel, and a somewhat old-fashioned radical positivist, believing that humanity will not come of age until divested of superstition like religion. He is especially hostile to the monotheistic, Abrahamic faiths of Judaism, Christianity and Islam. Such a perspective originates chiefly in the rationalist sector of the eighteenth-century Enlight-

---

[13] Martin 1997, pp. 7–9. Cf. Mojzes 1994.

enment. It was argued then that all religion based on the authority of divine revelation is sheer fantasy that does not stand up to any kind of empirical examination. Added to this was the moral argument that since religion has been associated with cruelty, killing and oppression, it scores badly in any ethical quality assurance exercise.

Further, since Dawkins affirms that anything scientifically wrong is morally evil, he considers religion to be like a virus, rather like the way in which medieval Christianity saw heresy as a virus. Dawkins' diagnosis concludes that a virus of the soul has infected whole populations, occasioning in them a pathology of irrationality. In a letter to the *Guardian* in 2001 (15 September) he asserted the following: 'To fill a world with religion, or religions of the Abrahamic kind, is like littering the street with loaded guns. Do not be surprised if they are used.' And in a radio interview with Sue Lawley on *Desert Island Discs* in 1995, he replied to her question whether God was irrelevant, a tooth fairy, or positively harmful, in this way:

> *Certainly* religion can be positively harmful in various ways, obviously in causing wars, which has happened often enough in history, causing fatwas, causing people to do ill to one another because they are so convinced that they know what is right. Because they feel it from inside – they've been told from within themselves what is right – anything goes – you can kill people because you know that they are wrong. That is *certainly* evil.[14]

Note his double use of the word *certainly*, a word he despises so much in the religious context. Richard Dawkins is no military man. Contrast his perception with another non-believer, but militarist *par excellence*, General Erich von Ludendorff of the German Third Supreme Command in World War One and later one of the first Nazi parliamentarians. Embodying a 'German spirit' infinitely remote from that of Goethe, and deploring

---

[14] Quoted Martin 1997, p. 24.

the diluting effect of Christianity on the martial spirit, he wrote: 'The Christian faith and the life shaped by it are the prime causes of national breakdown in the totalitarian war . . . Christianity has heaped rubbish on the national soul.'[15]

This is not the place to go down the inquisitorial road with Dawkins and identify his concepts of religion, causation and certitude. On the plane of history, there is undoubtedly a lot of truth in what he says.[16] Believers have conducted wars for religious reasons, or pretexts. But conviction atheists have also been war-mongers, and in our era even more consummately. That the murderous lust of Cain has been active with superabundant brutality well outside the mandates of religion was evident in Robespierre's Jacobin 'Terror' in the French Revolution, Stalin's Soviet Russia, Hitler's Nazi Germany, Ceaucescu's Romania, Castro's Cuba, Hoxha's Albania, Mengistu's Ethiopia, and Pol Pot's Cambodia. In those self-consciously secularist regimes, the elimination of religious faith was a specific objective. Accordingly, were Dawkins to say that *ideology* causes wars rather than the 'arbitrary pre-scientific illusions' of religion,[17] that would be less contentious.

On the Continent, in the German-speaking world, Dawkins' irate counterpart is the historically erudite (and privately sponsored) Karlheinz Deschner, described as the 'Nestor of Church critics'. He has iconic status among secularists for whom the Christian Church is anathema. His multi-volume and still unfinished *Criminal History of Christianity*,[18] embodies a spectacular,

---

[15] *The Nation at War*, translated from the German (*Der Totale Krieg*) by Dr A. S. Rappoport (London 1936), pp. 39, 40. Referring to 1 Corinthians 1. 26–9, the general deplored the role of what he saw as 'hysterical weaklings' in Christian witness, *ibid.* p. 46.

[16] Recent studies claiming to identify a pathology of belligerence in the one-God doctrine are, for example, Schwartz 1997; Dousse 2002. See also n. 18 below.

[17] Martin 1997, p. 159. Martin also observes, p. 160: 'Secular ideologies, like religions, find themselves fighting for peace' – since the germ of large-scale wars is competing universalist claims.

[18] Published by Rowohlt in Reinbek near Hamburg 1986–. Cf. Horst Herrmann, *Die sieben Todsünden der Kirche. Ein Plädoyer gegen die*

alternative Church history. Not yet translated into English, this *oeuvre* is a massive chronicle of crimes, big and small, against humanity and each other committed by Christians throughout the ages. That 'war is the Christian path to eternal life' is the *leit-motiv* of the book. Deschner's vilification of Christianity (with Nietzschean vigour) is grounded in the reasoning that since the actions of Christians have very often been reprehensible, this is because their religion, like all religion, is a moral plague. He admits of no distinction between 'true faith' and actual behaviour. 'There is much I admire', he has written, 'between heaven and earth, but I admire nothing less than the miracle of religion.' And in 1991, Deschner, an ex-Catholic, teamed up with the Münster ex-Catholic theologian, Horst Herrmann, to publish an *Anti-Catechism*.[19]

The Historical Diversity of Christian Views

The aim in this discussion is to project a more sober picture, to illustrate and account for the fact that on war and peace, there has been from the start a variety of Christian views (and behaviour). It is conspicuous that within the domains of the history of religion and Church history, the topic of war and military service was virtually ignored by historians until the early twentieth century. It is true that since Antiquity some philosophers and Christian thinkers occasionally reflected on the matter, finding it obviously a problem. On the whole, however – and one must stress 'on the whole' – their efforts were not so much concerned with its ultimate ethical status as with the circumstances in which the option of war is permissible. Discussions revolved around the appropriate situation and the ethics of its conduct. Not war in itself was the issue, abolition or retention; rather,

---

Menschenverachtung (Munich 1992), pp. 68 ff. For one reaction see Hans Kung, *Christianity: Its Essence and History* (1994), translated by John Bowden (London 1995), pp. 5–6. See also n. 80 below.

[19] See also the Deschner website: *<www.deschner.info/index_en.htm>*. For Dawkins, see *<www.world-of-dawkins.com/Dawkins/Work/papers. htm>* and *<www.infidels.org/library/modern/richard_dawkins>*.

when is it permissible, when is it just or unjust, and how may it be conducted?

A utopian world without war and wars was, therefore, rarely seen as a realistic possibility. Like bad weather, famine, disease and sin, war has always been viewed as a regrettable fact of natural life that cannot be simply abolished. Remedies have been orientated to management rather than extirpation. Yet within the history of Christianity there has also been a tenuous tradition of conscientious objection, pacifism and absolute rejection of violence. This view, actually predominant in the Church of the first three centuries, tends to be seen as the 'true' Christian position. It has continued to express itself intermittently up to modern times, but very much as a minority, if now increasing, standpoint.[20] Some instances will be indicated below.

In the field of the history of Christianity, it was arguably the book by Adolf von Harnack in 1905 that brought the subject of war and military action to the forefront. This was entitled: *Militia Christi. The Christian Religion and the Military in the First Three Centuries.*[21] Undoubtedly it was Harnack's work that helped prise open the subject for the world of mainstream Church history and Christian ethics in the twentieth century, the century of Mothers of Wars. The effect was to place Christian attitudes to war and peace through the ages higher on the

---

[20] Cf. especially the manifold works of Peter Brock, such as *Pacifism in Europe to 1914*, Princeton 1972. Id. *Freedom from War. Non-Sectarian Pacifism 1814–1914*, London and Toronto 1991. Id. *Roots of War Resistance. A Brief History of Pacifism from Jesus to Tolstoy* (1981), 2nd edn, Toronto 1992. Id. *Varieties of Pacifism. A Survey from Antiquity to the Outset of the Twentieth Century*, Syracuse, NY 1998. Id. *Pacifism since 1914. An Annotated Reading List*, Toronto 2000. Co-edited with Nigel Young, *Pacifism in the Twentieth Century*, New York 1999. For the USA in particular, see Brock, *Pacifism in the United States from the Colonial Era to the First World War*, Princeton 1968. For France, cf. Jean Baptiste Barbier, *Le pacifisme dans l'histoire de France de l'an mille à nos jours*, Paris 1966. Luc Rasson, *Ecrire contre la guerre. Littérature et pacifismes, 1916–1938*, Paris 1997. For Britain, cf. Martin Ceadel, 'Christian Pacifism in the Era of the Two World Wars', in Sheils (ed.) 1983, pp. 391–408.

[21] English translation and introduction by David McInnes Gracie, Philadelphia 1981.

agenda, and provoke controversy. The book was exploited by contemporaries like, among many others, the Glaswegian scholar, James Moffatt (a translator not only of the Bible but also of other Harnack works), in order to feel comfortable about reconciling 'Christian values' to the Great War,[22] and to a perceived struggle against 'social Darwinism . . . the Nietzschean will to power . . . the worship of science, materialism, and the brute power of "blood and iron" '.[23]

Christian pacifists, however, reckoned that Harnack misrepresented the basis of early Christian refusal or reluctance to do military service. He had argued that the traditional link between the Roman army and pagan religious practice, that is, idolatry offensive to conscience, was the decisive factor behind unanimous early Christian inhibitions and prohibitions. In other words, according to his interpretation, the problem was religious, not moral. Objectors countered that Christian non-compliance was rooted rather in absolute renunciation of war, violence and killing, in accordance with the gospel and its non-negotiable ethical mandates. Pacifist Church historians embarked on further studies to rectify impressions given by Harnack. Authors sceptical of him were, for example, Cecil John Cadoux,[24] Jean-Michel Hornus,[25] Gerrit Jan Heering,[26] and subsequently the well-known Church historian and Quaker at Harvard, Roland H. Bainton. His book, *Christian Attitudes to War and Peace: An Historical Survey*[27] has been the near-standard, broad historical work on the topic. Though some people, tongue in cheek, might cite Deschner, it has not been replaced, though in need of revision and updating.[28]

---

[22] See his article on 'war' in *Dictionary of the Apostolic Church* (Edinburgh 1915–18), vol. 2, pp. 646–73.

[23] Brown 1994, p. 85.

[24] See Cadoux 1982. Cadoux later reaffirmed his position in *Christian Pacifism Re-examined*, Oxford 1940.

[25] See Hornus 1980 (excellent index of source-references).

[26] See Heering 1930.

[27] See Bainton 1961.

[28] For more recent studies on the early Christian period, see Helgeland 1974. Helgeland; Daly; Burns (eds.) 1987. Peter Brock, *The Military Question*

In the area of New Testament ethics, a pacifist gauntlet was thrown down by the Professor of Divinity and Biblical Criticism at Glasgow University, George H. C. Macgregor [the Younger].[29] His lucid study of the issue in relation to New Testament utterances was aimed at restoring positive theological backbone to the Christian pacifist position. Arguing for the priority of love over justice and righteousness in the modern context of 'total war', and not just for a simplistic renunciation of violence, he repudiated the 'bad theology' of the traditional revisionist interpretation of the gospel and the Sermon on the Mount – that is, the Christian 'just war' theory.[30] Subsequently, Macgregor engaged in disputatious literary exchanges[31] with the ex-pacifist American theologian, Reinhold Niebuhr (d. 1971), advocate of Christian political 'realism' and of the virtual duty not to turn the other cheek. He considered pacifists to be admirable, but politi-

---

in the Early Church. A Selected Bibliography of a Century's Scholarship, 1888–1987, Toronto 1988.

[29] *The New Testament Basis of Pacifism*, London [1936], reprinted in the USA several times in the latter half of the century. A German translation, *Friede auf Erden*, was published in Munich in 1955. Macgregor failed to make it as an entry in the *Dictionary of Scottish Church History & Theology* (Edinburgh 1993), though he appears in the article on 'pacifism'. In Glasgow University Divinity Faculty and Trinity College at the time, he was Honorary President of the divinity students' 'Pacifist Society'. He was also a leading light in the Church of Scotland Peace Society.

[30] 'The modern war-mentality is utterly heedless of morality, provided only that the desired end be attained. One must admit the cogency of the truth, expressed by Hegel in his *Logik*, that all things have their measure and that, when the measure is passed through quantitative alteration, there is a qualitative change also: "things cease to be what they were" '. In other words, in modern technological circumstances war is obsolete. Macgregor 1936, p. 139.

[31] For example: *On the Relevance of the Impossible. A Reply to Reinhold Niebuhr*, London 1941. See Niebuhr's tract earlier that year: *Why the Christian Church is not Pacifist*, accessible in A. Holmes (ed.) 1975, pp. 301–13. For some recent discussions of Niebuhr's stance, see R. Holmes, 1989, pp. 63–8, and the sharp critique in Stanley Hauerwas' St Andrews Gifford Lectures, *With the Grain of the Universe. The Church's Witness and Natural Theology*, Grand Rapids, Mich. 2001; London 2002.

cally irresponsible.[32] Retrospectively, Macgregor's position was 'tainted' due to its perceived association with British appeasement of, and American indifference to, the rise of Nazi German militarism and aggression.

Reactions to the wording of the topic of *War and Peace in Christianity* might be: Whose war? Whose peace? Whose Christianity? Whose morality? and When? Here, the intention is not so much to evaluate this or that doctrine as to corroborate and explain the fact that within historical Christianity there has been a spectrum of attitudes, both in theory and in practice.[33] To this end, and based on evidence over the centuries, the main attitudes and teachings will be adumbrated. Following that, there will be illustration of the operation and interaction of the various positions in the major typical eras in the history of Christianity from its origins.

First, as for the chief positions, one can specify four. *One* is pacifism proper, historically a fringe position from the fourth century onwards. This can be summed up as refusal to kill or bear arms due to conscientious objection.[34] The *second* is accommodating Christian subscription to the notion of 'just war', historically a majority position. This can be summed up as qualified assent and participation. It denies that the teaching of the Sermon on the Mount is or was intended to be politically applicable and considers aspects of the New Testament world-view as no longer relevant.[35] Roman Catholic, Protestant, and presumably Orthodox dogmatic traditions have been unanimous about this.

[32] Cf. McKeogh 1997. Niebuhr's double morality – moral individuals and immoral (or non-moral) collective entities – was articulated famously in his *Moral Man and Immoral Society*, first published in 1932.

[33] For a typical example, see John Highet, *The Scottish Churches. A Review of their State* (London 1960), pp. 196–7.

[34] It can also provide a non-traditional, and in one sense not very credible Christian critique of liberation theology's sanctioning of violence; see Martin Hengel, *Victory Over Violence* (1971), translated from German by David E. Green, London 1975.

[35] After Niebuhr, another influential twentieth-century Christian advocate of the doctrine in the Protestant world was the Princeton Christian ethicist, Paul Ramsey (cf. Ramsey 1983). For some recent reassessments and critiques of the just-war doctrine, cf. Aquino and Mieth (eds) 2001.

The *third* is offensive holy war or crusade, militarist Christianity targetting non-Christians or Christian deviationists, at various times enjoying majority support. Since the late seventeenth century this has been seen as untenable and so an aberration. Its root principle was theocratic, imperialist domination of the world by the Church aided with the force of arms. This is the feature that is marked out by hostile observers like Dawkins and Deschner as the ultimately real Christian aspiration. Currently, active holy war notions are associated more with the Islamic *jihad*.[36] The *fourth* is what one might call 'public, but non-doctrinaire Christian peace-witness and lobbying', the favoured view of many in the churches now.[37] It too does not exclude participation in hostilities, but displays extreme reluctance. This therefore is not qualified pacifism, rather pacific realism. It has also been described as *pacificism*, a neologism coined by the historian, A. J. P. Taylor, in 1957.[38] All war is somehow evil, it is morally dubious, and few want it. When it looms, the Christian vocation requires doing all one can to prevent it, and when it unavoidably happens, all efforts should be devoted to minimizing it. Confession to peace should be reinstated as the Christian priority. Such a position has, for example, long been identified with – among other groups – the Iona Community since 1938 (though its founder, George MacLeod, represented a doctrinaire pacifist position).

Proactive Christian peace witness is a stance (now quasi-orthodox in what used to be the 'West') that up to recent times was frowned upon in ecclesiastical and political circles. Traditionally, the churches on the whole identified themselves with the various ideologies and symbols of the nation and the state,

---

[36] See Johnson 1997.

[37] This trend was already discernible in the last World War, cf. Sittser 1997. See also Reuver 1988; The World Council of Churches, *The Gulf War*, Geneva 1991; Harvey 1999. For a version urging more active, but non-violent 'resistance fighting', see Dorothea Sölle, *Of War and Love* (1981), translated from German by Rita and Robert Kimber, New York 1983.

[38] For a clarifying discussion, see Ceadel, 'Christian Pacifism', in Sheils (ed.) 1983, pp. 391–6.

irrespective of their moral quality. Christ and (any) Culture were predominantly neither especially distinct nor separate, rather simply fused. In respect of war, the ecclesiastical role was to provide added value by means of spiritual benediction. The trend in the current situation therefore suggests the following idea: there is a paradoxical correlation between, on the one hand, the decline of organized, institutional Christianity in the West along with its increasingly diminished social and political status, and on the other hand its rediscovered critical, admonitory and quasi-oppositional role – even if this involves dancing on eggs. In short, the 'Church's voice' is increasingly articulated from without the higher echelons of national and political establishments rather than from within them.

In the history of Christianity overall, therefore, there has been no immutable consensus on the ethics of force and war – doctrinal homogeneity is elusive, though ecclesiastical tradition attempted to claim it, and some modern commentators have been keen to identify it. Is war a permissible option reconcilable with the gospel or law of God? That is the question! Mainstream Church traditions enjoying privileged relations with the State answer affirmatively, provided the cause is just. But how can the justice of any war be established? On the perception of 'justice', Christian opinion is even more likely to fragment (as on many other moral issues), so that Christians can enthusiastically fight each other in any war. Sometimes this has been in the name of one or other understanding of Christianity, as in the Christian Wars of Religion of the late sixteenth and seventeenth centuries in Europe.[39] Modern Northern Ireland is never a good current example of such a thing, since any genuinely religious factors have long since been subsumed within secular politics and 'cultural traditions'. *Mutual* invocation of the deity in the conflict there as a strategic support mechanism has been redundant for several generations. Obviously one of the most notorious examples in living memory of two sides in a non-religious war self-consciously invoking the Christian deity was World

---

[39] Cf. Sproxton 1995.

War One. This produced an impressive corpus of war sermons on both sides.[40] World War Two reveals less of this phenomenon, though practical and moral support by the churches for the respective warring nations was generally undiminished.[41]

Turning now to illustrations from history of the various Christian positions. One can take samples from first, the Bible; second, the Early Church, phase I (up to about 320); third, the Early Church, phase II (from about 320 to 600); fourth, medieval Christendom (from about 600 to 1500); fifth, the Renaissance and Reformation era (from 1500 to about 1650); and sixth, the Enlightenment (from about 1650 to 1750). By the eighteenth century, attitudes to the question of war and religion were essentially differentiated and re-formulated in the modern sense of no war for the sake of theological dogma.

Testimonies in Scripture

First, the Bible: taken as a whole, it is problematic, and this was always the case. The 'problem' of the Bible is not an invention of modern scholars, text critics and sceptics. Arguably, the chief crisis in the history of the Bible as we know it occurred in the second half of the second century at a time when many Christian doctrines were still undefined. This was when a radical Christian thinker and writer, Marcion (c.85–c.160), from Sinope in the Black Sea region, urged the Church to throw out the Hebrew scriptures, or Old Testament, on the grounds that it was both irrelevant and unedifying. He argued that the God of Israel was unworthy, a war god, capricious, unstable, addicted to venge-

---

[40] Cf. Peter Matheson, 'Scottish war sermons', *Records of the Scottish Church History Society* 17 (1972), 203–13. Pressel 1967; Missala 1968.

[41] Cf. Alan Wilkinson, *Dissent or Conform? War, Peace and the English Churches 1900–1945*, London 1986. Arlie J. Hoover, *God, Britain and Hitler in World War 2. The View of the British Clergy, 1939–1945*, Westport, CT and London 1999. Heinrich Missala, *Für Volk und Vaterland. Die kirchliche Kriegshilfe im 2. Weltkrieg*, Königstein 1978. Leonore Siegele-Wenschkewitz, 'Die Evangelische Kirche Deutschlands während des 2. Weltkriegs', *Evangelische Theologie* 39 (1979), 389–409. Xavier de Montclos *et al.* (eds) 1982.

ance and punitive justice, imperfect, and devoid of the consistently highest ethical standards. Such a deity, ultimately responsible for the pains and tribulations inherent in his defective Creation, could not possibly be the father of Jesus Christ, the personification of moral perfection and harbinger of the gospel of love, grace, mercy, peace and forgiveness. His father must be an otherwise unknown supreme god.

The Church eventually expelled Marcion and placed him in the lineage of arch-heresy because of his rejection of monotheism and his associated view that fleshly humanity and the secular world were damned and irredeemable. Reaffirmed too was the idea of the fundamental unity of, and continuity between, the old and the new covenants, as well as the conviction that the historical faith of the Jews was the preparation for the full revelation of God through Jesus Christ, the Messiah. Therefore the Old Testament must be irrevocably incorporated in the Christian scriptures.

One can identify some of the bases of Marcion's position. His evaluation of Judaism and the Old Testament according to the ethical standards of the utopian Kingdom of God preached by Jesus and Paul was reminiscent of analogous reflections among writers of pagan antiquity about the moral qualities of the deities. For example, in his book, *The Republic*,[42] Plato speculated on whether the gods of Greek mythology were ethically virtuous, worthy of being images of the Supreme Good. Marcion provocatively transposed this debate on to the (Jewish-) Christian context. A true god had to be absolutely good and just, so that the Christian God, the father of Jesus Christ, should exhibit only the purest Christian morality. He claimed that Yahweh manifestly did not, so that Christianity should disassociate itself from him and all other vestiges of Jewish tradition.[43] Marcion's logic, grounded in ethical criteria, was cogent.

---

[42] See Section 378c f.

[43] Cf. Winrich Löhr, 'Did Marcion distinguish between a just god and a good god?', in *Marcion und seine kirchengeschichtliche Wirkung/Marcion and His Impact on Church History*, edited by Gerhard May and Katharina Greschat in Gemeinschaft mit Martin Meiser, (Texte und Untersuchungen

The consequence of the Church's decision to retain the Old Testament had therefore massive implications for our topic. For this meant that in the whole Christian Bible, all the four basic attitudes, arguably irreconcilable, that were mentioned earlier, are found in it. These were:

1. the mandatory holy war or crusade against non-compliant or intrusive idolaters or unbelievers;
2. pacifism, the way of absolute non-violence and non-resistance;
3. permissible war in good conscience, or at least accommodation to measured responses of force in the interests of order and security – 'just war';
4. practical peacemaking or disinterested mediation as a religious obligation, not just prudential politics.

The last three are discernible in the New Testament, though they, including the pacifist option, are not necessarily absent from the Old Testament, as the well-known pacific passage Isaiah 2.4 and the just war idea in Deuteronomy 20.10–15, 19–20 suggest.[44] The holy war (largely defensive wars of survival) is obviously confined to the Old Testament, though if it was truly God's war, its successful pursuit was not necessarily dependent on military means.[45] Further, an authentically divine war as an instrument of religious justice and righteousness could be instigated by means of unwitting foreign armies against Israel itself. The purpose was spiritual chastisement and recall to holiness.[46]

Later militarist Christians from the early Middle Ages onwards believed, however, that divine mandate for war or force could be found in the New Testament too. They cited Christ's

---

zur Geschichte der altchristlichen Literatur, vol. 150) Berlin and New York 2002, p. 146.

[44] Cf. Enz 1972. Lind 1980.

[45] Cf. von Rad 1991. Id., *Old Testament Theology* (1957), translated by D. M. G. Stalker (Edinburgh 1962), vol. 1, pp. 328–9; vol. 2, pp. 120–5, 159–61. See also Niditch 1993.

[46] Cf. J. Alberto Soggin, article 'Krieg' in *Theologische Realenzyklopädie*, gen. ed. Gerhard Müller (Berlin and New York), vol. 20 (1990), p. 23.

remark about bringing not peace, but the sword;[47] his breach of the peace in protesting about the Temple being used as a *bureau de change* and pigeon market;[48] his remark to the disciples that if they had no sword, they should buy one[49] – though he warned the disciple who offensively cut off the ear of the High Priest's servant that the way of the sword is the way of death.[50]

Those few passages can hardly be used to justify a Christian theory of just war. Paul argues that if there is a religious war, it is the spiritual warfare against sin and demons within believers that is relevant, the life-and-death conflict between 'flesh' and 'spirit'.[51] James, the only biblical writer to explicitly ask the question: 'What causes wars and fighting?', affirms that external hostilities reflect internal dysfunction and disorder.[52] And Paul's remark that 'the weapons of our warfare are not worldly',[53] mirrors Christ's remark to Pontius Pilate: 'If my kingship were of this world, my followers would fight.'[54] New Testament allegorical use of military imagery involving words like 'armour', 'battle-shield', 'fight', 'battle', 'destroy', 'sword', 'victor', 'soldier', 'captive', 'bulwark', 'wounds', 'kill', 'stronghold', 'arms', 'banner', 'standard', 'conquerors', 'legions of angels', etc. accordingly permeates classical Christian literature from the outset – perfectly understandable in societies that were heavily militarized and were to remain so indefinitely. The imagery of combat has been specifically and effectively employed by monastic orders and Christian organizations such as the Jesuit Order (Soldiers of Christ), the Boys' Brigade (Drill, Discipline and Obedience), and the Salvation Army (Blood and Fire, Swords of War against Sin), as well as in hymns, like the Psalms before them.

However, although New Testament imagery also provided adaptable language resources, it was the concrete paradigms

---

[47] Matt. 10.34. The expression was a metaphor for 'stirring it', not a threat of violence.

[48] Matt. 21.12.

[49] Luke 22.36. Anyway, swords were used for purposes other than slaying.

[50] Matt. 26.52.   [51] Rom. chapters 7, 8.   [52] James 4.1–12.

[53] 2 Cor. 10.4.   [54] John 18.36.

of military religious action against paganism, desecration and false worship in the Old Testament that were used primarily by the medieval Crusaders. They were also used in other measures of Christian military response and use of capital penalties. Examples were the resort to coercion in the evangelization programmes of the Christian Roman Empire and early medieval Europe;[55] measures against medieval heretical communities like Bogomils and Cathars, and against Anabaptists in the sixteenth century; intermittent persecution of Jews; the militarization of the Catholic–Protestant conflict in the Wars of Religion; and the religious policies accompanying Europe's colonial expansion into other non-Christian continents in the sixteenth and seventeenth centuries.

What happened, then, to the massively non-violent teaching of Jesus in the Sermon on the Mount,[56] and echoed in Paul?[57] That teaching was about moral life in the Kingdom of God. This, sponsored by the messianic Son of God, was about to break over the earth, establishing a new world of ethical perfection, ruled by God through Christ the King. However, in the New Testament, this Kingdom is somewhat elusive. Paradoxically, it is presented as both here already, and yet not quite here. In other words, the New Testament reflects a world of apparent transition – except that the transition has never been completed.

Consequently, in respect of the interim or halfway house situation reflected in most of the New Testament, there is in fact no mandatory renunciation of force, violence and war as a credal prerequisite. Christ praises the faith of the centurion in Capernaeum, whose servant he had healed[58] – he does not ask him to leave the army. Similarly, during the dialogue recorded in the Book of Acts between the pious Roman army officer, Cornelius, and Peter (who refers to the good news of peace), there is no

---

[55] Cf. Ramsay MacMullen, *Christianity & Paganism in the Fourth to Eighth Centuries* (New Haven and London 1997), pp. 12 ff.

[56] Matt. 5–7,29.

[57] For example, Rom. 12.14–21. Cf. Macgregor 1936, *passim*. Desjardins 1997.

[58] Matt. 8.5–13.

demand made of Cornelius to resign his commission.[59] Moreover, Paul accepted a military escort on his journey from Jerusalem to Caesarea[60]– he did not plead that the Lord would look after him. And lastly, we know that Jesus and Paul did not withhold tax payments to the civil authority, to which obedience is due in all matters not offensive to conscience – which most likely refers to idolatry. Accordingly, it was on this element of *de facto* accommodating realism in the New Testament, seen as permissive, that later Christian doctrines of lawful force and just war were partly based. It evolved out of the original context of having to balance two things: First, expectation of an imminent new celestial order of perfection on earth, and second, prudential Christian citizenship in the old and continuing sinful order of imperfection that was on the way out.

This, though, did not exempt believers from pursuing peace and trying to act in a Christ-like manner, as if their holiness and calling should be suspended on the grounds that the world is still an imperfect and tough place. Yet as unworkably romantic is how the notion of 'meekness' – cited by Christ in the Beatitudes,[61] and employed in some expressions of Christian spirituality – has been assessed. This is reinforced by the word's anodyne connotations in modern English. It is indeed associated in the Beatitudes with 'peacemaking', a sign of the 'peace of God' and the expected non-militant approach of disciples of Jesus. But it was subsequently linked in traditions of piety with Christ's supposedly lamb-like qualities, engendering a caricatured image of compliant passivity, evasion of conflict, tameness and submissiveness – all marks of a 'saint', of an ideal and 'true' Christian. Some pacifists have espoused this debased notion of meekness as a course of action (or inaction). The earlier wider range of meaning of the word in English comprehended better the scope of the word's meaning in Greek – 'gentle' indeed, but in the classical sense of 'equitable', 'reasonable', 'fair', 'moderate', 'restrained',

---

[59] Acts 10.1–35.
[60] Acts 23.23–35.
[61] Matt. 5.5.

'non-partisan', 'peaceable', 'impartial', 'courteous', 'cool-headed', etc. Such a sense is captured by James with his comment on the 'meekness of wisdom from above', so that 'whoever knows what is right to do and fails to do it, for him it is sin'.[62] Does this rule out physical coercion and even military action *a priori?*

All subsequent, and often conflicting, Christian varieties of opinion up to the present day on matters of civil duty including war have earthed their positions in one or other strand in the Bible. The scale of its markers, collectively ambiguous and conveying a mixed message, determined future developments, positive and negative. What does appear like a dichotomous morality derives from the longstanding *modus vivendi* between the inaugural Christian peace ethic on the one hand (theoretically normative), and a contingency ethic of legitimate recourse to force in self-defence on the other (theoretically exceptional).[63] The idea appears to sit comfortably with the Aristotelian distinction between 'absolute noble actions' (securing harmony and the common good) and 'necessary conditional actions' (like judicial removal of the manifestations of evil).[64]

Rejection of War by the Early Church up to the Fourth Century

The *second* period to review is that of Early Church, phase I, up to about 320 CE. In this phase, essential teaching simply prohibits Christian involvement in war and violence, though as was noted above, the reasons for this are disputed. One cannot be a soldier of Christ and a soldier of the Emperor at the same time. Divine attributes cannot be ascribed by Christians to the Emperor; their *Imperator*, lord, ruler or 'commander' in that regard is God or Christ,[65] to whom an oath of exclusive loyalty (*sacramentum*)

---

[62] James 3.13–18; 4.17.
[63] See Aquino and Mieth (eds), pp. 7–8, 52–60. Cf. Athanasius quotation in n. 68 below.
[64] See Aristotle, *The Politics*, Book VII, 13.
[65] E.g. Cyprian of Carthage, *Epistle* 15,1, in *The Ante-Nicene Fathers*,

is made at baptism. This is the age of Christian doves – one can cite Justin Martyr, Irenaeus of Lyons, Clement of Alexandria, Origen, Cyprian, Lactantius, and especially Tertullian as well as other writers.[66] Orientation to the pacifism of the Sermon on the Mount was viewed as mandatory, and despite the Harnack interpretation, obedience to the sixth commandment was considered as unqualified – for Christians, that is. In practice, however, Christians actually serving in the Roman army (as conscripts presumably, or as new converts) presented the problem of *de facto* accommodation, as already in the New Testament. In this connection, the Church did grant a degree of concession: soldier converts can remain in the army if they confine themselves to policing or non-combat duties. It is hard to imagine the Roman military accepting such casuistry.

Renunciation of this world and counter-cultural witness, therefore, was the keystone of the Church in these centuries, when it existed only as a small minority of the population, a fellowship of conviction Christians. This was the 'sectarian' phase of Christianity, when it was not concerned with having an influence on public 'policy' or participating in the organs of the State. There was no heroic Christian 'peace movement', only witness to the right not to conform to the expectation of military or even civil service. No Christian can serve in two kingdoms, those of God and of Caesar, so that Christians mostly did not hold public office either. As people who opted out, they were accordingly seen as 'atheists' (despisers of the traditional deities), disloyal citizens, subversive of social order and convention, and irrational enemies of humanity, worthy of contempt. Being a member of the Church in that era was often life threatening.

That being the case, how did Christians survive? One might

---

vol. V, p. 291, col. 1. *The Fathers of the Church* (Washington edn.), vol. 51. And Lactantius, *Divine Institutes*, Books VI, 8 and VII, 27, in *The Ante-Nicene Fathers*, vol. VII, p. 171, col. 1; p. 222, col. 2; p. 223, col. 2. *The Fathers of the Church* (Washington edn), vol. 49.

[66] For a convenient anthology of patristic quotations (pre-300 CE) on the subject of war and military service, see David Bercot (ed.) 1998, pp. 676–82. See also Swift 1983.

well ask. Only with difficulty, is the answer. For this was the age of intermittent bloodletting of Christians, persecution, and martyrdom, even if not so much for 'religious' reasons as on the grounds of bad 'citizenship'. The experience was, however, considered by them as redemptive – a glorious opportunity to share in the suffering, sacrificial life of Christ, despised by the 'world', and in the ultimate victory over death.

Change in the Attitude of the Christian Church as Official State Religion

The *third* era to consider is phase II of the Early Church (320–600). This reveals a transition from Christian abstentionism to Christian participation. Emperor Constantine (280–337) provided the obvious stimulus and ultimate legitimation. An upwardly mobile soldier, he converted to Christianity on the eve of a battle in 312. Later on, he superimposed Christian symbols on the regimental standards of the Roman army. In 325 he presided over the first general Church Council at Nicaea. The authorities now privileged the Christian faith. Inevitably, the Church fastly assimilated herself to secular concerns, including war and security. The legislation and attitude of Emperor Theodosius (346–395) made this development irreversible when he declared Christianity to be the sole religion of the Roman State. Rome (political authority), Athens (philosophy), and Jerusalem (revealed faith) became metaphorically fused in the Christian Roman Empire, whose army was now composed exclusively of Christians.[67] Increasingly, being Roman meant being Christian, and being Christian meant being Roman – the ways of faith and the ways of the world were now soldered together. The Roman Emperor became the guarantor on earth of the triune God.

This resulted in a farewell to the commitment to pacifism and non-violence of earlier Christianity, though the Council of

---

[67] In 416, non-Christians were barred from the army. See the *Theodosian Code* XVI, x. 21 (edited by Jill Harries and Ian Wood, Ithaca, NY 1993).

Nicaea (325) in its canon 12 had taken a hard line with Christian ex-soldiers who had returned to the army and effectively apostatized. Christian thinkers welcomed and endorsed the emerging *volte-face*, such as Eusebius of Caesarea, Athanasius,[68] and the ex-Roman senator, Bishop Ambrose of Milan. However, some others, like Basil of Caesarea in the late fourth century, were much less enamoured of the idea, considering military arks of triumph as symbols of murder.[69] A reductionist version of the early Christian refusal to bear and use arms was adopted, when from the Council of Chalcedon (451) onwards right up to the present day, the prohibition was restricted to clergy. A double standard? The sea change that occurred in the Church's thinking at that time is the ultimate source, for example, of a comment made 1,600 years later in 1935 by the English prelate and later Archbishop of Canterbury, William Temple. Like Reinhold Niebuhr after him, he described pacifism as 'heretical',[70] though he subsequently back-pedalled somewhat.

In the train of this development, which was indeed seen by some other contemporary Christians as questionable, there emerged a famously influential book both of critique and of qualified accommodation to the new situation. It was the classic composed by the North African bishop-theologian, Augustine (354–430), entitled *The City of God*.[71] In this *magnum opus*, he

---

[68] Athanasius, Bishop of Alexandria, was one of the first theologians to sanction lawful or official killing (as in the Old Testament), and so adapt Christian ethics to secular norms. See his letter to a monk, Ammonios (or Amun): 'It is not lawful to kill. But to destroy opponents in war is lawful and worthy of praise. Those who distinguish themselves in war are counted worthy of great honours, and monuments are erected celebrating their achievements. Thus the same act when unseasonable is unlawful, when seasonable, however, is appropriate and permitted', in J.-P. Migne (ed.), *Patrologia Graeca* 26, col. 1173.

[69] Cf. Hornus 1980, p. 126.

[70] *The Church of England Newspaper*, 1 November 1935. Cf. Niebuhr, in A. Holmes, 1975, p. 305.

[71] The most recent English translation is by R. W. Dyson, *The City of God Against the Pagans* (Cambridge Texts in the History of Political Thought) Cambridge 1998. Other accessible translations are in the Loeb Classical Library, vols. 411–17; Penguin Classics; Everyman's Library, nos.

devoted some sections to a realistic re-evaluation of Christian thinking on war, revealing strongly pacific, though not pacifist, leanings.[72] He primarily envisages correctional war, one occasioned by the exigencies of basic law and order in society and external relations. He is not granting theological sanction to pre-existing notions (once shared by him) of Christian imperialism maintained by the force of arms. His stance that war for reasons of natural justice has a legitimate place in Christian ethics became, in one form or other, mainstream Christian teaching up to our own times, at least theoretically.[73]

Admittedly, for most subsequent Christian leaders the element of 'justice' in any given war enterprise was usually very elastic indeed. It is notwithstanding very wrong to depict Augustine as a fountain of war-theology. On the contrary, he was primarily a theologian of peace. His utterances on the subject of war and peace in the *City of God* [74] are designed not to give war-making by Christians an unchangeable green light, and certainly not to authorize holy war; rather to sanction war only when all other possibilities were exhausted. As a last resort, it can only be adjudged as a 'tragic necessity'[75] for the sake of morality in immoral society, for the sake of the 'tranquillity of order',[76] as a remedy for collective sin, and as action not motivated by sheer enmity and hatred, rather responsible love.

The *City of God* included Augustine's response to the international terrorism of his age. The climax of this makes '11 September' look rather ephemeral in significance. That was when the figurehead of barbarian, that is, non-Roman Europe, Alaric the 'Hun', led an army of Visigoths into the capital and heart

---

982–3; The Fathers of the Church (Catholic University of America Press), vols. 8, 14, 24.

[72] See especially Robert A. Markus 1983. For examples of more conventional portrayals of Augustine's thinking on the matter, cf. Russell 1975, pp. 16–26; A. Holmes, 1975, pp. 114–45.

[73] Cf. Battenhouse (ed.) 1955, pp. 42–3, 82, 271–5.

[74] Particularly in Books XV, chaps. 4ff.; XIX, chaps. 7ff.

[75] Cf. Markus 1983, p. 12.

[76] *City of God*, Book XIX, chap. 13 (first paragraph).

of the civilized and now Christian world, Rome, in 410 and 'sacked' much of it. According to Augustine, this was actually in a manner more restrained than might have been expected – not a little due to the ironic fact that this barbarian task force was largely (Arian) Christian![77] Nonetheless, the impact of the wider, multi-front barbarian invasions resulted in the Mediterranean being not just a sea of water, but also a sea of refugees and runaway slaves. The trauma of the sack of Rome itself was, however, more symbolical and psychological, for it challenged not just the power of Rome, but its self-understanding as 'eternal', especially in 'these Christian times'. The foreboding was justified, since Alaric's strike heralded the collapse of the Roman Empire in western Europe and North Africa.

Augustine's book was largely a response to the question: where does Christianity stand in the middle of this debacle? 'Are we being punished for having abandoned the old gods?' people asked quite naturally.[78] It had been as recently as 384 that Emperor Theodosius, capping the work of Constantine, definitively 'established' Christianity as the exclusive legal religion and as a corollary, proscribed worship of the ancient gods with which Rome's 'identity' was so connected. However, vulnerability was exposed by Alaric, the antitype of Constantine, the inaugurator of the Christian Empire.

In view of Augustine's massively seminal influence on the Western mind, both in general and in relation to doctrines of war and peace, we will consider the evolution of his thinking. Often he has been applauded by some and denounced by others for his prototype Christian (or Christianized) theory of just war (*iustum bellum*[79]) – an ethical device designed primarily to inhibit war and restrict its licensing by means of prescriptive prerequisites such as its declaration by legitimate authority, just cause, and right intention. Detractors can, however, cite certain texts to

---

[77] The frontier West Goths had been converted by Wulfila (Ulfilas).

[78] *City of God*, Book I, chap. 1; Book III, chap. 31.

[79] The expression originates in Cicero, *De officiis* (*On Obligations*) I, 11, 36, where he restricts war options in accordance with principles of natural law. Similarly in his *Republic*, Book 3, 22–3.

depict Augustine as a godfather not only of crusading holy wars, but also of the Inquisition, all seen as illegitimate, unjust and intentionally wrong. Some even cast him as the virtual patent-authorizer of indiscriminate, super-destructive weapons of modern technological warfare.[80]

That later generations indiscriminately cited proof-texts from Augustine to support contrasting points of view, whether hawkish or dove-like, is explicable by the fact that his thought evolved through various stages, of which the *City of God* is the climax. Initially, Augustine believed that earthly society should reflect the divine and cosmic order of peace and harmony, based on a synthesis of rationality, morality and goodness. Any breach of these virtues on earth is subject to correction, and by force, military or otherwise, if necessary. Some years later, he modified his position slightly. In the face of evil and aggression, individual Christians are counselled to show non-resistance in self-defence. Exercise of force is the task of the security forces. No taking of the law into one's own hands, no lynch law nor community reprisals. This is the source of the Christian teaching reflected, for example, in the *Westminster Confession* (1647),[81] and in general legal theory up to modern times, that any taking of life must be 'lawful' and 'just', that is, as the outcome of judicial enquiry. This principle has been perceived as reconcilable at least with the ideas of responsible Christian citizenship that are found in the New Testament, Romans 13.1–7 in particular. There, Paul asserts that offences incurring the anger of God will be liable to punitive measures by those entrusted with the sword of justice, namely, the secular authorities.

---

[80] A splendid example of the current culture of ideological blame and contempt in this respect is the satirical tract by the Glasgow fiction writer, Tom Leonard: *On the Mass Bombing of Iraq and Kuwait, commonly known as the 'Gulf War', with Leonard's Shorter Catechism, or 'And now would you please welcome St. Augustine of Hippo, who's come along this evening to talk about "The Concept of the Just Fuel-Air-Explosive Bomb"'*, Stirling 1991.

[81] See its Chap. XXIII, 1–2, and the accompanying *Larger Catechism*, Answer to Question 136.

After this, Augustine adopts what looks like the more bellicose attitude of the Imperial Christian establishment. This arose out of his debates with Faustus, a leader of the rival Manichean religion and sharp opponent of orthodox Christianity. Faustus, like Marcion before him and other thinkers associated with dualistic 'Gnosticism',[82] had used the New Testament to condemn the Old on moral grounds. Augustine was then forced to base his notions of legitimate war and military service on more exclusively biblical, Judaeo-Christian grounds.[83] The unity of the Old and the New Testaments, a non-negotiable article of orthodox Christian doctrine, made this approach compelling and well nigh inescapable.

Anyway, he is now convinced that for all the beauty of divine order, it cannot be replicated in the world of endemic disorder by means of piety, reason, and appeals to a moral sense. For the autonomous power of sin and human inadequacy is radically subversive. Inspired by God's occasional commands in the Old Testament to make war, avenge, and redress, Augustine now puts his faith in the theocracy of the Christian Empire, God's instrument to establish righteousness and eradicate idolatry by force and coercion. Non-violence, he says, was appropriate in the Apostolic era, but now, in the political Christian era, there is prophetic, that is, biblical sanction for the use of violence by the State on Christ's behalf. In this then, one can clearly see ideas approximating to holy war and religious totalitarianism. Those who dislike Augustine most focus on this phase of his thought, and the discussion in *Against Faustus* is indeed a classical statement, availed of by Christian rulers up to the early modern era.

However, it is precisely in the *City of God*, a huge work composed in his sixties and seventies, completed in 426, that

---

[82] A nebulous way of thinking at the time to which the reality of the created natural order was repugnant.

[83] See his *Against Faustus* (AD 398), where Book XXII, chaps. 74–8 embody his most extensive discussion overall of warfare, before his revisionist adjustments in the *City of God*. English translation in *A Select Library of the Nicene and Post-Nicene Fathers*, series I, edited by Philip Schaff (New York 1890–1900), vol. IV.

Augustine moves beyond such thinking. Christians have a dual citizenship, terrestial and celestial, they are pilgrims in a foreign and miserable land. They live at the intersection of the human and the divine, the finite and the infinite. The ultimate goal of their pilgrimage is not attainable in this life. God does not normally exercise his hand directly in human affairs, not because he is not almighty, but because he chooses not to, inscrutably. The world, if not quite a blazing house in the Buddhist conception, is a theatre of war between God and Satan, angels and devils, heaven and hell, Jerusalem and Babylon. Wayfaring Christians, the Elect, are caught in the crossfire, although inwardly and spiritually, they too experience such a struggle in their own persons. There is no lasting security or stability here and now. Periods of earthly peace, like the *pax romana*, are ephemeral and fragile, and only dimly reflect the *pax Christi*, the eternal Peace of Christ.[84]

Augustine's thinking on life and society – the miseries and hazards which he described as like 'hell on earth'[85] – and the Christian role in it, is now shaped by realism and pragmatism. He no longer envisages a Christian society or body politic, a contradiction in terms. Rather, he posits a disturbed and dysfunctional society in which Christians should participate publicly in order to exercise a mitigating influence. His concept is governed, not by out and out pessimism, but by reflection on the art of the possible. Human society is and will remain a melting pot of conflicting interests, of antinomies, tensions and contradictions, an arena of realpolitik where rationality is not sovereign. Good government, however, prevents anarchy, it is conflict management by means of checks and balances, and Christians can contribute. Just government involves coercion at various levels, and sometimes at junctures of extreme tension, inescapable war. At that point, Christians cannot simply opt out. Augustine's ultimate moral position is that just war is preferable to unjust peace in which wrong becomes infrastructural and canonical.

---

[84] Cf. Wengst 1987.
[85] *City of God*, Book XXII, chap. 22 (*ad fin.*).

Finally, the Numidian bishop is convinced that while war is of utilitarian moral value, it should *not* be invested with special spiritual or religious significance. War is a thing of humans, not of God. Anyway, the Christian Church, the gateway to eternity, ought not to identify itself inwardly with any socio-political structure and its ideologies due to their intrinsic obsolescence. Her Master is Christ, not the Emperor. If war is often inevitable – after all there will always be 'wars and rumours of wars' (Matt. 24.6) – the wise (and Augustine hopes that Christians will be among them) will do what they can to prevent it. The paradox is expressed in some of his letters, where he says: 'War is waged that peace may be obtained – but it is a greater glory to kill war with words than men with swords, to gain and maintain peace by means of peace, not by means of war.'[86] In the first part of this quotation, there are echoes of Aristotle's famous remark: 'We make war that we may live in peace',[87] which has become the virtual self-justifying motto of current United States foreign policy. That apart, while future Christian tradition was zealous in quarrying Augustine to justify various points of view on the matter, one has to say there is limited evidence of addiction to his mature and ultimate position, embodied in the second part of the above quotation. He may have sanctioned war, but he definitely did not glorify or sanctify it in the way most churches have done up to the twentieth century.

Meanwhile, Christian purists and idealists retreated into monasteries and convents to pursue the private life of Christian perfection undisturbed by external, secular trials and tribulations. Their wars and battles were primarily with invisible but potent enemies within their own psyches.

---

[86] See *Epistles* 47, 5; 189, 6; 229, 2.

[87] *The Nicomachean Ethics*, Book X, 7 [= 1177^{b}14]. See also *The Politics*, Book VII, xiv, 13. The notion was prefigured by Plato's idea of 'war for the sake of peace'; see his *Laws*, Book 1. See also Cicero, *On Obligations* I, 11, 35; I, 23, 79. The chief vehicle of the idea's transmission in the Latin West was Gratian's *Decretals,* incorporated in Canon Law.

Theory and Practice in Medieval Christianity

To turn to the *fourth* era, namely medieval Christendom (600–1500): possibly as a consequence of the adaptation of European Christianity to the belligerent militarism of barbarian culture – especially Germanic – the Middle Ages experienced the acceleration of Christian imperialist wars on pagans and the emergence of the special form of holy war, the 'crusade' against the progress of Islamic powers. This included enterprises against anti-Catholic heretics like Bogomils, Cathars or Albigensians, and pagan Slavs like the Wends.[88] Holy warriors and Christian knights, often monastic, like the Knights Templar, soldiers of Christ, became role models for the disciplined military élite. In fact, therefore, notions of just war were often suspended, so that 'total war', brutality, atrocities, annihilation and demonization of the enemy, especially if non-Christian or heretical, became the norm. The great Cistercian preacher and inspiration for the Knights Templar, Bernard of Clairvaux (1090–1153) – well known as an activist for the Peace of God among Christians – was the chief religious polemicist for the Second Crusade (1147–49). 'Be killed or be converted' was the rather unevangelical concept he allegedly supplied in respect of not only Eastern Moslems but also European pagans.[89] At least the option of conversion was offered, though to be fair to Bernard, he urged that the subdued be spared and did not foresee immediate conversion.

The Islam-policy of the Church was not unremittingly about repelling, liquidating or subjugating Moslems; it was also associated with mission and evangelization, and not always coercive.[90] As already mentioned above, a later (lay) Catholic and more radically Christian voice suggesting it might be better to throw away swords as instruments of Christian witness and mission was that of the ex-holy warrior, Francis of Assisi (d. 1224).

---

[88] Cf. Erdmann 1977. Mastnak 2002, pp. 167–8.

[89] Cf. Mastnak 2002, pp. 154–68 (subsection entitled: 'Sanctification of Crime').

[90] See Elizabeth Siberry, 'Missionaries and Crusaders, 1095–1274: Opponents or Allies?', in Sheils (ed.) 1983, pp. 103–10.

Lest the whole of Christianity in these centuries should be tarred with the same brush of moral opprobrium from a modern human rights and ethically fundamentalist perspective, it should be pointed out that on the matter of the militarist ethos culminating in the Crusades, 'theology' did not always accord with popular religious sentiment and praxis. The Crusades, governed by the 'will of God', were militantly theocratic rather than theologically motivated wars. The just war concept of classical and theological traditions was ignored as irrelevant in religiously heterogeneous contexts. Voices of theological dissent from the trend were in vain, such as Peter Damian (1006–72), and Anselm of Canterbury (1033–1109). Both had denounced the culture of 'Blessed be war', the superimposing of the sword on the cross.

Furthermore, of little impact was later scholastic recycling of the just war idea of Augustine. This was re-articulated, synthesized and supplemented by Thomas Aquinas (*c.*1224–74) in a university context. The conditions in which Christians may opt for war (*jus ad bellum*) are: declaration of war by a legitimate civil authority; just cause; and the right intention of promoting good that qualifies the licence to kill, confining it to regrettable necessity.[91] Though related to Augustine's notion of 'compassionate killing' out of higher 'love' and divorced from personal hatred and animosity, the third requirement was relatively innovative. It reflected an attempt to reconcile Christian teaching more explicitly with the ethical and political theory of Aristotle[92] – determinative of true justice is the 'common good', the good of 'another', 'one's neighbour', and even ultimately of an enemy. Thomas was particularly concerned about the ethics of the conduct of war (*jus in bello*), and the issue of proportionality. In reality, this was all rather academic in the Crusading era, when the 'normal rules' were *de facto* suspended. Yet from a post-Enlightenment perspective, it may be hard for some people to credit that (discounting the matter of abominable conduct)

---

[91] Cf. Russell 1975, pp. 259–91. Barnes 1982.
[92] See especially Books V & VI of *The Nicomachean Ethics*. Cf. nn. 64 and 79 above.

the Crusades did in the minds of Christian theologians qualify as a just war. To Thomas, they could be vindicated as an imperative of the natural order occasioning a 'humanitarian intervention'[93] to save those oppressed by the tyrannical Turks, the Saracens (who were incidentally Moslems and who oppressed Arab Moslems as well).

Anyway, his great work, the *Summa theologiae*,[94] devotes only five out of 4,000 pages to the topic (though elsewhere in the *Summa* and in other writings, he does address related issues). Some critics have declared, somewhat harshly, that with Thomas, the Peace (or Truce) of God was declared bankrupt by scholastic theology.[95] There was certainly no resonance among contemporaries. Be that as it may, the essential theoretical features of the standard Christian doctrine of just war synthesized with Classical natural law thinking were cumulatively provided by Augustine and Thomas. Subsequent reiterations or reformulations derive from their reasoning.[96]

On the religious fringes, the old Christian pacifist tradition, now seen as virtual heresy, was upheld by disempowered dissenters like the Waldensians,[97] the Bohemian Brethren,[98] as well as by the Spiritual Franciscans and others.[99] In sum: by the Middle Ages, Christian thinking and practice on war and peace had mutated from pacifism to just war, and then to the totally hostile Crusading spirit, detached from ethical norms, a spirit which could be invoked not just against Muslims, but also against

---

[93] *Summa theologiae*, secunda secundae, quaestio 40 a 1. Cf. Gerhard Bestermöller, *Thomas von Aquin und der gerechte Krieg. Friedensethik im theologischen Kontext der 'Summa theologiae'*, (Theologie und Frieden 4) Cologne 1990, pp. 167ff.

[94] Secunda secundae, quaestio 40 and quaestio 41.

[95] Cited by Maron 1996, p. 27, n. 1.

[96] Cf. Johnson 1981. Lisa S. Cahill, 'Christian Just War Tradition: Tensions and Development', in Aquino and Mieth (eds) 2001, pp. 74–82.

[97] Cf. Peter Biller, 'Medieval Waldensian Abhorrence of Killing pre-c.1400', in Sheils (ed.) 1983, pp. 129–46.

[98] Cf. Peter Brock, *The Political and Social Doctrines of the Unity of Czech Brethren in the Fifteenth and Early Sixteenth Centuries*, 's-Gravenhage 1957.

[99] Cf. relevant works by Brock at n. 20 above.

heterodox Christians, Jews and others. This is the conventional picture, one of uncompromising tyranny and oppression. Yet it is perhaps not the full one. It can be argued that had it not been for the Christian leaven in society with its elements of mitigating, civilizing and restraining influence based on the higher law of God, medieval Europe would have been much more 'barbaric', 'dark', and 'primitive' than it is supposed to have been.[100]

Controversy and Diversity During the Renaissance and the Reformation

The *fifth* era to draw attention to is that of the Renaissance and Reformation (1500–1650). This reflects, in new manifestations, the uneasy co-existence clash of the various traditional concepts. Christian Humanists – thinkers and scholars devoted to the study of Antiquity and concerned with the restoration of origi-nal biblical and Early Church values – stressed the precedence of right Christian living over right formulaic doctrine and helped revive the ideal of *pax Christi*, Christian Peace.[101] Examples were Thomas More in his *Utopia*, but more especially Erasmus of Rotterdam (1469–1536) in his *Complaint of Peace* (1517). Pre-viously, in the 1515 edition of his famous collection of *Adages*, Erasmus had published a long excursus[102] on a dictum originat-ing in the ancient Greek poet, Pindar.[103] In its Latin reception this was: *dulce inexpertis bellum* ('war is lovely for those who have never experienced it').[104] Erasmus made much use of the restrain-

---

[100] Cf. Peter Brown, *The Rise of Western Christendom*, Blackwell Publishers 1996.

[101] Cf. Robert P. Adams, *The Better Part of Valor. More, Erasmus, Colet and Vives on Humanism, War and Peace*, Seattle 1962.

[102] English translation in Margaret Mann Phillips, *The 'Adages' of Erasmus. A Study with Translations* (Cambridge 1964), pp. 308–53. See also pp. 112–14.

[103] *Fragment* 110. Cf. *The Odes and Selected Fragments – Pindar*, edited by Richard Stoneman, London and Vermont 1997.

[104] Cf. Roland H. Bainton, 'The *Complaint of Peace* of Erasmus, Classi-cal and Christian Sources', in id. *Early and Medieval Christianity* (London 1965), pp. 227–8.

ing moral argument, particularly in respect of indiscriminate destruction and innocent suffering, what is now called 'collateral
damage'.[105]

The *Complaint of Peace*, which underwent 32 editions in the
sixteenth century, has been translated many times into English,
particularly at times of war fever, such as the Napoleonic Wars
(1799–1815) and the twentieth-century World Wars. Much of
it appeared in a collection published in the early nineteenth century by the *Society for the Promotion of Universal and Permanent Peace*.[106] It has been the most widely read peace-tract ever
written.[107] Erasmus raised doubts about the viability at least of
the just war doctrine, though both here and more explicitly in a
later writing, *On the War Against the Turks* (1530),[108] he disa-
vowed absolute pacifism. In this case, defensive military action
is permissible provided a spirit of repentance and a higher commitment to mission by persuasion accompanies it. (This position
means, of course, that even Erasmus forfeits high esteem in the
Olympian high ground of some modern multi-culturalist thinking, since he clearly believed in world Christian mission, seen
by some as 'Christian imperialism'.) More pertinently, on the
general issue of war the *Complaint* raised a recurrent problem:
since there is no actual provision for impartial adjudication, no
international tribunal, how can the justice of a war be credibly
established?

Widely quoted (or paraphrased) examples of Erasmus' tone
on the matter of the ethical scandal of inter-Christian war making are:

How can you say 'Our' Father, if you plunge steel into the guts
of your brother? Christ compared himself to a hen. Christians

---

[105] Id. *Erasmus of Christendom* (London 1970), pp. 150–8.

[106] *Extracts from the Writings of Erasmus in the Subject of War*, (Tract
no. 4) London 1830.

[107] Translation of full text in *Collected Works of Erasmus* (Toronto
1974–), vol. 27. Long extract in *The Erasmus Reader*, edited by Erika
Rummel (Toronto 1990), pp. 287–314.

[108] In *Collected Works of Erasmus*, vol. 64. Extracts in *Erasmus Reader*,
pp. 315–33.

behave like hawks. Christ was a shepherd of sheep. If the flock tears itself to pieces, what is there left for wolves to do? [109]

Such polemic was directed less at war or military action in itself than at internecine strife between parties that are 'Christian'. The problem is not just moral, but a religio-ethical scandal: 'The cross is displayed in both camps, and the sacraments are administered on both sides. The cross fights the cross and Christ makes war on Christ.'[110] In other words, Erasmus was highlighting internal Christian moral degeneration and morbidity, and so a double calamity. In the last analysis however, much lauded Christian Humanist thinking does not substantively advance on the best of mainstream medieval precedent.

The mainstream Reformers, Catholic and Protestant, adhered essentially to traditional theories of legitimate force and just war against external enemies or internal revolution, though the early Zwingli flirted with Erasmian pacifist ideas. Reflection on the issue in this era was far from abstract or academic. For the context in Balkanized Europe was not just one of regular 'international' or 'inter-kingdom' wars, but also endemic civil wars arising from regional baronial feuds, ecclesiastical militarism, private armies and a widespread culture of mercenary service. Over and above this, there were manifestations of serious sedition, rebellion and apocalyptic terrorism, social and religious, Moslem Turkish aggression, civil secessionism and total pacifist renunciation of coercion and force urged by radical religious thinkers like some 'Anabaptists'. The situation was exacerbated by advances in military technology occasioning an 'arms race'.

Normative for Reformation theology's subscription to the exclusive competence and authority of civil government was Luther's *On Temporal Authority* (1523).[111] This reaffirmed the divinely legitimated obligation of rulers to exercise the sword, if

---

[109] See *Erasmus Reader*, pp. 298–9. Bainton, *Erasmus of Christendom*, p. 155.

[110] *Erasmus Reader*, p. 303.

[111] In *Luther's Works* (gen. eds. J. Pelikan and H. T. Lehmann), vol. 45, pp. 81–129. Original German in Weimar edn, vol. 11.

necessary, in the administration of justice. It distinguished between the impersonal office and the personal holder of it. In contentious matters threatening the peace of society, 'no one should
be his own judge' urged Luther, thereby invoking a notion of
arbitration. He addressed the more concrete issue of the place
of genuine Christians in the army in *Whether Soldiers Too Can
Be Saved* (1526/27).[112] Such a career, he reaffirms, is compatible
with a good Christian conscience, provided the military activity
is defensive and not aggressive, 'pre-emptive' or retaliatory. He
is not averse to appealing to Aristotelian ideas of justice and self-
defence: war is only an option of last resort, it must be judicially
regulated, and the ethical standing of the soldier must be safe-
guarded. Moreover, on religious grounds, the right of conscientious objection can be exercised if the cause is unjust, as the fear
of God overrides the fear of men.

It was in his tract on military action against the Islamic Turks
that Luther broke controversial new ground: *On War Against
the Turks* (1529).[113] In this he startlingly rejects the old concept
of religious crusade. This was based on his innovative notion that
war on the grounds of religion was not permissible, since coercion in spiritual matters is unchristian. The Kingdom of heaven,
the realm of the Spirit, and the kingdoms of earth, the realms of
the flesh, should not be confused. Luther shared Erasmus' abhorrence at the obscenity of flaunting Christian symbols in battle
situations. Excluded also was any idea of initiating a 'Protestant'
war against the Catholic Emperor and Estates (a notion that was
not reciprocated!).

The specifically 'Christian' input to coping with the Turkish
menace should be, Luther maintained (echoing Erasmus), repentance, amendment of life, and prayer, since God was using the
Turks to chastise unfaithful Christianity. Earlier, he handed a
propaganda gift to the Catholic establishment when, in pass-

---

[112] *Luther's Works*, vol. 46, pp. 93–137. Weimar edn, vol. 19. The bulk
of the text is also in A. Holmes (ed.), 1975, pp. 140–64.

[113] *Luther's Works*, vol. 46, pp. 161–205. Weimar edn, vol. 30/2.

ing, he had expressed such an idea in an even more radical form. Going beyond Erasmus, he remarked that fighting against the Turk is to resist the corrective rod of God on sin.[114] In the papal condemnation of Luther in 1520, this was one of the 40 errors (no. 34) cited against him. In his 1529 writing, however, he arrives at a compromise position. Faced with the Turks, Christians' primary response should still be spiritual self-examination. In terms of divinely approved natural law, however, Christians may participate in a defensive Turkish war, but only as subjects of the Emperor, the responsible authority, not as crusaders led by the Church or an irresponsible Christian prince in search of a dramatic guarantee of personal salvation. Such a perspective helped reinforce the Catholic view that the Protestant Reformers were soft on Islam and lukewarm about mission in general. It certainly represented a new division within Christian attitudes.

Though Calvin dedicates no specific writing to the subject, his general discussion of civil government in the *Institutes*[115] devotes some brief sections to the issue of judicial violence and legitimate war. His way of thinking on the matter is essentially within the parameters of Luther and Augustine, though he is more attuned to natural law thinking (as would be expected from one with a legal training). Calvin takes little for granted. The ethical dilemma for a Christian to reconcile the divine commandment not to kill with the killing required or necessitated by the course of justice is 'a hard and difficult question'. Also, 'since Christ's coming has changed nothing' (in regard to the reality of sin), and since the New Testament 'is not about civil government, rather the spiritual kingdom of Christ', violence and war may be resorted to 'in extreme necessity' if mayhem and anarchy are not to hold sway. Yet this doctrine, insists Calvin, should provide

---

[114] The offending statement was made by Luther in his *Explanation of the Ninety-five Theses* (1518); see *Luther's Works*, vol. 31, pp. 91–2 (citing Isa. 10.5).

[115] Book IV, 20, 10–12. See *Institutes of the Christian Religion*, ed. John T. McNeill (Library of Christian Classics 21), Philadelphia and London 1960, vol. 2, pp. 1497–1501. Text is also in Holmes, *War and Christian Ethics* (see n. 31 above), pp. 165–9.

no comfortable justification or grounds for complacency among pro-war Christians, since their obligation is 'to do more than wage war to seek peace'.[116] The well-being of communities and populations, 'public tranquillity', must be paramount, so that the option of war should only be invoked after all other means of conflict resolution have been exhausted.

However, within the slipstream of Christian reform thinking at the time, radically alternative views emerged that challenged mainstream Catholic and Protestant conceptions of war and peace, and of Christians in the world. Two antithetically opposed positions can be referred to. Both of them derived from a rejection of the dominant view that Christian existence functions partly in the spiritual kingdom of Christ and partly in the worldly kingdom of earth where witness expresses itself in interim sin-management – not just individual, but also collective. This is because sanctification of the 'world' is a long-term objective, to be completed by Christ himself after the 'last days'.

One extremist alternative to such thinking was represented by Thomas Müntzer, the socio-political and religious revolutionary, mystical-spiritualist theologian of sanctification by sacrifice, catastrophe and violence, and a self-declared instrument of divine righteousness and wrath against sin, corruption and Spirit-killing 'book' religion. He consequently abolished the conceptual distinction between earthly and heavenly kingdoms in his zeal to convert the world into a sinner-free paradise of saints. The Kingdom and Peace of God are achievable here and now by apocalyptic tumult, blood and physical suffering, like that of Christ. Müntzer's analysis of worldly society as institutionalized oppression was not without merit, but his liberating solution – the Elect should exterminate sinners, especially rulers and clergy, all 'men of the flesh'[117] – helped lead to the holocaust of the Peasants' Revolt (1525). His notions of a theocratic regime

---

[116] Cf. to n. 87 above.

[117] See his 'Sermon to the Princes' in Michael G. Baylor (ed.), *The Radical Reformation*, (Cambridge Texts in the History of Political Thought) Cambridge 1991, pp. 11–32.

of terror and sacred violence administered by God's own agents like himself also re-emerged in the equally traumatic, so-called 'Anabaptist' thousand-year *Reich* of Christ in Münster in West-phalia in 1534.

At the other end of the dissenting spectrum were manifestations of complete pacifist renunciation of violence. This was found among many Anabaptist and other radical religious groups, inheriting to some extent ancient and medieval traditions on the matter. Like Müntzer, they rejected the view that the 'world' of 'flesh' and the 'spirit' of heaven were in any way compatible, even provisionally. Unlike Müntzer, rather than seek to abol-ish the 'world', they seceded from it and its 'ways', preferring to live cocooned within the 'perfection of Christ'. This separation-ist theology was the basis of their pacifism, non-resistance, and rejection of physical coercion and violence. A truly revolutionary position (secular 'Christian society' is pure fantasy), they were inevitably harshly persecuted, more for such thinking than their rejection of infant baptism. Their understanding is affirmed in parts of the chief summary statement of Anabaptism at the time, the *Schleitheim Confession* (1527):[118] 'As Christ is, so too must his members be', and further: 'Worldly people are armed with spikes and iron, Christians with the armour of God – truth, jus-tice, peace, faith, salvation and the Word of God.' Accordingly, not only clergy should not wield the sword (as taught by Catho-lic and Protestant theology), but also the Christian laity. Thereby one limitation of the Reformation doctrine of 'the priesthood of all believers' was exposed!

Despite persecution, this way of thinking survived on the fringes among the Mennonites, Hutterites and later the Quakers.[119] The chief Quaker apologist in this respect was the influential Scot, Robert Barclay (1648–1690),[120] who received little honour in his own country during the Covenanting era and beyond.

---

[118] *Ibid.*, pp. 172–80, especially articles 4 and 6.
[119] Cf. Peter Brock, *Freedom from Violence. Sectarian nonresistance from the Middle Ages to the Great War*, London and Toronto 1991. Id. *The Quaker Peace Testimony 1660–1914*, York 1990.
[120] See his *Apology for the True Christian Divinity* (s.l.) 1678, English

Despite slightly unjustified attempts to accord the distinction to Erasmus' *Complaint of Peace*, the only book published in the Reformation and Renaissance era devoted to an unrestricted anti-war case was by the anti-ecclesiastic spiritualist and religious eclectic, Sebastian Franck (1499–1542) – *Warbook of Peace* (1539).[121] This work, written under the pseudonym of Friderich Wernstreyt ('Pacific Fightstrife') was denounced widely as subversive. Franck's concern was not just with the degrading effect of war on society, but on the damage it does to the human soul. He is one of the first to reinterpret the role of Christian conscience in the matter, by refusing to accept both Roman Catholic and Reformed appeal to the distinction between person (agent) and office. This had been the escape route enabling the Christian conscience to feel uncompromised in performing nasty official business. 'I was only obeying orders.' Franck's position, like that of the pacifist Anabaptists, therefore resembles that in phase 1 of the Early Church: the only war that is just is a spiritual war. For all that, Franck had little to say on the process of practical peacemaking in this world, so that he has been criticized in modern times for having little vision beyond quietist inaction.

In the meantime, thinking about and articulation of just war theory made significant advances in Roman Catholic circles – ultimately in such a way as to transcend confessional differences and become embedded in general jurisprudence and political theory from the late sixteenth century onwards. This was an outcome of the Thomist and Aristotelian revival in the century, and with it, a more informed reappropriation of the just war doctrine both in Thomas and in classical natural law ideas. Two names

---

translation of Latin original (1676). There were to be 14 editions, the last in Glasgow in 1886. It was also translated into French, German, and Spanish.

[121] *Krieg Büchlin des Friedes.* A 1550 edn was reprinted in 1975. See also Bruno Quast, 'Krieg Büchlin des Friedes'. Studien zum radikalreformatorischen Spiritualismus, *Bibliotheca Germanica* 31 (1993). Sigrid Looß, 'Sebastian Francks Aufassungen zu Frieden und Krieg im historischen Kontext', in Jan-Dirk Müller (ed.), *Sebastian Franck (1499–1542)*, (Wolfenbütteler Forschungen 56) Wiesbaden 1993, pp. 119–30.

stand out. Firstly, Francis de Vitoria (1485–1546), a Thomist scholastic theologian in Salamanca. Vitoria's utterances recall the original objective of the just war notion, namely, to restrict the causes and moderate the conduct of war, as well as to restrain the claims of the triumphant party (unlike what happened at Versailles in 1918). He expressed these ideas with exceptional clarity in his *The Law of War*,[122] lectures first published in 1586 – in which he also polemicizes against perceived pacifism of Protestant 'heresy'.

The second figure of significance was Francis de Suarez (1548–1617), a Jesuit theologian and scholastic philosopher. His thinking, based on cues taken from Thomas and Vitoria on the putative precedence of 'law of nations' over individual natural and civil law systems, anticipates modern universal 'international law' as the framework in which war should be adjudicated and managed. The lack of this had been particularly lamented by Erasmus. In addition, like some largely Calvinist theologians and thinkers, Suarez foresaw extending the validity of the war option to the eventuality of popular revolution against a tyrannical ruler, as well as to pre-emptive military strikes if the outcome is good. Such ideas are expounded particularly in Suarez' *On the Three Theological Virtues, Faith, Hope and Charity* (1621).[123]

Signs of Partial Theoretical Breakthrough in the Enlightenment Era

Lastly, despite the strictures of the Reformers on aggressive war for the sake of the religion, late sixteenth- and seventeenth-century Europe demonstrated that rulers and churches were not shy about pursuing internecine religious wars and crusades for

---

[122] Text in Anthony Pagden and Jeremy Lawrance, *Francisco de Vitoria. Political Writings*, (Cambridge Texts in the History of Political Thought) Cambridge 1991, pp. 295–327. Brief extract in A. Holmes 1975, pp. 118–19.
[123] Section on 'Charity: Disputation 13'. See *Selections from Three Works by Francisco de Suarez*, (The Classics of International Law) Oxford 1944, vol. 2, pp. 800–65. Much of text also in A. Holmes 1975, pp. 199–225.

their version of the gospel. Eventually, two factors helped determine a new way of thinking. First, Christian confessional war-
fatigue and aversion emerged from the largely inconclusive wars
of religion. Secondly, the Enlightenment. The cumulative outcome was that killing for the sake of theological dogma became
widely unacceptable (as Luther had urged in the 1520s), so that
religion was ultimately eliminated as an ostensible *casus belli*
undertaken by a civil power.

The formative thinkers in this process of relative neutraliza-
tion were not so much theologians or church leaders (though
Suarez too had questioned the legitimacy of religious war), but
lay Christian philosophers and thinkers. To be cited in particular is the influential and enlightened Dutch Calvinist jurist and
strong advocate of the prerogatives of 'international law' and
arbitration mechanisms in the sphere of military hostilities,
Hugo Grotius (1583–1645). His *On the Laws of War on Peace*
(1625)[124] included an exposition of the conviction that among the
valid causes of just war, religion has no place. Religious belief, as
personal conviction, belongs to the realm of private conscience,
not civil law. Articles of faith cannot be judicially or militarily
imposed with any degree of justification. This excludes, therefore, internal persecutions as well as external religious wars
against other Christian confessions, heretics and 'infidels'. It implied 'freedom of religion'. The book became very relevant during the Thirty Years War of religion (1618–48), though in 1627
it was placed on the Index of Prohibited Books of the Catholic
Church. Its ideas became widely accepted in principle throughout most of civil Europe during the eighteenth century – even
though few established churches explicitly acclaimed them. Prudential acceptance or grudging compliance was what prevailed.

Not that this impetus towards the formal secularization of
the causes of war prevented people on both sides in future conflicts from claiming that God was on their side. But by the end of
the seventeenth century at least, explicitly religious war among

---

[124] Text in The Classics of International Law (Washington 1913–1925),
vol. 2.

Christians became largely a thing of the past, even if inflamed sentiment survived much longer. Thereby, the dawn of the 'modern era' was reached, though wars of increasing magnitude continued to be pursued. This has often been not so much according to just war principles (apart from pure defence) as to motives of greed, ambition, rivalry, aggrandizement, might rather than right, and increasingly, universalist claims of a non-religious sort and so on. This is the point at which one should recall Richard Dawkins' maxim that 'religion causes war'.

Conclusion

Everyone likes simplicity and clear guidelines. However, to reiterate the chief thesis of this essay – biblical and historical evidence suggests that one should not speak of *the* Christian attitude to war, rather, Christian attitudes to war. Christians are not immutably unanimous about the legitimacy of force, violence and war, nor were they in the past, going back to early times. As a corollary, they have in practice disagreed about peace too, even if everyone subscribes to it. In Vergil's *Aeneid*, Book 8, there is an account of a monstrous, fire-breathing giant called Cacus (the very name means 'trouble'), the ultimate neighbour from hell. He terrorized the neighbourhood with atrocious deeds, and then retreated to his mountain cave, an ante-room of the nether world. However, what roused the fury of Cacus most of all was any interference in the peace in his own cave. Even ogres like him appreciated the value of repose, just as society was heartily grateful for his eventual assassination by Hercules.[125]

Nearly everyone fears war and loves peace, yet wars occur regularly. The last word can be given to the seventeenth-century English Presbyterian writer, Richard Baxter. In his book, *The Reformed Pastor* (1657), he stated in another context that 'I have

---

[125] Augustine cites the example of Cacus in his *City of God*, Book XIX, chap. 12, summarized in the Cambridge translation as 'That even the ferocity of war and all human discords have as their goal the peace that every nature desires.'

hardly ever met anyone who will not speak for concord and peace, or at least who will not speak expressly against it. Yet it is not common to encounter those who are addicted to promoting it'.[126]

Select Bibliography

Abrams, R. H., 1969, *Preachers Present Arms: The Role of the American Churches and Clergy in World Wars I and II*, Scottdale PA: Herald.

Aquino, M. P., and Mieth D. (eds), 2001, The Return of the Just War, *Concilium, International Journal for Theology* (No. 2).

Bainton, R. H., 1961, *Christian Attitudes toward War and Peace. A Historical Survey and Re-evaluation*, London: Hodder and Stoughton.

Barbier, J.-B., 1966, *Le pacifisme dans l'histoire de France de l'an mille à nos jours*, Paris: La Librairie Française.

Barnes, J., 1982, The Just War, in: *The Cambridge History of Later Medieval Philosophy*, ed. N. Kretzmann, A. Kenny, J. Pinborg and Eleonore Stump, Cambridge: Cambridge University Press, pp. 771–84.

Battenhouse, R. W. (ed.), 1955, *A Companion to the Study of St Augustine*, Oxford and New York: Oxford University Press.

Bercot, D. (ed.), 1998, *A Dictionary of Early Christian Beliefs: A Reference Guide to more than 700 Topics Discussed by the Church Fathers*, Peabody, Mass.: Hendricson Publishing.

Brock, P., 1981, *Roots of War Resistance: A Brief History of Pacifism from Jesus to Tolstoy*, Nyack, NY: Fellowship of Reconciliation.

Brock, P., 1998, *Varieties of Pacifism: A Survey from Antiquity to the Outset of the Twentieth Century*, Syracuse, NY: Syracuse University Press.

Brock, P. and Young, N. (eds), 1999, *Pacifism in the Twentieth Century*, Syracuse, NY: Syracuse University Press.

Brown, S. J., 1994, A Solemn Purification by Fire. Responses to the Great War in the Scottish Presbyterian Churches, *Journal of Ecclesiastical History* 45, pp. 82–104.

Cadoux, C. J., 1982, *Early Christian Attitudes to War: A Contribution to the History of Christian Ethics*, New York: Seabury Press (reprint of 1940 edn).

Deschner, K., 1986–2000, *Kriminalgeschichte des Christentums*, vols 1–7, Reinbek: Rowohlt.

Desjardins, M. R., 1997, *Peace, Violence and the New Testament* (The Biblical Seminar 46), Sheffield: Sheffield University Press.

---

[126] In Chapter 3.

Dousse, M., 2002, *Dieu en guerre. La violence au coeur des trois mono-théismes*, Paris: Edition Albin Michel.

Enz, J. J., 1972, *The Christian and Warfare: The Roots of Pacifism in the Old Testament*, Scottdale, PA: Herald.

Erdmann, C., 1977, *The Origin of the Idea of Crusade*, trans. by M. W. Baldwin and W. Goffart, Princeton: Princeton University Press.

Ferguson, J., 1977, *War and Peace in the World's Religions*, London: Sheldon Press.

Girard, R., 1977, *Violence and the Sacred*, trans. from French by Patrick Gregory, Baltimore and London: Johns Hopkins University Press.

Harnack, A. von, 1981, *Militia Christi. The Christian Religion and the Military in the First Three Centuries*, trans. from German and introduced by D. McInnes Gracie, Philadephia: Fortress Press.

Harvey, A. E., 1999, *Demanding Peace: Christian Responses to War and Violence*, London: SCM.

Heering, G. J., 1930, *The Fall of Christianity: A Study of Christianity, the State and War*, trans. from Dutch by J. W. Thompson, London: Allen and Unwin.

Helgeland, J., 1974, Christians and the Roman Army, A.D. 173–337, *Church History* 43, pp. 149–61.

Helgeland, J., Daly, R. J. and Burns, J. P. (eds), 1987, *Christians and the Military: The Early Experience*, London: SCM.

Holmes, A. F. (ed.), 1975, *War and Christian Ethics: Classic Readings on the Morality of War*, Grand Rapids, Mich.: Baker House.

Holmes, R. L., 1989, *On War and Morality*, Princeton, NJ: Princeton University Press.

Hoover, A. J., 1989, *God, Germany and Britain in the Great War: A Study in Clerical Nationalism*, London and New York: Praeger Publishers.

Hornus, J.-M., 1980, *Évangile et labarum. Etude sur l'attitude du christianisme primitif devant les problèmes de l'Etat, de la guerre et de la violence* (Geneva: Labor et Fides, 1960), revised by the author and translated into English by Alan Kreider and Oliver Coburn as *'It is not lawful for me to fight'. Early Christian Attitudes toward War, Violence and the State*, Scottdale, PA: Herald.

Johnson, J. T., 1981, *Just War Tradition and the Restraint of War: A Moral and Historical Enquiry*, Princeton: Princeton University Press.

Johnson, J. T., 1997, *The Holy War Idea in Western and Islamic Traditions*, Pennsylvania State University Press.

Lind, M. C., 1980, *Yahweh is Warrior: The Theology of Warfare in Ancient Israel*, Scottdale, PA: Herald.

Macgregor, G. H. C., 1936, *The New Testament Basis of Pacifism*, London: James Clarke.

Macquarrie, J., 1973, *The Concept of Peace*, London: SCM.

Markus, R. A., 1983, St Augustine's Views On the Just War, in: Sheils, W. J. (ed.), *The Church and War* (Studies in Church History 20), Oxford: Blackwell, pp. 1–15.

Maron, G., 1996, Frieden und Krieg. Ein Blick in die Theologie und Kirchengeschichte, in P. Herrmann (ed.), *Glaubenskriege in Vergangenheit und Gegenwart*, Göttingen: Vandenhoeck & Ruprecht, pp. 17–36.

Marrin, A., 1974, *The Last Crusade: The Church of England in the First World War*, Durham, NC: Duke University Press.

Martin, D., 1997, *Does Christianity Cause War?*, Oxford: Oxford University Press.

Mastnak, T., 2002, *Crusading Peace. Christendom, the Muslim World, and Western Political Order*, Berkeley, Los Angeles and London: The University of California Press.

McKeogh, C., 1997, *The Political Realism of Reinhold Niebuhr: A Pragmatic Approach to Just War*, Basingstoke: Macmillan.

Missala, H., 1968, '*Gott mit uns*'. *Die deutsche katholische Kriegspredigt 1914–1918*, Munich: Kösel.

Mojzes, P., 1994, *Yugoslavian Inferno. Ethnoreligious Warfare in the Balkans*, New York: Continuum.

Montclos, Xavier de *et al.* (eds), 1982, *Eglises et chrétiens dans la IIe guerre mondiale*, vol. 2: *La France*. Lyon: Presses Universitaires de Lyon.

Müller, G. (ed.), 1983, Frieden, in: *Theologische Realenzyklopädie*, vol. II, Berlin and New York: De Gruyter, pp. 599–646.

Müller, G. (ed.), 1990, Krieg, in: *Theologische Realenzyklopädie*, Berlin and New York: De Gruyter, pp. 11–55.

Niditch, S., 1993, *War in the Hebrew Bible. A Study in the Ethics of Violence*, Oxford and London: Oxford University Press.

Niebuhr, R., 2001, *Moral Man and Immoral Society: A Study in Ethics and Politics* (1932), London 1963. (New edn with introduction by L. B. Gilkey) Louisville and London: Westminster John Knox Press, 2001.

Nuttall, G. F., 1958, *Christian Pacifism in History*, Oxford: Blackwell.

Piper, J. F., 1985, *The American Churches in World War I*, Athens, Ohio and London: Ohio University Press.

Pressel, W., 1967, *Die Kriegspredigt 1914–1918 in der evangelischen Kirche Deutschlands*, Göttingen: Vandenhoeck & Ruprecht.

Rad, G. von, 1991, *Holy War in Ancient Israel*, trans. and edited by M. J. Dawn, Grand Rapids, Mich: Eerdmans.

Ramsey, P., 1983, *The Just War. Force and Political Responsibility*, new edn Lanham and London: University Press of America.

Reuver, M., 1988, *Christians as Peacemakers. Peace Movements in Europe and the USA*, Geneva: World Council of Churches.

Russell, F. H., 1975, *The Just War in the Middle Ages*, Cambridge: Cambridge University Press.

Schwartz, R. M., 1997, *The Curse of Cain: The Violent Legacy of Monotheism*, Chicago and London: University of Chicago Press.

Scott-Craig, T. S. K., 1938, *Christian Attitudes to War and Peace*, Edinburgh: Oliver & Boyd.

Sheils, W. J. (ed.), 1983, *The Church and War* (Studies in Church History 20), Oxford: Blackwell.

Sittser, G. L., 1997, *A Cautious Patriotism: American Churches and the Second World War*, Chapel Hill and London: University of North Carolina Press.

Smith, W. K., 1972, *Calvin's Ethics of War: A Documentary Study*, Annapolis MD: Annapolis Academic Fellowship.

Sproxton, J., 1995, *Violence and Religion: Attitudes towards Militancy in the French Civil Wars and the English Revolution*, London and New York: Routledge.

Swift, J. L., 1983, *The Early Fathers on War and Military Service*, Wilmington, Delaware: Michael Glazier.

Wengst, K., 1987, *Pax Romana and the Peace of Jesus Christ*, trans. from German by J. Bowden, London: SCM.

Wilkinson, A., 1978, *The Church of England and the First World War*, London: SPCK.

7. War and Peace in Islam

LLOYD RIDGEON

Introduction

Writing a chapter on 'War and Peace in Islam' is fraught with difficulties because in the course of 14 centuries of Islamic history there have been so many interpretations on the topic, each of which is inextricably bound up in a particular historical context. There has been and is no single, true Islamic understanding of war and peace; rather there exists a range of perspectives that reveal more about the historical context and psychological make-up of the interpreter. However, fully conscious of the dangers of essentializing Islam, or denominations within Islam, it is possible to provide a simplistic categorization of two groups of Muslims based on their perspectives of pluralism, which, as we shall see, has important implications for war and peace. The first group consists of those Muslims who advocate a *universalist* Islam, that is, an Islamic order that is destined to predominate throughout the whole world and in which non-Muslims can participate but without enjoying the same privileges as Muslims. Such an Islam is hardly pluralistic and does not endorse the principle of reciprocity, that is, one should treat other people as he or she wishes to be treated by them.[1] Examples of universalist Muslims from the modern era include the Pakistani scholar and founder of the political party, the *Jama'at-i Islami*, Abu Ala Mawdudi who died in 1979, and who advocated one Islamic government for the whole world in which non-Muslims have limited rights.[2]

---

[1] See An-Na'im 1990.

Also worthy of note as a universalist is Sayyid Qutb, the radical Egyptian Islamist who was executed in 1966. His universalist message is clear in the following:

> It may happen with the opponents of Islam that, deeming it expedient, they may not commit aggression against Islam provided it [Islam] allows them to continue the leadership of human being[s] over others within their geographical limits, leaves them to their lot and does not force them to follow its [Islam's] message and its declaration of freedom. But Islam cannot declare a 'cease-fire' with them unless they surrender before the authority of Islam and they will no more place impediments in its way by virtue of any political power.[3]

The universalist message is brought up to date with Hamas, a Palestinian offshoot of the Muslim Brotherhood that in 1988 declared that one of its aims was for Muslims to recapture Islamic lands that had been lost in the course of history which would include not only Palestine but also Spain, India and much of the Balkan region.[4] At the other end of the spectrum lie the *pluralists*, a group that does not see the necessity or even desirability

---

[2] See Mawdudi 1980. Originally an address at Lahore Town Hall in 1939, this work attests to the universalism of his interpretation of Islam. 'The objective of the Islamic "Jihad" is to eliminate the rule of an un-Islamic system and establish in its stead an Islamic system of State rule. Islam does not intend to confine this revolution to a single State or a few countries; the aim of Islam is to bring about a universal revolution' (p. 22). Moreover his views concerning the rights of non-Muslims in such 'Islamic' states hardly conform to Western notions of pluralism (pp. 27–8).

[3] Qutb 2000, p. 243.

[4] Hamas does not explicitly endorse Islamic universalism, although many of the articles in its covenant of 1988 can be understood as a defence of Islam, including article 7 which is entitled 'The Universality of the Islamic Resistance Movement'. This defence is, however, problematic from a pluralist perspective, especially article 31 which states 'Under the wing of Islam, it is possible for the followers of the three religions – Islam, Christianity, and Judaism – to coexist in peace and quiet with each other . . . It is the duty of other religions to stop disputing the sovereignty of Islam in this region.' Moreover article 11 comments that all land conquered by Muslims is consecrated land, and therefore belongs to Muslims until the Day of Judgement.

Lloyd Ridgeon

of universal Islam. Included in this group are Fazlur Rahman, Abdullahi Ahmad an-Na'im and Abdulaziz Sachedina. The arguments of these three thinkers will be examined in due course.

Between these two extremes, the universalists and pluralists, lie many shades of grey,[5] but the pluralists' willingness to advocate tolerance, reciprocity and denial of supersessionism (that Islam is the perfect religion which re-establishes an exclusive truth in society) enables them to fit comfortably within the international laws established by the United Nations. Unfortunately, the voices of the pluralists are all too often unheard, and it is the anger and animosity of the universalists that receives media attention. Consequently, perceptions of Islam in the West are all too often unbalanced, epitomized by Jerry Falwell, the conservative American Baptist minister, who remarked in October 2002, 'I think Muhammad was a terrorist . . . he was a violent man, a man of war.'[6] A month later Pat Robertson, the American televangelist and former Presidential candidate stated 'Adolf Hitler was bad, but what the Muslims want to do to the Jews is worse.'[7] Such opinions, although extreme, reflect perhaps the underlying fears and unspoken views of many Americans and Europeans. Given the media attention on the Taliban, Osama bin Laden, Hamas

---

[5] One example, albeit of a personal nature, may be useful to provide an insight into a more 'moderate' form of Islam. In April 2003, I took a group of students from Stirling University to visit the large Edinburgh mosque (funded in part by a £4 million donation from Saudi Arabia) for a question and answer session. On being asked about pluralism, one of our hosts answered that Judaism, Christianity and Islam are all divine religions, but Hinduism and Buddhism are man-made. Despite this non-pluralistic attitude, none of the Muslims advocated the spreading of Islam around the world in the manner of Sayyid Qutb, rather, the Muslims in the mosque advocated education and instruction, and did not believe that force could be used to prevail in any circumstance.

[6] Jerry Falwell, interviewed for *60 Minutes* (CBS News programme) on 6 October 2002. Although Falwell later retracted his comments, it was too late to stop Muslim–Hindu riots in India in which five people were killed.

[7] Pat Robertson added: 'The Koran teaches that the end of the world will not come until every Jew is killed by Muslims.' Cited by Buchanan 2002. Anyone who has read the Qur'an will know that there is no such passage therein.

and the 'War on Terror' such perceptions of Islam and Muhammad are perhaps not surprising among uncritical observers. Yet the current Islamophobia (a fear of Islam) is not confined to certain unsophisticated religious individuals but has penetrated into political establishments. When George W. Bush commented that 'Islam, as practised by the vast majority of people, is a peaceful religion, a religion that respects others', a senior advisor of his admitted that this was the 'right political argument, but . . . a harder intellectual argument to make'.[8] Moreover, a form of Islamophobia seems to have spread into academic circles. I have heard an academic observe that the only democracies in the Middle East are Israel and secular Turkey. This statement, which was made in the context of a discussion concerning Islam, implies that there is something inherent within Islam that prevents the growth of democracy and promotes authoritarian regimes that are more likely to resort to military measures to settle conflicts than pursue peaceful negotiations. Such a simplistic evaluation of the Middle East and Islam ignores the historical legacy and socio-economic circumstances of the region (such as the effects of westernization, rapid modernization, globalization and the legacy of colonialism).[9] I do not wish to suggest that Islam, or Muslim perceptions of Islam, can be bracketed out of the equation; merely that a more balanced and nuanced analysis of Islamic approaches to pluralism and war and peace is required. Much ink has been spilled in dispelling the myth of 'Islamic confrontation',[10] yet antipathy is still directed against Muslims as a result of populist soundbites and hasty assumptions about what Islam really is. Justification enough, perhaps, for yet another discussion about 'War and Peace in Islam'.[11]

It has been recognized by pluralist Muslims that what is com-

---

[8] Remarks of Kenneth Adelman who serves on George Bush's Pentagon's Defence Policy Board. See Milbank 2002.

[9] For socio-economic problems in the region see Humphries 1999.

[10] See for example Lawrence 1998, and Halliday 1996.

[11] The literature on war and peace in Islam is huge. Some of the literature that is worthy of mention includes Khadduri 1979, Watt 1976, Ayoub 1992. Other references to the literature are made in the footnotes of this chapter.

monly called 'Islam' is in fact not an unchanging reified entity, but individual interpretations that respond to historical contexts. Such Muslims argue that the modern period requires new reflections from Islamic intellectuals so that Muslims can accommodate the inevitable societal changes brought by modernity and globalization. Moreover, pluralist Muslim academics attempt to undermine the universalist standpoint by highlighting the contextual foundation of universalism. This is a major point, and one that needs to be discussed in more detail in order for the general western perception of Islam to change. This chapter builds upon the ideas of such Islamic intellectuals along with those of non-Muslim historians in an attempt to demonstrate that the universalist perspective of radical Muslims such as Qutb and Mawdudi has its foundation in the works of the Islamic jurists of the eighth–ninth centuries CE. The universalist position of the jurists is typified in the writings of Shaybani (d. 804). In the first page of his work entitled *Traditions Relating to the Conduct of War*, he cites a *hadith* (a saying of Muhammad) that states:

> Fight in the name of God and in the 'the path of God'. Combat only those who disbelieve in God. Do not cheat or commit treachery, nor should you mutilate anyone or kill children. Whenever you meet your polytheist enemies, invite them to adopt Islam. If they do so, accept it and let them alone . . . If they refuse [to accept Islam] then call upon them to pay the jizya (poll tax); if they do, accept it and leave them alone.[12]

The conclusion that is omitted by Shaybani is that if the polytheist enemies refuse to pay the poll-tax, they should be fought and killed. The writings of another prominent jurist of the period in question, Shafiʻi (767–820), reveal a similar perspective that cites passages in the Qur'an that command believers to fight polytheists, and also those that offer the chance of security by paying the poll-tax. Although the universalism is not explicit, it is not difficult to see how it could be read in such a manner.[13]

---

[12] *Siyar* of Shaybani, translated by Khadduri 1966, p. 76.
[13] See Shafiʻis Risala, translated by Khadduri 1987, for the passages on jihad, see pp. 82–7.

However, universalist although the jurists were, in the context of their times, their writings reveal an Islam that was in theory remarkably tolerant. Indeed, many of the jurists of the eighth and ninth centuries believed that an indefinite peace treaty could be made with the unbelievers so long as it served the interests of the Muslim state, and the People of the Book (the Jews and Christians) who lived within the Islamic world were guaranteed both security (by paying the poll-tax) and the right to practise their own religion.[14] It is unfortunate, however, that the modern universalists have not embraced the relative tolerance that was expressed by their eighth- and ninth-century counterparts.

Despite such relative tolerance, the views of the jurists of this period must be reconsidered in the present age if the peoples of the world are to live in a more harmonious fashion.[15] Such a reconsideration has been in progress for some time, but is not widely recognized. First, I will reflect on some of the ways in which it is possible to question the universalist legacy left by the jurists. Having exposed the weaknesses of the universalist idea, I will then proceed to offer alternative visions by summarizing the views of several leading 'pluralist' Muslims.

Islamic Universalists of the Eighth–Ninth Centuries

Islamic universalism and its reasons

Beginning the investigation of Islamic perspectives on war and peace by analysing the Qur'an is problematic because it contains verses that often seem contradictory. Compare for example the two following verses:

> Kill them wherever you find them and turn them out from where they have turned you out. (2.191)

> Invite to the way of your Lord with wisdom and beautiful

---

[14] See Zaman 2002, p. 93, and Johnson 1997, pp. 68–72.
[15] Of course, the obligation to rethink one's heritage and perspectives lies not solely with some Muslims but also with many non-Muslims too.

ways; and argue with them in ways that are best and most gracious. (16.125)

Many jurists believed that the answer to discovering the reason for apparent contradictions lay in discovering the Qur'an's final pronouncement on war and peace. However, discovering this final command is problematic because the Qur'an is not a chronological account of revelations given to Muhammad. Indeed, many modern scholars have rejected the legitimacy of searching for Qur'anic chronology to justify adopting certain legal norms because such a method does not reflect the totality of the Qur'anic message. This is an argument to which we shall return later.

If it is not useful to start the investigation of the Islamic perspective of war and peace with the Qur'an, then perhaps a better approach would be to analyse the first systematic explanations of *jihad*[16] which were composed by the jurists of the Sunni schools of law of the eighth–ninth century CE when the Islamic empire had already been established, and stretched from the Pyrenees to the Punjab. What is interesting about this period is that the jurists agree that the aim of *jihad* is Islamic universalism, which is legitimized by the Qur'anic verse that states 'We have sent you [Muhammad] to the whole of mankind, as a warner' (34.28), and until Islam prevails, the world is divided into two spheres, the realm of Islam (*dar al-Islam*) and the realm of war (*dar al-harb*). Why did the jurists accept such a perspective when it is possible to read an ethic of pluralism and religious tolerance, epitomized in 5.48, 'For every one of you, We [God] have appointed a path and a way. If God had willed, He could have made you but one community; but that [He has not done in order that] He may try you in what has come to you. Be then forward in good deeds.' The acceptance of Islamic universalism was a significant factor towards the next stage of advocating a more aggressive form of Islam, utilizing both verbal persuasion and military force. The

---

[16] Sometimes rendered into English as 'Holy War', but as many Muslims point out, it means striving in God's way. The Qur'an never associates 'jihad' with war (*harb*).

following offers four reasons why the Sunni jurists endorsed the belief in Islamic universalism.

1. As already mentioned, the Qur'an contains verses which could be understood as a command to spread Islam throughout the world, such as 34.28 'We have sent you [Muhammad] forth to all of mankind' and 2.193 'fight them until there is no sedition and the religion becomes God's'. Given the context in which the jurists were writing, the very expansion of the Islamic empire must have seemed to vindicate the truth of the Qur'an and the prophethood of Muhammad, and verses such as these perhaps served to legitimize an expansionist policy, or at least they strengthened the idea of an Islamic 'manifest destiny'.[17]

2. The promotion of Islamic universalism would have been very difficult to challenge because by the eighth–ninth centuries the Islamic empire had already been created, and its history, myths and heroes were firmly entrenched in the collective memories of the believers. To question the legality of universalism would have been tantamount to belittling some of Islam's greatest champions, some of whom were companions of the prophet Muhammad. Therefore it would have been inconceivable to cast aspersions on Islamic universalism. In effect the only task the jurists could perform was to provide 'legal justification for the rapid expansion of the Islamic empire that occurred in the decades following the Prophet's death, [and for this reason the] . . . connotations [of *jihad* in their works] are offensive rather than defensive'.[18]

3. The sources from which the jurists derived their legal opinions on war and peace included the Qur'an and the so-called *maghazi* literature, a form of literature that focused on the military campaigns of the prophet. The historicity of this literature has been questioned by both Muslim and non-Muslim scholars, as the earliest collections of such works exist only in fragments, and the first substantial

---

[17] Analogy suggested by Humphries 1999, p. 178.
[18] Hashmi 2002, p. 205.

work appears in a biography of the prophet written by Ibn Hisham (d. 834).[19] This work contains the *Sira Rasul Allah* ('Biography of the Prophet of God') written by Ibn Ishaq (704–67) whose 'objectivity' has been questioned by Jacob Lassner: 'A systematic analysis of the work reveals it to be a revisionist history that was most likely written with the encouragement, if not the active support of the ruling house. In any event, the text, which Ibn Ishaq presented to the Caliph al-Mansur, provided the historical evidence necessary to trumpet Abbasid claims, and thus insured the author a place of prominence at the court of his new-found patron.'[20]

There are several points concerning this literature that have a bearing on the appropriateness of the jurists' universalism. The first is that the *maghazi* works appear to have been the first attempts to trace the historical outlines of Muhammad's life. These writings were based on the old Arab model of describing battles and military events in detail,[21] but this method of writing history was not suitable for conveying a picture of Muhammad's general life. Thus Shibli Nu'mani (a late-nineteenth-century Indian scholar) claimed that the *maghazi* literature emphasized Muhammad's military campaigns at the expense of his 'piety, sanctity, forbearance, generosity, love of humanity, and altruism'.[22] In addition to the single

---

[19] This has been translated by Guillaume 1955.

[20] Lassner 1986, p. 16.

[21] See W. Raven, 'Sira' in *Encyclopedia of Islam* (second edition) who states that the *maghazi* literature was a 'continuation of the profane accounts of the *ayyam al-'arab*'.

[22] This argument and the quotation is from 'Allama Shibli Nu'mani (a nineteenth-century Indian Muslim scholar who taught in Ahmad Khan's school in Aligarh), 'Methodology of Historical Writing', from his *Sirat al-Nabi*, translated by M. Tayyib Bakhsh Budayuni (Delhi: Idarah-i Adabiyat-i Delhi, reprint, 1983). This section appears in Moaddel and Talattof (eds) 2000, p. 67. Shibli's point appears valid, especially when considering that section two of Ibn Hisham's work, entitled 'Muhammad's Call and Preaching at Mecca' covers this ten-year period in about 100 pages (pp. 109–218), whereas section three, called 'Muhammad's Migration to Medina, His Wars, Triumph and Death' covering 13 years, is included in just under 500 pages (pp. 219–690).

dimension of Muhammad portrayed in the *maghazi* literature, the problem of the trustworthiness and reliability of the
hadiths used by the authors has been called into question.[23]
Yet, the *maghazi* literature must have been popular for the
Muslims of the Umayyad period (661–750), as it was a form
of devotional literature that portrayed an idealized golden
period when the community was united under the brave and
courageous leadership of Muhammad. It stood in contrast to
the conditions prevalent in the latter years of the Umayyad
empire, which was finally toppled in 750 CE by the Abbasids,
and never again was the Islamic empire to be united. The
expansion of the empire had virtually come to a halt in the
final years of the Umayyad dynasty, and the Caliph paid
more attention to preserving order within the empire than
extending its boundaries.[24] Therefore, the *maghazi* literature
provided the Muslims with a myth of unity and expansion,
reflecting the aims of the new dynasty, the Abbasids. One
may speculate that the jurists of the subsequent generation
were influenced by this literature, as their own treatises on
jihad and international law establish similar goals, namely,
Islamic universalism, and a united, expanding empire.[25]

4. The ideal of the unity and equality of Muslims was important
   for the Abbasids because it provided the *raison d'être* for their
   dynastic rule. Although the Umayyads were successful (at
   least initially) in maintaining order and security, it was at the

---

[23] See 'Allama Shibli Nu'mani (previous footnote) who points out that
many of the *hadiths* contained in the *maghazi* literature do not have complete *isnads* (chains of transmission) (p. 61). An indication of the unrelia-
bility of the *Sira* authors such as al-Waqidi has been stressed by Shibli
Nu'mani who stated that the works of al-Waqidi 'deserve no notice' as he
'coined and fabricated traditions' (p. 59).

[24] See Kennedy 1986. 'The reign of al-Walid (705–15) also saw the furthest
extension of the geographical frontiers of the Umayyad state', p. 103.

[25] It is difficult to assess the influence of State pressure upon individual
jurists. The case of Shaybani is instructive in this respect, for it seems that he
preferred the life of an independent scholar to that of a state judge (Khadduri
1966, pp. 32–6). However, he was 'forced' to accept the position, although
he was later dismissed by the Caliph for not giving an 'appropriate' judgement.

expense of the ideal of equality, for one of the key elements
of Umayyad rule was its dependence on Arab tribes over non-
Arabs. The Muslim Arabs were rewarded through taxation
and official posts within the administration,[26] which contrasts
with the Qur'anic message that Islam transcends blood and
tribal affiliations,[27] and naturally resentment against Arab
nepotism increased as the empire and the number of non-Arab
converts expanded. The Abbasids therefore were keen not to
repeat the mistakes of the Umayyads and so stressed Islamic
universalism which would render any distinction based on
race invalid. By extension, Islamic universalism also implied
the propagation of Islam into the *dar al-harb* (the non-Islamic
territories) with the possibility that the Muslims might have
to resort to force to achieve this objective.[28]

The role of abrogation

The above four reasons arguably contributed to the jurists adopting a universalist stance, yet it is necessary to move beyond 'why'
and explain 'how' the jurists justified this position. The key to
the 'how' question lies in the theory of abrogation (*naskh*).[29] The
formative jurists believed that abrogation answered the question
to all Qur'anic verses that contained contradictory meanings. To
appreciate the theory of abrogation it is necessary to say something about the process of Qur'anic revelation.

---

[26] An example of discrimination is apparent in the *mawali* system, under
which non-Arab Muslims were obliged to become clients of Arab Muslims.
In some areas and during some periods of Umayyad rule, *mawalis* were
taxed as if they were non-Muslims (Kennedy 1986, p. 106) and excluded
from military power and positions of influence (Kennedy 1986, p. 105).

[27] See 9.24: 'If it is your father, sons, brothers, wives, tribe, wealth that
you have gained, and the commerce that for which you fear decline, and
dwellings which you love more than God and his messenger and jihad in his
way, then wait until God brings about his command. God does not guide
the wrongdoing tribe.'

[28] For the theory that the Abbasids adopted this universalist approach to
Islam in contrast to the Umayyad policy, see Khadduri 1966, pp. 19–20.

[29] For an explanation of the theory of *naskh* see Burton 1977.

According to Islamic tradition the Qur'anic revelations were received by Muhammad over a period of 23 years; for 10 years in Mecca and subsequently for 13 years in Medina, during which time Muhammad was successful in establishing Islam over most of Arabia. It is accepted by Muslims and non-Muslims that the *general* nature of Meccan Qur'anic revelations stands in contrast to the Medinan revelations. The Meccan revelations emphasized the unity of God, human resurrection and judgement, that Jews and Christians are 'People of the Book' and their religions are to be respected as precursors to Islam, and that the idolatrous religious practices and the inhumane social ethics of the Meccans are abhorrent to God. As a result of Meccan opposition to criticisms of them in these revelations (opposition which took the form of a trade boycott, and verbal and physical abuse), Muhammad was forced to flee, and he found a degree of security in the city of Medina.[30] The revelations he received there reflect the changing context of the fledgling Islamic community, namely the continuing threat from the Meccans, the hostility from some Jewish tribes in Medina, and the economic instability of the Muslim community. It was under these circumstances that some Muslims attacked a Meccan trade caravan and in the skirmish killed one of the Meccans.[31] This escalated the hostility, and ultimately there was a series of battles between the Muslims and the Meccans during which hundreds of men were killed. The death of Muslims resulted in new social problems that were dealt with in the Medinan revelations that discuss the need to care for widows and orphans, to write wills, to obey the leader of the community, and to engage in the *jihad* with one's wealth and body in battle. The Muslim community eventually triumphed, as the Meccans surrendered, and by the time of Muhammad's death most of Arabia had in some way recognized the supremacy of Islam.

---

[30] For a general background see Watt 1961, pp. 56–82.

[31] That the Muslim community was weak is not accepted by all commentators. Muhammad Haykal, a modern Egyptian biographer of the Muhammad, claimed that the early military expeditions and skirmishes were intended to demonstrate to the Meccans the new power of the Muslim community. Cited in Hashmi 2002, p. 202.

The Qur'anic revelations ceased with Muhammad's death and Muslims were posed with the problem of how to understand the relationship between Qur'anic verses that appeared contradictory, such as those that advocate tolerance and peace and those that urge believers to fight.

One method to resolve this apparent contradiction was to utilize the concept of abrogation, a Qur'anic term (2.106) by which early verses (such as the more inclusive Meccan verses) are made null and void by subsequent verses (namely the exclusive Medinan verses). Thus, it is claimed by some Islamic scholars that verse 9.5 ('kill the idolators wherever you find them') abrogated as many as 120 verses of warfare that had been revealed at an earlier stage of Muhammad's life.[32] According to such an interpretation even the Jews and Christians were treated with an increased degree of severity in the 'perfected' version of Islam: 'Fight those among the People of the Book who do not believe in God and the Last Day, do not forbid what God and his messenger have forbidden, and do not profess the true religion, till they pay the poll-tax out of hand submissively' (9.29). The problem facing the Muslim jurists in finding the 'perfected religion' of Islam is that utilizing the abrogation principle means that it is necessary to know the order in which the verses were revealed. Now, Muslim scholars argue that the Qur'an as we have it today was assembled in the generation after Muhammad's death. If we accept this dating, Islamic scholars are still faced with a huge problem of interpretation because the Qur'an does not provide a chronological or linear depiction of events; its structure is based upon other factors.

In an attempt to solve the problem of identifying the historical context in which the verses were revealed, Muslim scholars made reference to Muhammad's sayings and biographies. Still, an accurate dating of Qur'anic verses through reference to these sources has been questioned by both western and Islamic scholars because not all of the literature is considered genuine. Some of the traditions were fabricated in the first century after Muham-

---

[32] Firestone 1999, p. 151, n. 21.

mad's death to justify certain political and theological doctrines, and this is expressed in no uncertain terms by Firestone: 'There can be no question that some of the material was forged in order to fill gaps in his [Muhammad's] biography, provide appropriate historical contexts for certain qur'anic revelations, extol the miracles associated with the Islamic Prophet par excellence, and promote certain partisan ideas or views by associating them with Muhammad himself.'[33] Other aspects of Islamic tradition as recorded in books must also be questioned, as G. R. Hawting has observed concerning the oral material of the prophet's life:

> The material thus collected was then transmitted to later generations which treated it in a variety of ways. It might be again broken up and put together with material from different sources in order to make it relate to a different theme; long narratives might be abridged by omitting material considered irrelevant; short narratives might be filled out by interpolation or by linking material together without making it clear where the link occurs or even that it has been made; material might fall out of circulation or it might be reshaped consciously or subconsciously by substitution of words or phrases, by the addition of glosses, or even by formulating entirely new material. It is obvious therefore, that there was plenty of scope for the material to change in the course of its transmission, and it would be natural that it should change in accordance with changing political, social and religious circumstances. Generally speaking, the material would have been constantly revised to make it relevant and acceptable, and the original significance and context of the material would come to be forgotten.[34]

The theory of abrogation that was utilized in the period following the establishment of the Islamic Empire to justify offensive *jihad* is not an accurate method to determine the dates and occasions of Qur'anic revelations. What is remarkable about

---

[33] Firestone 1999, p. 105.
[34] Hawting 1986, p. 16.

the texts of the jurists is that there is no *explicit* mention of abrogation in the context of *jihad*. Shaybani does not discuss the
relationship between the 'peaceful' and 'hostile' verses, and there
is only one reference to abrogation in his *Siyar* when he states:
'The prohibition of fighting during the sacred months [2.214]
was abrogated by God, the Most High (in another text of the
Qur'an) which says: "Slay the polytheists wherever you may find
them." '[35] And likewise, Shafi'i's discussion of abrogation in his
Risala fails to note that the positive Qur'anic verses concerning
Jews and Christians are abrogated by subsequent verses com-
manding *jihad*. The *Risala* was written for purposes other than
explaining relations between Muslims and non-Muslims, but
Shafi'i's brief description of the duty of *jihad* suggests that his
readers were already familiar with the abrogation of the positive
verses. It had become part of the ideology of the ruling élite.

A complex picture

The classical period in which the Sunni perspective on Islamic
universalism was systematically discussed and presented as
normative Islamic belief is grounded on foundations that need
further examination. Questioning the Islamic tradition (including the *hadiths* and the *maghazi* literature) is problematic for
many Muslims because it is through such traditions that the
historical validity of the Qur'an is vouchsafed.[36] I do not wish
to discount the possibility that there was a premeditated, religious impulse to establish Islam throughout the known world,
and it is unlikely that the number of *hadiths* that suggest that
this was indeed the case were all fabricated.[37] Muslim scholars
were scrupulous in authenticating the sayings of Muhammad,

---

[35] Shaybani, translated by Khadduri 1966, p. 94.

[36] See Rahman 1955, p. 873.

[37] Harald Motzki argues that from one perspective the *hadith* and *sira*
material 'may be considered as pieces of a broken mirror which reflect what
really happened and therefore can be used to reconstruct historical reality'. See 'The Murder of Ibn Abi l-Huqayq: On the Origin and Reliability
of some Maghazi Reports,' in Motzki, 2000, p. 170. The problem with

none more so than Bukhari, whose works include the episode of Muhammad sending letters to neighbouring rulers, calling them to accept Islam.[38] However, there are also sayings of Muhammad that do not accord with the social reforms that he strived so hard to implement, including the *hadith* uttered on his death bed that states: 'If I survive, God willing, I'll expel the Jews and the Christians out of the Arabian Peninsula.' (Incidentally, this was the justification for Osama bin Laden's declaration of war in 1998 against the USA, whose military forces were based on Arabian territory.) In short, questions concerning the motivation for the creation of the Islamic empire remain, and so the idea of Islamic universalism must be subject to greater scrutiny.

Stephen Humphries speculates that the initial aim for the spread of Islam was merely to capture Jerusalem, a sacred city for the Muslims, and which passed to Islamic control in 638 CE, only six years after Muhammad's death. He then adds that the successes achieved in Iraq and Iran at the same time that Jerusalem was taken were opportunistic and began as an alliance with local rulers who contested Iranian supremacy. Following early victories, a snowball effect resulted in greater Islamic victories.[39]

Another possible reason for the initial expansion of Islam outside of Arabia has more to do with maintaining the internal stability of the nascent Islamic community rather than an ideological, religious commitment to universalism. On the death of Muhammad the leadership of the Islamic community recognized the danger of some Bedouin tribes withdrawing their allegiance to Islam, typified in the so-called *ridda* wars (or wars of

Motzki's argument is to identify which pieces are mirrors and which are stones. Andrew Rippin argues that 'the close correlation between the *sira* and the Qur'an can be taken to be more indicative of exegetical and narrative development within the Islamic community rather than evidence for thinking that one source witnesses the veracity of the other.' Rippin 2000, p. 307.

[38] Bukhari, *Sahih*, Vol. 1, Book 1, no. 6. It has been argued by Fatima Mernissi that not all the *hadiths* recorded by Bukhari should be regarded as 'authentic'. See Mernissi 1991; see also various references in the index to Abu Hurayra.

[39] See Humphries 1999, p. 180.

apostasy). Thus, Hugh Kennedy suggests that the expansion of Islam was a means by which leadership was preserved over the Bedouin tribes. [40] Raiding and warfare were essential for the economic survival of the Bedouin tribesmen, but the *pax Islamica* guaranteed security to all Muslims. In the words of M. Khadduri: 'It would, indeed, have been very difficult for the Islamic state to survive had it not been for the doctrine of jihad, replacing tribal raids and directing the enormous energy of the tribes from an inevitable internal conflict to unite and fight against the outside world in the name of the new faith.'[41]

Once the universalism of Islam had been accepted by the jurists, the principle of a *jihad* to expand the realm of Islam became enshrined in the practice of the Caliph calling for a *jihad* at least once every year.[42] Yet the fracture of the united empire into independent territorial units with rival caliphs and sultans meant that the actual practice of engaging in *jihad* often ground to a halt, and on many occasions Muslim rulers entered into peaceful relations with neighbouring Muslims. There was even the precedent, set in 678, of Muslims making peace with the Byzantines and paying a financial tribute. Indeed, there have been occasions when Muslims were allied in wars with non-Muslims against Muslims. In the modern period there is the example of Arab Muslims fighting with the British against the Ottoman Turks during World War One.

In addition to the practical impossibility of establishing a universal form of Islam, there have been Muslims who have advocated a pluralist, less militarist and more inclusive world-view. Perhaps most noteworthy in this respect are the Sufi mystics. The poetry of the thirteenth-century Persian mystic Rumi, associated with the whirling dervishes, indicates that he believed all faiths to be manifestations of the truth, and that God appeared in various guises to all. Yet even Rumi, despite his inclusive message and verses advocating toleration, penned some verses which endorse *jihad* and describe Islam as the religion of 'war and terror' while

---

[40] Kennedy 1986, p. 59.
[41] Khadduri 1979, p. 62.
[42] Peters 1996, p. 3.

Christianity is the religion of solitude in caves and mountains.[43]

Perhaps the most remarkable example of Islamic inclusivism and its rejection of universalism came with Akbar, the ruler of the Moghul dynasty in India during the second half of the sixteenth century. Among his reforms Akbar abolished the *jizya* poll-tax on non-Muslims, established an institution to discuss theological questions of interest to Muslims, Hindus, Christians and other religious faiths, sacred texts of the various religious traditions were translated into Persian and there was freedom to build places of worship.[44] These reforms were reversed by subsequent rulers of the Moghul dynasty, but nevertheless the precedent of an inclusive Islam that is tolerant and pluralist is not that difficult to discover in Islamic history.

Mention also needs to be made of the Shiʿ-ite tradition in Islam, which has had a major impact on the development of Islamic intellectual thought, and today Shiʿ-ites comprise some ten per cent of all Muslims. From the tenth century at least, the Shiʿ-ites considered the doctrine of an offensive *jihad* impermissible, which meant that only defensive *jihad* was legitimate. In recent years the Shiʿ-ites of Lebanon (in the form of Hezbollah) and Iran since the 1978 revolution have been quite vocal in their denunciation of the West. The news of hostage-taking, suicide bombings and children marching through minefields fostered the image in the West of an intolerant and belligerent Islam. However, much of the rhetoric and the policies advocated by such Shiʿ-ites must be seen in the context of increasing cultural erosion, globalization, modernization, the marginalization of such groups in their respective societies and the political insensitivity of the West. It is indeed unfortunate that such political insensitivity continues at the highest levels of international politics as George W. Bush included Iran within his 'axis of evil', apparently because some factions in Iran were supplying weapons to Palestinian groups. It is not hard to see why many Muslims perceive such a denunciation of Iran as an embodiment of American double standards, as the USA has consistently armed Israel despite the latter ignoring

---

[43] Rumi, *Mathnawi*, VI, 490–5.
[44] For Akbar see Choudury 1952, and Sharma 1988.

resolution 242 of the United Nations, passed in 1967, calling for Israeli withdrawal of the occupied territories, namely the West Bank, Gaza and the Golan Heights. But this American ambivalence towards the United Nations should come as no real surprise, especially in the light of the conflict in Iraq during 2003.

Modern Islamic Pluralists

Having shown that the position of the Islamic universalists is based upon tenuous sources, space has been opened to present the arguments of the modern pluralists. The Islamic world was forced to take pluralism seriously (that is, not a patronizing form in which Muslims enjoy privileged positions) once the nineteenth-century European powers became fully committed to their imperialist aims. As a result of European pressure the Ottoman Empire (which ruled most of the Middle East and North Africa) implemented the so-called Tanzimat reforms in which all people within the Empire were considered equal, regardless of race or religious identity. A bolder step was taken by Ahmad Khan, an Indian Muslim, who wrote in the aftermath of the 'Mutiny' of 1857, declaring that it was perfectly legitimate for Muslims to serve under non-Muslim rulers, and that offensive *jihad* was not the answer to India's problems. For Ahmad Khan, British rule in India was 'the most wonderful phenomenon the world has ever seen'.[45] And the revolution that occurred in Iran in 1907 established a constitution which declared in article 8 that 'all the people of Iran . . . have equal rights before the laws of the state', and article 97 stated that 'everyone . . . [will] be treated equally in matters pertaining to the payment of taxes'.[46] Pluralism therefore is not something that has suddenly arrived on the doorsteps of Muslims.

The past 30 years or so have witnessed dramatic changes in society, and the world is indeed shrinking while the volume of interaction between Muslims and non-Muslims is expanding.

---

[45] Cited in A. Ahmad, 'Sayyid Ahmad Khan, Jamal al-Din al-Afghani and Muslim India', *Studia Islamica*, XIII–XIV, p. 65.

[46] See Banani 1961, pp. 17–19.

Moreover, the number of Muslims living in the West is growing and this has caused Muslims to re-examine their Islamic heritage, including notions of Islamic universalism and *jihad*. In the following I will present a summary of the ideas of three Muslim thinkers (Fazlur Rahman, Abdullahi Ahmed an-Na'im and Abdulaziz Sachedina) who have offered an inclusive and pluralist Islam. Some of these ideas have resulted in much opposition from more conservative interpretations of Islam, and it will be interesting to see whether or not Islamic communities in the West and also in traditionally Islamic regions adopt some of these views.

Rahman ended his career teaching at the University of Chicago from 1969 to 1988, an-Na'im is a Professor of Law at Emory University, and Sachedina teaches at the University of Virginia. It might therefore be asked to what extent are their views known by the Muslims living in areas where the concentration of Muslims is high, or whether these views are confined to pockets of Muslims in the West and academics of Islam.

Fazlur Rahman was the Director of the Central Institute of Islamic Research in Pakistan from 1961 to 1968. Some of the issues that Rahman investigated included the authority of the *hadith*, prophetic practice, and the nature of revelation. Demonstrations against Rahman took place when sections of his book *Islam* were translated into Urdu. The protestors disliked Rahman's suggestion that somehow Muhammad was involved in the transmission of the Qur'an to humans. As a result Rahman was forced to resign and subsequently found work in North American academic institutes. Having become such a 'notorious' figure his works, which were written in English, would have been well known by Muslim academics, but it is debatable how much the average Pakistani Muslim would have been familiar with books such as *Islam and Modernity*[47] and *Revival and Reform in Islam*.[48]

An-Na'im is of Sudanese origin and was a follower of the re-

---

[47] Rahman 1982.
[48] Rahman 2000.

formist scholar Mahmoud Mohamed Taha.[49] In 1985 an-Na'im left Sudan, as Taha was accused of apostasy and executed,[50] and since then he has taught in a variety of western academic institutes. Presently, he is the Charles Howard Candler Professor of Law in the Faculty of Emory Law School. The main elements of his thought (individualism and feminism) are features that reflect the concerns of his mentor, and so therefore these kinds of issues are well known in Sudan, although it is difficult to assess their popularity.

Sachedina was born in Tanzania in 1942 and was educated in India, Iran and Canada. At present he is Professor of Religious Studies at the University of Virginia. His writings have been published in English, and so it is unlikely that Muslims of the traditional Islamic areas of the world are familiar with them. However, Sachedina notes the difficulties he has faced in expressing his views in the USA, including an attempt to silence him through a *fatwa* to prevent Muslims in North America listening to his 'plea for improved inter-communal relations through mutual tolerance, respect, and acceptance of religious value in all world religions'.[51]

It is probably fair to say that these kinds of views are known to some extent in the Muslim world, and it is perhaps inevitable that such ideas will become more known as levels of education and contact with the West increase. These three thinkers, Rahman, an-Na'im and Sachedina, have been selected because of the diversity between their views. It would have been possible to select other Muslim thinkers who contemplate Islam's position in relation to pluralism, democracy and war and peace. Examples include the Egyptian scholar and former jurist, Muhammad Sa'id al-'Ashmawi[52], and the Iranian writer Abdolkarim Soroush.[53]

---

[49] For Mahmoud Muhammad Taha see Taha 1986. The original Arabic was published in 1967. For a critical analysis of Taha's work see Mahmoud 1998.

[50] See An-Na'im 1986.

[51] Sachedina 2001, p. xi.

[52] For al-'Ashmawi's thought see Al-'Ashmawi 2001. Al-'Ashmawi's
[*See opposite page for n. 52 cont. and n. 53*]

Fazlur Rahman

Rahman asserts openly and boldly that the stand of modern Muslim apologists who have tried to explain the *jihad* of the early Islamic community (presumably after the death of Muhammad) in purely defensive terms is unacceptable.[54] Rahman's understanding of the Qur'anic verses that deal with non-Muslims (such as 5.48) endorses a modern perspective of pluralism. He adopts a literal understanding of 2.112 as evidence: 'Whoever surrenders himself to God while he does good deeds as well, he shall find his reward with his Lord, shall have no fear, nor shall he come to grief'.[55] Rahman would also have recognized that some Qur'anic verses (understood literally in the way of medieval Islamic jurists), do not conform to modern pluralism. However, he offered a method by which pluralism emerges from the Qur'anic text when the reader looks at the specific, historical context of any single verse, and then comprehends the general principle behind that verse. One could argue that in the case of Muslim relations with non-Muslims, the specific context of verses which appear hostile to non-Muslims reflects a need to defend Islam, and so the general principle to be drawn from other verses is one of pluralism and co-existence.[56] So this general principle, argues Rahman,

---

inclusive Islam and denunciation of 'fundamentalist' tendencies have resulted in him receiving government protection since 1980. Despite attempts by official Islamic institutions (al-Azhar) to have his books banned at the Cairo International Book Fair, his writings are readily available in Egypt (p. 4).

[53] For Soroush see Soroush 2000. Soroush is a well-known 'dissident' in Iran. For more information, biographies and articles see the website www.seraj.org.

[54] Rahman 1966, p. 37.

[55] Rahman 1994, pp. 166–7.

[56] This is not a new argument, as it was expressed (somewhat opaquely) by Ahmad Khan (the nineteenth-century Muslim reformer from India) who remarked: '. . . any person seeking a true interpretation of scriptural passages . . . should first, by a careful regard to the context, and by study of contemporary history, make himself acquainted with the special circumstances – the times, seasons, and purposes, for which the ordinances were sent down from Heaven. – Our worthy commentators have however

must then be applied in the present age in the form of specific legislation to take into account the existing circumstances.[57] His writings reveal that he believed the general ethic of the Qur'an is humanitarian and pluralist. 'Something can still be worked out,' he insisted, 'by way of positive cooperation, provided the Muslims hearken more to the Qur'an than to the historic formulations of Islam and provided that recent pioneering efforts continue to yield a Christian doctrine more compatible with universal monotheism and egalitarianism.'[58]

Abdullahi Ahmed An-Na'im

An-Na'im's main concern is for Islamic law to accord with the norms of modern international law which is based on the idea of reciprocity. One dimension of traditional Islamic law that violates this centres on Islam's relations with non-Muslims. He cites examples of discrimination against non-Muslims in the spheres of both public law (such as denying or restricting non-Muslims' testimonial competence before the law)[59] and personal law (such as the prohibition on non-Muslim men marrying Muslim women). An-Na'im recognizes that in many Islamic societies such discrimination has largely been supplanted by the introduction of secular law; however, the problem remains that such laws still exist according to the *shari'a*, Islamic law, and can be implemented should circumstances arise.[60] The solution to this problem is for Muslims to 'set aside' the Medinan revelations and practices which form the basis of Islamic law, and implement the

---

scorned to go to work so tediously, and in their eager haste, have chosen the simpler course of collecting together *all* the verses relating to war and slaughter they could find, without the smallest regard to their peculiar and special application to times and to peoples long departed!' Khan 1993, p. 240.

[57] Rahman 1982, p. 20.
[58] Rahman 1994, p. 170.
[59] An-Na'im 1990, p. 123.
[60] An-Na'im 1990, p. 172.

verses of the Meccan stage which 'preached the solidarity of all humanity'.[61]

> The only way to achieve the necessary degree of reform is to substitute as bases of Islamic law those clear and definite verses of the Qur'an and related Sunna that sanction the use of force in propagating Islam among non-Muslims with texts of the Qur'an and Sunna that enjoin the use of peaceful means in achieving those objectives. In accordance with the fundamental premise that both the Qur'an and Sunna must be understood in their historical context, the proposed reform would replace those elements of Shari'a based on the Qur'an of Medina and related Sunna, and on the practice of that stage, with modern Islamic law based on the Qur'an of Mecca and related Sunna.[62]

An-Na'im's position is startling for its radicalism, and his views would surely meet stiff opposition from most Muslims, purely because acceptance of them would be tantamount to casting aside more than half of God's word, the Qur'an. Moreover, his view that the Meccan revelations 'preached the solidarity of humanity' is not entirely accurate, as there are some Meccan verses that criticize Christianity and Judaism.[63]

Abdulaziz Sachedina

The third Muslim scholar and one who has made a profound contribution to the promotion of peace from an Islamic perspective is Abdulaziz Sachedina. A book of his published in 2001, entitled *The Islamic Roots of Democratic Pluralism*, depicts an inclusive, tolerant and peaceful Islam that is established upon a reading of the Qur'an that 'extracts relevant passages that deal with the vision of a universal humanity and of interfaith relations

---

[61] An-Na'im 1990, pp. 179–80.

[62] An-Na'im 1990, p. 158. Chapter 6 entitled 'Shari'a and Modern International Law' is of particular relevance in the context of this chapter.

[63] See Rahman 1994, Appendix II, pp. 162–70, and Marshall 2001, pp. 3–29. See also the comments of Firestone 1999, pp. 90–1.

[and] treats the entire Qur'an as a unified text'.[64] The significance of his work is the weaving together of various strands of thought to present a coherent world-view, founded upon the Qur'an, that promotes pluralism and inclusion, even of secularists and atheists.

Sachedina's world-view is grounded upon three principles: first, the unity of humankind; second, a common morality and freedom of conscience which is based upon an inherent quality bestowed by God upon all individuals; and third, forgiveness and mercy. The essence of the first of these, the unity of humankind, is contained in 2.213 of the Qur'an: 'The people were one community; then God sent forth the Prophets, good tidings to bear and warning, and He sent down with them the Book with the truth, that He might decide the people touching their differences.' For Sachedina, this verse endorses pluralism, and Muslims should engage in building bridges between the once unified human community. One method is to recognize that Islam actually means 'submission', that is, submission to God. Therefore, when the Qur'an states in 3.85 'Whoso desires another religion other than Islam, it shall not be accepted of him', the verse should be read as 'Whoso desires another religion other than submission (islam) it shall not be accepted of him', and this therefore includes individuals of other religious traditions.[65] Such an interpretation stands in contrast to many of the jurists who reified the term 'Islam' and understood that the previous verse refers to a whole set of rituals and acts of worship that are specific to Islam.

---

[64] Sachedina 2001, p. 26. Chapter 3 of this work (which discusses *fitra*) is taken from Chapter 3 of Little, Kelsay and Sachedina (eds) 1988, pp. 53–90. Sachedina avoids the accusation of 'selective retrieval' because his approach considers the totality of the Qur'an and extracts its universal message. But it is here that one could criticize Sachedina, because drawing universal themes from the Qur'an is done by examining particular Qur'anic verses, the understanding of which is always within the framework of historicity and language. Such an argument implies that 'universals' are contingent, and in reality do not exist.

[65] As Sachedina acknowledges, this is not a new interpretation but can be found in the writings of Wilfred Cantwell Smith (cf. Smith 1962). For Sachedina on *islam*, see Sachedina 2001, pp. 38–40.

The second major theme in Sachedina's work, the universalism of human morality and freedom of conscience in Islam, is based on his understanding of the Qur'anic term *fitra*, translated by Sachedina as 'original human nature'. The word *fitra* appears in 30.30–31 of the Qur'an: 'So set thy purpose for religion (*din*), a human by nature upright – God's original nature upon which He created humankind.' Sachedina understands this original nature to be a rational faculty, ingrained in the human personality that can discern the objective value of good and evil. In other words, this faculty, if properly nurtured, provides humans with a form of prerevelatory guidance.[66] This initial guidance allows the individual to become morally and spiritually aware, and the guidance then offered through the prophets helps the individual to become 'unshakable when encountering unbelievers and hypocrites'. But what is essential is Sachedina's claim that the idea of *fitra* is a form of universal guidance and reason which bears with it human responsibility to act in a good manner. Conforming to the demands of this original human nature for Sachedina is an act of submission (*islam*) to God, so that even atheists and agnostics may be rewarded by God on Judgement Day if they have responded according to the whisperings of their *fitra*. Since *fitra* requires humans to choose between right and wrong, it follows that humans must have freedom of conscience, and it is for this reason that the Qur'an states 'there is no compulsion in religion' (2.256), which Sachedina understands as a Qur'anic guarantee of human rights. *Moral* obligations, he argues, may have to be enforced through compulsion if people do not conform or accept the standards demanded by *fitra*. It is not legitimate, however, for *religious* obligations to be enforced, a stance that undermines the so-called Islamic fundamentalists' position.[67]

The third theme in Sachedina's work concerns forgiveness and

---

[66] Sachedina 2001, p. 85.
[67] For Sachedina and the concept of *fitra* and its implications see Sachedina 2001, pp. 63–96.

restorative justice, and he begins his discussion by citing 2.178 of the Qur'an which states:

> O believers, the law of fair retribution is prescribed for you in cases of murder: a free man for a free man; a slave for a slave; and a woman for a woman. But if [one of those seeking to avenge the victim] should wish to pardon the murderer, then let the pursuing be honourable, and let the payment be with kindness. This is a manifestation of the mercy and compassion of your Lord [for the murderer].

Sachedina justifies the Qur'anic ideal of mercy and forgiveness by claiming that it is through such acts that membership in society is restored and wounds are healed. Indeed, 'retributitive punishment is worth pursuing only to the extent that it leads to reconciling the victim and the wrongdoer, and rehabilitating the latter after his or her acknowledgement of responsibility',[68] something that Palestinians and Israelis might need to consider more.

Sachedina's writings represent a determined effort to present an interpretation of the Qur'an that can accommodate the major religions of the world and also agnosticism and atheism, and it certainly provides evidence that Islam possesses the roots for pluralism and democracy. However, it remains to be seen whether his views are embraced by Muslims, or whether his writings will be considered a watered-down version of Islam that smacks of humanism. Certainly, the arguments that Sachedina presents would not require Muslims to lose their identity, as distinctive ritual and worship are maintained through his belief in the efficacy of following the revelations given to the prophets. However, one may rightly ask, if humans are to find salvation through following the prompting of their *fitra*, then what is the need for Muslims to obey particular laws such as those relating to food and drink or clothing that make Islam so identifiable. Perhaps a more serious problem in Sachedina's writings concerns the ability to identify those morals which the individual's *fitra*

---

[68] Sachedina 2001, p. 111.

can distinguish in an innate fashion, and where the difference lies in moral and religious obligations. Sachedina's arguments are too abstract to provide specific examples of good and evil, and one wonders whether this issue was purposely avoided because in the modern age universal morals and rights are difficult to determine. The Salman Rushdie episode demonstrated this, and it is noteworthy that article XII.e of the Universal Islamic Declaration of Human Rights (agreed upon by an Islamic Council in Paris in 1981) states that 'No one shall hold in contempt or ridicule the religious beliefs of others or incite public honesty against them; respect for the religious feelings of others is obligatory on all Muslims.'[69] What is a right to freedom of speech for one person (allegory, metaphor or irony not withstanding) infringes the right to the protection of honour and reputation (article VIII).

Conclusion

This study on war and peace in Islam has been an attempt to advance from a survey of what the Qur'an, *hadith*, and commentaries of religious texts say about the topic to an analysis of why some Muslims have and continue to advocate a universalist form of Islam. It has been argued that the basis for universalist Islam rests on unverifiable foundations, and the last section of this chapter has presented the arguments of some modern Islamic scholars who believe that Islamic universalism is untenable in the contemporary age. The adoption by Muslims of any of the views of the three scholars summarized in this chapter is most probably contingent upon a number of factors. Re-reading of scripture caused much heartache for nineteenth-century Christians in Europe and the USA, but reform was undertaken from within, as there were no real challenges to the Christian cultures of Europe and the USA. European Christians enjoyed technological and military strength, and therefore were able to set meta-narratives for the international world that reflected their cultural and moral

---

[69] Cited in Noorani 2002, p. 137.

'superiority', such as the creation of nation-states. In the contemporary Islamic case, it is difficult to say that reform is a result
of forces from within or outside of the tradition. Whatever the
case, many Islamic reformers, while recognizing the economic
and technological backwardness of many Islamic countries, may
feel that Islam is one area where there is no reason to feel in-
adequate to the West. Change or reinterpretation of scripture
is, therefore, a great challenge. However, the call for change has
been embraced by reformers who recognize the need to jettison
the Islamic imperialist legacy, that salvation is not exclusive to
Islam, and that there are universal standards that do not always
match those of traditional Islam.[70] One of the difficulties facing
reformers is how to present Islamic reform without diminishing
Muslim identity, a feat problematic enough given the cultural
erosion that is concomitant with globalization. Accusations of
the 'Americanization of Islam' are frequently found in 'Islamic'
books, pamphlets and newspapers.

Which direction will Muslims turn? Tradition and the certain-
ties offered therein (including universalism) are always comfortable. Yet it is probably the case that universalism represents a
minority view among Muslims today, and the radical views of
Sayyid Qutb, the Muslim Brotherhood, and members of Hamas
have arguably been adopted because of the corners into which
they have been fenced. Alternatively, Muslims may be able to
open space for a pluralist understanding of Islam, one which
perhaps draws on the Islamic mystical tradition for precedents,
or one which re-reads the Qur'an, or at least reinterprets the text
in the ways suggested by Rahman, Sachedina and an-Na'im. At
stake is Islamic identity, and no doubt this identity will manifest
many regional variations as it responds to changing contexts –
something that has been witnessed throughout Islamic history.
The non-Muslim world and western powers are in a position
to influence the directions to which Muslims turn. Surely, a

---

[70] Standards too, that are sometimes ignored by western powers, such as
the decision of the USA and Britain to go to war with Iraq despite not being
able to secure the agreement of the United Nations Security Council.

more even-handed policy by the USA and Britain in the Israel–Palestine dispute would offer a positive symbol of co-existence, but unfortunately Muslims all too frequently witness negative responses from the West.

During the Iraq War, I read an article in the *Guardian* newspaper that typifies such negative symbols. As US forces advance on Baghdad, poised behind the troops are American evangelists, ostensibly providing humanitarian aid:

> Muslim worries have been heightened because the man leading the charge into Iraq is the Revd Franklin Graham, who delivered the invocation at President Bush's inauguration, the son of Billy Graham and a fierce critic of Islam. He is on record as calling it a 'wicked, violent' religion, with a God different from that of Christianity. 'The two are as different as lightness and darkness', he wrote.
>
> [The evangelical groups] . . . are causing alarm among Muslims, who fear vulnerable Iraqis will be cajoled into conversion, and Christians, some of whom warn that the missionaries will be prime targets in an unpacified Iraq.[71]

Select Bibliography

Ahmad, A., Sayyid Ahmad Khan, Jamal al-Din al-Afghani and Muslim India, *Studia Islamica*, XIII–XIV.

Al-'Ashmawi, S. M., 2001, *Against Islamic Extremism*, ed. and trans. by C. Fluehr-Lobban, University Press of Florida.

An-Na'im, A. A., 1986, The Islamic Law of Apostasy and its Modern Applicability: A case from the Sudan, *Religion* 16, pp. 197–224.

An-Nai'im, A. A., 1990, *Towards an Islamic Reformation*, New York: Syracuse University Press.

Ayoub, M., 1992, Jihad: A Source of Power and Framework of Authority in Islam, in: *Bulletin of Middle Eastern Studies*, Niigata, Japan: International University of Japan.

Banani, A., 1961, *The Modernisation of Iran, 1921–1941*, Stanford: Stanford University Press.

---

[71] Matthew Engel, 'Bringing aid and the Bible, the man who called Islam wicked', *The Guardian*, 4 April 2003, p. 6.

Buchanan, P., 2002, Is Islam a Religion of Peace?', in: *The Washington Dispatch*, 1 December.

Burton, J., 1977, *The Collection of The Qur'an*, Cambridge: Cambridge University Press.

Choudury, M. L. R., 1952, *The Din-i-Ilahi or the Religion of Akbar*, Delhi: Munshiran Manoharlal Publishers Pvt Ltd.

Firestone, R., 1999, *Jihad: The Origins of Holy War in Islam*, Oxford: Oxford University Press.

Guillaume, A. (trans.), 1955, *The Life of Muhammad: A Translation of Ibn Ishaq's Sirat Rasul Allah*, Karachi: Oxford University Press.

Halliday, F., 1996, *Islam and the Myth of Confrontation: Religion and Politics in the Middle East*, London: I.B. Tauris.

Hamas, 1988, *The Covenant of the Islamic Resistance Movement* (18 August 1988). Found on the web at www.yale.edu/lawweb/avalon/mideast/hamas.htm. This forms part of The Avalon Project at the Yale Law School.

Hashmi, S. H., 2002, Interpreting the Ethics of War and Peace in Islam, in: S. H. Hashmi (ed.), *Islamic Political Ethics*, Princeton: Princeton University Press.

Hawting, G. R., 1986, *The First Dynasty of Islam*, London: Croom Helm.

Humphries, S. R., 1999, *Between Memory and Desire: The Middle East in a Troubled Age*, Los Angeles: University of California Press.

Johnson, J. T., 1997, *The Holy War Idea in Western and Islamic Traditions*, Pennsylvania: The Pennsylvania State University Press.

Kennedy, H., 1986, *The Prophet and the Age of the Caliphates*, London: Longman.

Khadduri, M. (trans.), 1966, *The Islamic Law of Nations: Shaybani's Siyar*, Maryland: The Johns Hopkins Press.

Khadduri, M., 1979, *War and Peace in the Law of Islam*, New York: AMS Press.

Khadduri, M. (trans.), 1987, *Al-Shafi'i's Risala*, Cambridge: The Islamic Texts Society.

Khan, A., 1993, An Account of the Loyal Mohomedans of India, in: H. Malik (ed.), *Political Profile of Sir Sayyid Ahmad Khan*, Delhi: Adam Publishers Limited.

Lassner, J., 1986, *Islamic Revolution and Historical Memory: An Inquiry into the Art of Abbasid Apologetics*, New Haven: American Oriental Society.

Lawrence, B., 1998, *Shattering the Myth: Islam Beyond Violence*, New Jersey: Princeton University Press.

Little, D., Kelsay, J. and Sachedina, A. (eds), 1988, *Human Rights and the Conflict of Cultures*, University of South Carolina Press.

Mahmoud, M., 1998, Mahmud Muhammad Taha's Second Message of Islam and his Modernist Project, in: J. Cooper, R. Nettler and M. Mahmoud (eds), *Islam and Modernity: Muslim Intellectuals Respond*, London: I.B. Tauris, pp. 105–28.

Marshall, D., 2001, Christianity in the Qur'an, in: L. Ridgeon (ed.), *Islamic Interpretations of Christianity*, London: Curzon Press.

Mawdudi, A. A., 1980, *Jihad in Islam*, Lahore: Islamic Publications Ltd.

Mernissi, F., 1991, *The Veil and the Male Elite*, trans. M. J. Lakeland, New York: Addison-Wesley Publishing.

Millbank, D., 2002, Hawks Chide Bush over Islam, in: *Washington Post*, 2 December 2002.

Moaddel, M. and Talattof, K. (eds.), 2000, *Contemporary Debates in Islam*, London: Macmillan.

Motzki H., 2000, The Murder of Ibn Abi l-Huqayq: On the origin and reliability of some maghazi reports, in: H. Motzki (ed.), *The Biography of Muhammad*, Leiden: Brill.

Noorani, A. G., 2002, *Islam and Jihad: Prejudice Versus Reality*, London: Zed Press.

Nu'mani, 'A. S., 2000, Methodology of Historical Writing, from his *Sirat al-Nabi*, trans. by M. Tayyib Bakhsh Budayuni (Delhi: Idarah-i Adabiyat-i Delhi, reprint, 1983), reprinted in M. Moaddel and K. Talattof (eds), *Contemporary Debates in Islam*, London: Macmillan.

Peters, R., 1996, *Jihad in Classical and Modern Islam*, Princeton: Markus Wiener Publishers.

Qutb, S., 2000, War, Peace and Islamic Jihad, (Chapter 21 of *Milestones*, trans. by S. Badrul Hasan, included in Mansoor Moaddel and Kamran Talattof (eds), *Contemporary Debates in Islam*, London: Macmillan.

Rahman, F., 1955, Internal Religious Developments in the Present Century Islam, *Cahiers d'histoire mondiale/Journal of World History*, 2.

Rahman, F., 1966, *Islam*, Chicago: Chicago University Press.

Rahman, F., 1982, *Islam and Modernity: Transformation of an Intellectual Tradition*, London: University of Chicago Press.

Rahman, F., 1994, *Major Themes of the Qur'an*, Minneapolis: Bibliotheca Islamicca.

Rahman, F., 2000, *Revival and Reform in Islam: A Study of Islamic Fundamentalism*, Oxford: Oneworld.

Rippin, A., 2000, Muhammad in the Qur'an: Reading Scripture in the 21st Century, in: H. Motzki, *The Biography of Muhammad*, Leiden: Brill.

Rumi, J. al-Din, 1373, *Mathnawi*, VI, 490–5, Tehran: Pizhman.

Sachedina, A., 2001, *The Islamic Roots of Democratic Pluralism*, Oxford University Press.

Sharma, S. R., 1988, *The Religious Policy of the Moghul Emperors*, Delhi: Munshiram Manoharlal Publishers Pvt Ltd.

Smith, W. C., 1962, *The Meaning and End of Religion*, New York: Macmillan.

Soroush, A., 2000, *Reason, Freedom, and Democracy in Islam: Essential Writings of Abdolkarim Soroush*, trans. and ed. by M. Sadri and A. Sadri. Oxford University Press.

Taha, M. M., 1986, *The Second Message of Islam*, trans. by Abdullahi Ahmed an-Na'im, New York: Syracuse University Press.

Watt, W. M., 1961, *Muhammad: Prophet and Statesman*, Oxford: Oxford University Press.

Watt, W. M., 1976, Islamic conceptions of the Holy War, in: Thomas Patrick Murphy (ed.), *The Holy War*, Columbus: Ohio State University Press.

Zaman, R. M., 2002, Islamic Perspectives on Territorial Boundaries and Autonomy, in: S. H. Hashmi, *Islamic Political Ethics*, Princeton: Princeton University Press.

PART III

INTER-RELIGIOUS FOUNDATIONS FOR PEACE

8. Global Ethic: Development and Goals

HANS KÜNG

The Long History of Humanity

The history of our globe shows 'grandeur' and 'misery', and the history of humanity is great and sublime, but also infinitely cruel. Human beings and nations, with all their inventions, creations and achievements, with all their disputes, conflicts and wars, are sometimes in danger of taking themselves too seriously. Would it really make any difference to the universe if the human race destroyed itself? Our globe is a very insignificant star on the periphery of one of 100 million Milky Ways. Just as the human race came into being, so it can pass away again – and our generation is the first in the long history of the earth which proves to be technically able to destroy itself, by nuclear weapons or by eroding the ecological basis of its survival.

According to a number of scientists the world has existed for at least 13 billion years. There has been human life on our planet for perhaps 1,500,000 years. So 99.9 per cent of human history will have been primal history: a history without writing, without the name of a people or a religion, a political or a religious leader. But since the early Stone Age the *homo sapiens*, as present-day human beings proudly call themselves, have been distinct from the animal world by their consciousness of themselves. *Homo sapiens* invented tools and weapons, learned to control fire, and seized the dens occupied by marauding beasts; at that time already they buried their dead and offered sacrifices, and were able to produce cave paintings, carvings and statues, motivated by magic and religion.

Only about 5,000 years ago, at the beginning of the third millennium BCE, the early historical high cultures and high religions developed in Mesopotamia, the Nile valley, the Indus valley and the Huangho valley in China. That brings 'prehistory' without writing to an end and written 'history' into being, which is able to speak to us for itself in a living way through its literary documents. The real 'historical' period of the human race begins, in which an increasing number of specific peoples, religions and historical persons emerge into history. Now, not only information about administration and trade, but later also myths and sagas, customs, laws and morals are recorded.

From a historical perspective the concrete ethical norms, values, insights and key concepts of religions and philosophies have been formed in a highly complicated social and dynamic process. Where the basic human needs and concerns emerged, there was from the beginning of human history pressure for regulations for human conduct: priorities, conventions, customs, commandments, instructions and laws, in short particular ethical norms. Much therefore that is proclaimed in the Bible as God's commandment is already found in the ancient Babylonian Code of Hammurabi from the eighteenth and seventeenth centuries BCE.

Human beings had to test and still have to test ethical norms and ethical solutions in projections and models, often practising them and proving them over generations. After periods of proving and acclimatization, such norms finally come to be recognized by a group, tribe, people or nation, but sometimes – if the times have changed completely – they are also diluted and replaced. Are we perhaps living in such a time of change?

Given the reality of our modern technological society which is so many-layered, changeable, complex and often impenetrable, nobody can avoid making use of scientific methods in order to investigate as far as possible without prejudice the material laws and future possibilities of this society. Certainly not every average person needs to make use of these scientific methods.

Even today, of course, the pre-scientific awareness of particular ethical norms, insofar as it still exists, retains basic significance for a high proportion of people. And happily, many people still 'spontaneously' act correctly in particular situations without ever having read a treatise on moral philosophy or moral theology. Nevertheless, the wrong verdicts (for example in connection with war, racism, the situation of women or the significance of birth control) which have found their way into many religions in the course of more recent history have shown that modern life has become too complex for defining specific ethical norms – particularly with regard to sexuality or aggression, economic or political power – in a naïve blindness to reality, which overlooks empirical data and insights confirmed by science.

In positive terms, this means that nowadays a modern ethic is depending on contact with the sciences: psychology and psycho-therapy, sociology and social science, behavioural research, biology, cultural history and philosophical anthropology. Also the religions, their responsible leaders and teachers, should not show any anxiety in becoming involved in all these: the human sciences in particular offer them a growing wealth of relatively certain anthropological insights and information which is relevant to action, and these can be used to facilitate decisions in a way that can be justified.

A Coalition of Believers and Non-Believers for a Common Ethic

Over the millennia the religions were the systems of orientation which laid the foundation for a particular morality, which legitimated it, motivated it and often also sanctioned punishments. But does that need to be the case even now, in many largely secularized societies? Religions, like all historical entities which have been ambivalent for men and women, have perceived their moral function for better and for worse. The religions have contributed a great deal to the spiritual and moral progress of the peoples. But undoubtedly also non-religious people can have a basic ethical orientation and lead a moral life without religion.

Indeed, in history there have often been non-religious people who pioneered a new sense of human dignity and did more for human emancipation, freedom of conscience, freedom of religion and other human rights than their religious allies. Many non-religious people have also developed and pursue goals and priorities, values and norms, ideals and models, criteria for good and evil.

In our days many religious and secular people around the world are pioneering together a morality which takes its bearings from the human dignity of all men and women, and according to present understanding this human dignity includes reason and responsibility, freedom of conscience, freedom of religion and the other human rights which have been established over the course of a long history. And it is of utmost significance for peace among the peoples, for international collaboration in politics, economics and culture, and also for international organizations like the UN, that religious people – whether they are Jews, Christians or Muslims, Hindus, Jains, Sikhs, Buddhists, Confucians, Taoists or whatever – and non-religious people, who call themselves 'humanists' or by whatever name, can in their own way advocate and defend human dignity and human rights, in short a humane ethic. In fact both believers and non-believers advocate what stands as Article I in the United Nations Declaration of Human Rights which was passed on 10 December 1948 – after World War Two and the Holocaust: 'All human beings are born free and equal in dignity and rights. They are endowed with reason and conscience and should act towards one another in a spirit of brotherhood.'

A coalition of believers and non-believers in mutual respect is indispensable for a common global ethic. Non-believers can join believers in resisting all trivial nihilism, diffuse cynicism and social apathy and devote themselves with conviction to the following aim: that the basic right of all human beings to a life worth living (no matter what sex, nation, religion, race or class they belong to) is not largely ignored, as it used to be, but is increasingly being realized. This is not pure utopia, but a realistic vision. A society without war has become a reality since 1945, at least in the OECD world in which the material imbalances are slowly reduced by strengthening democratic structures and institutions and by raising the standard of living of the poor.

Globalization Needs a Global Ethic

Globalization concerns not only internal and special issues of the economy: it concerns universal social, highly political, and ultimately also ethical issues. In concrete terms it is about the question of whether profit, and therefore the pursuit of profit that is justified in principle, should be the one and only purpose of the economy, of a bank, or an enterprise. The phenomenon of economic globalization makes it clear that along with globalization the question of what is ethical should also be posed, and ethics should also be applied to globalization. We need also a *globalization of ethic.*

Globalization is therefore much more than just an economic concept. In order to lend *sustainability* to the globalization of markets, technology and communication, the profits of the economy must be produced in such a way that they are society- and environment-friendly. The globalization of the economy, technology and the media means also the globalization of problems: from financial and labour markets to the environment, organized crime and terrorism. For this reason reflection on global ethical standards is essential. In order to ensure that economic performance remains subordinate to human and social goals, globalization needs a political foundation and an ethical framework. What is needed is not a uniform ethical system ('ethics' in the strict sense), but only a necessary minimum of shared ethical values, basic attitudes and standards to which all regions, nations and interest groups can subscribe – in other words, a shared basic 'ethic' for humankind, an 'ethos' in the sense of a moral attitude.

'Global ethic' is therefore not a new ideology or superstructure. It will not make the specific ethics of the different religions and philosophies superfluous. It is therefore no substitute for the Torah, the Sermon on the Mount, the Qur'an, the Bhagavadgîta, the Discourses of the Buddha or the Analects of Confucius. Global ethic is nothing but the necessary minimum of common values, standards and basic attitudes. In other words: a minimal basic consensus relating to binding values, irrevocable standards and moral attitudes, which can be affirmed by all religions despite their 'dogmatic' differences, and can also be supported by non-believers.

There is a need for the rediscovery and reassessment of ethics in politics and economics, a need for morality (in the positive sense), but not for moralism (morality in the negative sense). For moralism and moralizing overvalue morality and ask too much of it. Moralizers make morality the sole criterion for human action and ignore the relative independence of various spheres of life like economics, law and politics. Speaking out for a few basic ethical standards does not mean deciding every controversial issue on which an ethical consensus cannot be reached in the present situation.

On the other hand, ethics excludes also a libertinism which claims rights without any responsibilities. The dignity of the human person is the basis of both rights and responsibilities. Article 29 of the Universal Declaration of Human Rights affirms the importance of 'duties' and of the 'just requirements of morality':

1. Everyone has duties to the community in which alone the free and full development of his personality is possible.
2. In the exercise of his rights and freedoms, everyone shall be subject only to such limitations as are determined by law solely for the purpose of securing due recognition and respect for the rights and freedoms of others and of meeting the just requirements of morality, public order and the general welfare in a democratic society.

A Global Process of Growing Ethical Awareness

There are already several important international documents which explicitly speak of human rights and human responsibilities, indeed which programmatically call for a global ethic and even attempt to identify specific areas of application:

1. The 1995 report by the UN Commission for Global Governance calls for an ethic of neighbourhood in all areas: 'global values must be the core of a world political order'.
2. The equally important report by the World Commission on Culture and Development, also of 1995, calls in the very first chapter for 'a New Global Ethic', an ethic of humankind, a global ethic 'to cope with the global problems mentioned'.
3. This request also found support in the UNESCO Universal Ethics Project of 1997, the World Economic Forum at Davos in 1997 and the Indira Gandhi Conference at Delhi in 1997.

Such international conferences and commissions not only stress the need for a global ethic but also in part call for a formulation of human responsibilities. This was first done in 1993 by the Parliament of the World's Religions in its Declaration Toward a Global Ethic, and later by the InterAction Council, made up of former heads of state and government, which in 1997 published a proposal for a Universal Declaration of Human Responsibilities. In 1999, the Third Parliament of the World's Religions meeting at Cape Town issued a 'Call to our Guiding Institutions'. Let me first recall the main thrust of the 1993 Declaration Toward a Global Ethic.

Two Basic Ethical Principles of Humanity

We have not to re-invent the wheel of ethic again. In the often millennia-old cultural traditions of humanity we find very elementary ethical standards which are convincing and practicable also today for all women and men of good will. Of course, these cultural traditions differ in many ways from each other in their understanding of what is helpful and what is unhelpful for the human being, what is right and what is wrong, what is good and what is evil. It is absolutely impossible to gloss over or to ignore the very serious differences among the civilizations. However, these differences should not be obstacles to perceiving and appreciating those ethical values and standards which are already held in common and which can jointly be affirmed, on religious or non-religious grounds. On the basis of all the scholarly work in this field done so far, it is now possible to outline the content of a global ethic.

Now, as before, women and men are treated inhumanely all over the world. They are robbed of their opportunities and their freedom; their human rights are trampled underfoot; their dignity is disregarded. In the face of all inhumanity ethical traditions demand strongly that *every human being must be treated humanely*. 'Humanity', 'Humaneness' (Chinese: *ren*) in the sense of benevolence is already a central ethical term in the Analects of Confucius and can be found in most cultures and religions.

There is a broad ethical consensus worldwide, that every human being, without distinction of age, sex, race, skin colour, physical or mental ability, language, religion, political view, or national or social origin, possesses an inalienable and untouchable dignity. And everyone, the individual as well as the State, is therefore obliged to honour this dignity and protect it. Humans must always be the subjects of rights, must be ends, never mere means, never mere objects of commercialization and industrialization in economics, politics and media, in research institutes, and industrial corporations. No one stands 'above good and evil' – no human being, no social class, no influential interest group, no cartel, no police apparatus, no army, and no state. On the contrary: possessed of reason and conscience, every human is obliged to behave in a genuinely human fashion, to do good and prevent evil.

There is another principle which is found and has persisted in many cultural traditions of humankind for thousands of years: *What you do not wish done to yourself, do not do to others.* This 'golden rule' is already attested by Confucius (*c.*551–489 BCE); it is also expressed in Judaism by Rabbi Hillel (60 BCE to 10 CE), and in Christianity (Sermon on the Mount): 'Whatever you want people to do to you, do also to them.' Kant's categorical imperative could be understood as a modernization, rationalization and secularization of this 'golden rule': 'Act in such a way that the maxims of your will at any time can be taken at the same time as the principle of a universal legislation', or, 'Act in such a way that you always use humankind, both in your person and in the person of anyone else . . . , at the same time as an end, never as a means.'

These two principles of humanity can serve as the irrevocable, unconditional norms for all areas of life, for families and communities, for races, nations and religions. Racism, nationalism, sexism or religious fanaticism prevent humans from being authentically human. Self-determination and self-realization are legitimate so long as they are not separated from human self-responsibility and global responsibility; that is, from responsibility for fellow humans and for the planet earth.

On this basis four irrevocable directives are developed, four imperatives of humanity (extensively in the Declaration of the Parliament of the World's Religions, in a more condensed and juridical form in the proposal of the InterAction Council):

1. 'Have respect for all life!' The ancient precept, especially urgent in a time of children killing children: 'You shall not kill!' That means today the responsibility for a culture of non-violence and respect for life.

2. 'Deal honestly and fairly!' The very old commandment, important more than ever in the age of globalization: 'You shall not steal!' That means today the responsibility for a culture of solidarity and a just economic order.

3. 'Speak and act truthfully!' The ancient axiom, valid also for politicians and the media: 'You shall not lie!' That means the responsibility for a culture of tolerance and a life of truthfulness.

4. 'Respect and love one another!' The age-old directive, even more important in an age which seems to be without taboos: 'You shall not abuse sexuality, not commit sexual immorality!' That means the responsibility for a culture of equal rights and partnership between men and women.

Recent Developments of the Global Ethic Project

During the first week of December 1999 the Third Parliament of the World's Religions convened at Cape Town, following those held in Chicago in 1893 and in 1993. One of the main tasks of the 1999 Parliament consisted in building upon the process of the past six years and in concretizing further the Global Ethic Project. This was done on the basis of a 'Call to our Guiding Institutions', those institutions which play a decisive and influential role in society: religion and spirituality; government; agriculture, labour, industry, and commerce; education; arts and communications media; science and medicine; international intergovernmental organizations; organizations of civil society. They are invited to adopt the principles and directives of the Global Ethic and to apply them to concrete issues. The rationale focuses on the notion of 'creative engagement':

> When reflecting on the future of the human community, one must consider the world's most powerful institutions – institutions, whose policies, for better and for worse, influence every aspect of life on the planet. Clearly, the critical issues facing the world today present an acute ethical challenge to these institutions. What is urgently needed is a new opening to creative engagement among the guiding institutions – an active, attentive, and inventive collaboration, rooted in shared moral principles and expressed in mutually sustained programs on behalf of the peoples of the twenty-first century.

The 'Call' document is directly based on the Chicago Declaration of 1993, the related quotations of which are printed at the margin of each single call.

In addition, an increasing number of political and religious personalities have joined the calls for a global ethic. Some examples follow.

Václav Havel, former President of the Czech Republic, emphasized at the annual meeting of IMF and World Bank in Prague in 2000 that

> the crucial task is to fundamentally strengthen a system of uni-

versally shared moral standards that will make it impossible, on a truly global scale, for the various rules to be time and again circumvented with still more ingenuity than had gone into their invention. Such standards will truly guarantee the weight of the rules and will generate natural respect for them in the societal climate. Actions proven to jeopardize the future of the human race should not only be punishable but, first and foremost, should be generally regarded as a disgrace. This will hardly ever happen unless we all find, inside ourselves, the courage to substantially change and to newly form an order of values that, with all our diversity, we can jointly embrace and jointly respect; and, unless we again relate these values to something that lies beyond the horizon of our immediate personal or group interest.

Important support for this vision was given by the new Director General of the IMF, Horst Köhler. He recalled the appeal by President Václav Havel 'to reflect on the wider dimension of the task, to allow globalization to work for the prosperity of all, to seek new sources of a sense of responsibility for the world'. And Dr Köhler added: 'I fully share this call for generally recognized moral standards. Indeed, as Hans Küng says, a global economy needs a global ethic.'

The following statements reflect consent from a variety of civilizations:

Mary Robinson, High Commissioner for Human Rights:
What is clear is that for the first time ever the pursuit of a goal by humanity, the attempt to move in the direction of a minimal consensus of shared values, attitudes and moral standards, will require the same degree of commitment and equal contribution of women and men.

Prince Hassan Bin Talal of Jordan:
By providing a starting point that all can agree upon, a global ethic would begin to traverse the split between subject and object. It would identify the fundamentals that are common to all religious traditions, and distill from them the essence of

human belief. A global ethic should constitute a core of belief, acceptable to all. It should not seek to impose one vision, or to legislate away our differences. It should strive for unity, but seek neither to eradicate nor to compromise diversity. After all, in this global age, only a truly global ethic can be of real value.

Aung San Suu Kyi of Burma, Nobel Peace Prize Laureate:
The challenge we now face is for the different nations and peoples of the world to agree on a basic set of human values, which will serve as a unifying force in the development of a genuine global community.

The need for a global ethic is also confirmed by religious authorities. Pope John Paul II declared in his address to the Pontifical Academy of Social Sciences in Rome in 2001:

As humanity embarks upon the process of globalization, it can no longer do without a common code of ethics. This does not mean a single dominant socio-economic system or culture which would impose its values and its criteria on ethical reasoning. It is within man as such, within universal humanity sprung from the Creator's hand, that the norms of social life are to be sought. Such a search is indispensable if globalization is not to be just another name for the absolute relativization of values and the homogenization of lifestyles and cultures. In all the variety of cultural forms, universal human values exist and they must be brought out and emphasized as the guiding force of all development and progress.

The Moderator of the World Council of Churches Central Committee Aram I, Catholicos of Cilicia, underlined the global ethic idea in his Official Report to the 8th Assembly of the World Council of Churches at Harare, Zimbabwe, in 1998:

We are committed to the development of a basic common ethics that may lead societies from mere existence to meaningful co-existence, from confrontation to reconciliation, from degeneration of moral values to the restoration of the quality of life that restores the presence of transcendence in human life. Global culture must be sustained by a global ethics that will guide the relations of nations with each other and with the creation, and will help them to work together for genuine world community. Such a global ethics, the idea of which was launched by the Parliament of World Religions in 1993, should not reflect the Western Christian ethos; it must be based on a diversity of experiences and convictions. The Church, together with other living faiths, should seek a global ethics based on shared ethical values that transcend religious beliefs and narrow definitions of national interests. Human rights must be undergirded by ethical principles. Therefore, dialogue among religions and cultures is crucial as the basis for greater solidarity for justice and peace, human rights and dignity.

Let me conclude by mentioning a particularly exciting development: the global ethic on the UN level. The year 2001 had been proclaimed by the UN 'International Year of Dialogue Among Civilizations', taking up a proposal made by the President of Iran, Seyed Mohammad Khatami to the UN General Assembly in 1998.

At the end of that International Year of Dialogue among Civilizations a 20-person expert group of 'Eminent Persons' convened by UN Secretary-General Kofi Annan presented a report to him and to the General Assembly. I was privileged to be a member of this group, together with outstanding personalities such as Hanan Ashrawi, Jacques Delors, Nadine Gordimer, Prince Hassan of Jordan, Graça Machel, Amartya Sen, Dick Spring, and Richard von Weizsäcker, to name only a few of them. The main thrust of the report, with the title 'Crossing the Divide' is to develop a new paradigm of international relations able to meet the new challenges our world is facing. The horrible events of 11 September 2001 manifested in a cruel way that political thought and action today has to take the political, economic, cultural and religious aspects seriously into account. Let me now quote some sentences of the report which clearly show how strongly the contribution of a global ethic for a new paradigm of international relations is now perceived on the UN level:

It is reconciliation that may lead all of us, no matter how this reconciliation process is achieved, to discover and to establish a global ethic. A global ethic for institutions and civil society, for leaders and for followers, requires a *longing and striving for peace, longing and striving for justice, longing and striving for partnerships, longing and striving for truth*. These might be *the four pillars of a system of a global ethic* that reconciliation, as the new answer to the vicious circle of endless hatred, is going to provide us.

The new hegemonialism of the United States which found its striking expression in the illegal and immoral Iraq war of spring 2003 seems however to jeopardize seriously all attempts towards a new paradigm and is clearly a relapse into the old paradigm of confrontation. But let us not lose hope, and conclude these reflections with a forward-looking question:

How is a Global Ethic to be Established?

This is a question which is valid for all new ideas. An example could be the demands of the UN Global Compact, which have now attained UN status, at least as demands. But what a long process of conscientization has it taken for human rights, humane working conditions and environmental demands to reach the level of the UN! In all these issues, as in the cases of peace and disarmament and the partnership between men and women, a very complex and long process of growing awareness has been needed. As such, this is already a prerequisite for a change of human awareness towards an ethic for humankind.

Many people can help here: pioneer thinkers, activists and initiative groups, but equally the countless teachers, from kindergarten to secondary school, who are already committed to a new understanding of the world religions, universal peace and a global ethic. Reflection on the ethic that all men and women have in common is more than ever necessary for the peaceful coexistence of humankind, on the local level (in countless multi-cultural and multi-faith cities) and on the global level (in terms of global communication, global economy, global ecology and global politics). What happens in an individual's sphere of life, larger or smaller, depends therefore on that individual and his or her motivation.

In order to meet the challenges of the future, humanity needs not only science, but wisdom; not only technology, but spiritual energy; not only economy, but humanity. Humankind has to remain humane, has to become even more humane. And for a humane survival of humanity, human beings need an *ethic*! Ethical values and standards as mentioned above:

- non-violence and respect for life;
- justice and solidarity;
- truthfulness and tolerance;
- partnership and mutual respect and love.

Smartness and toughness are not enough. Professional and political competence is not enough. Ethical competence is required, based on moral values and standards. This is an insight of all the different civilizations: in 500 BCE Confucius said: 'If a man is not humane, what can he do with the rituals? If a man is not humane, what can he do with music?' And Mahatma Gandhi finds as the 'seven social sins of human kind', which can be overcome on the base of a global ethic:

> Politics without principles,
> wealth without work,
> enjoyment without conscience,
> knowledge without character,
> business without morality,
> science without humanity,
> religion without sacrifice.

SELECT BIBLIOGRAPHY

Council for a Parliament of the World's Religions, 1999, *A Call to Our Guiding Institutions*, presented on the occasion of the 1999 Parliament of the World's Religions, Cape Town, South Africa.

Dower, N., 1998, *World Ethics: The New Agenda*, Edinburgh: Edinburgh University Press.

Küng, H., 1991, *Global Responsibility: In Search of a New World Ethic*, London: SCM; New York: Crossroad.

Küng, H. (ed.), 1996, *Yes to a Global Ethic*, London: SCM; New York: Continuum.

Küng, H., 1998, *A Global Ethic for Global Politics and Economics*, London: SCM, 1997; New York: Oxford University Press, 1998.

Küng, H., 2001, *Crossing the Divide: Dialogue among Civilizations*, ed. by Seton Hall University, South Orange, NJ.

Küng, H. and Kuschel, K.-J., 1993, *A Global Ethic: The Declaration of the Parliament of the World's Religions*, London: SCM; New York: Continuum.

Küng, H. and Schmidt, H. (eds), 1998, *A Global Ethic and Global Responsibilities: Two Declarations*, London: SCM.

May, J. D'Arcy, 2000, *After Pluralism: Towards an Interreligious Ethic*, Münster, Hamburg, London: LIT Verlag.

Morgan, P. and Braybrooke, M. (eds), 1998, *Testing the Global Ethic: Voices from the Religions on Moral Values*, Oxford: The World Congress of Faiths; Ada, MI: CoNexus Press.

Runzo, J. and Martin, N. M. (eds), 2001, *Ethics in the World Religions* (The Library of Global Ethics and Religions, Vol. III), Oxford and New York: Oneworld Publications.

Swidler, L. (ed.), 1999, *For All Life: Toward a Universal Declaration of a Global Ethic: An Interreligious Dialogue*, Ashland, Or.: White Cloude Press.

Twiss, S. B. and Grelle, B. (eds), 1998, *Explorations in Global Ethics: Comparative Religious Ethics and Interreligious Dialogue*, Boulder, Col., Oxford: Westview Press.

Wentzel Wolfe, R. and Gudorf, C. E. (eds), 1999, *Ethics and World Religions:Cross-Cultural Case Studies*, Maryknoll: Orbis.

9. Peace and Multireligious Co-operation: The World Conference of Religions for Peace (WCRP)

NORBERT KLAES

The Demand for Global Peace as a Challenge for Multireligious Co-operation

The study known as *The Global 2000 Report to the President* was published in 1980 and was directed by Gerald O. Barney. It sold 1.5 million copies in eight languages. In 1999, this report was revised by Barney and was edited under the title *Threshold 2000* for the Parliament of the World's Religions, Capetown, 1999.[1] It is about the future of this endangered earth and the survival of humankind.

> Problems abound: poverty and starvation, consumerism and population growth, debt burdens and trade imbalances, crime, AIDS, drugs, war and refugees. Most ominously all of the bio-geochemical systems essential for life on Earth, the habitats essential for the survival of diverse species, and even the atmosphere and the oceans are now disturbed and threatened on a planetary scale, these problems are all interconnected . . . what we really have is a poverty-hunger-habitat-energy-trade-population-atmospheric-waste-resource-problem.[2]

---

[1] Cf. Barney 1999.
[2] Barney 1999, p. 25.

This megaproblem is the *global problematique*. On the other hand, the *global problematique* is only the negative factor of a process of globalization which, with its advancement of technology and communication, opens up fascinating chances for the responsible formation of a peaceful future for humankind.

Now, it is astonishing that, unlike in earlier editions, the authors of the millennium study no longer address politicians, experts of economy and institutions like the United Nations, but challenge the leaders of the world's religions.

> To do what must be done, earth's spiritual leaders of all faiths and all traditions must work together in ways previously unimagined and unimaginable. We must count on you to develop a community of earth's faith traditions that is an example of the kind of open communication, mutual respect, acceptance, co-operation and good will that should characterize the emerging global community of nations and peoples. Each tradition has at its core a vision of Divine harmony that urges its followers to embody it in the social sphere.[3]

Scientists as well as political leaders like Kofi Annan, Secretary-General of the UN, urge the religions to co-operate for a more humane future, in spite of the concerns that religions often promote conflicts rather then resolve them. At the European level, presidents of the European Commission such as Delors and Santer conceived a programme 'A Soul for Europe'. This 'has the aim of bringing together Humanists, Christians, Jews, Muslims and other traditions to reflect about the ethical and spiritual implications of European integration'.[4]

The religions themselves respond to this challenge only hesitantly. It is true, however, that most of the religious traditions have a universal vision which encompasses all human beings and their salvation. Hindus confess the ultimate unity of all reality in the divine Brāhman, Mahāyāna-Buddhists in the Buddha-nature, the Abrahamic religions in the God of Creation –

---

[3] Barney 1999, p. 108.
[4] Forward Studies Unit 1998, p. 11.

departing from God and returning into God. Very often these fundamental beliefs lead to social action, global responsibility and solidarity. Modern religious organizations like the International Network of Engaged Buddhists (INEB), the Hindu Rama-Krishna-Mission, the Gandhi Peace Foundation, the International Islamic Relief Organization or the numerous Christian development agencies take part in the struggle for a better, more humane world. However, in their concern for the one human family they seldom envisage inter-religious co-operation. Very gradually, in the context of growing globalization, the great religions have been developing structures of inter-religious dialogue like the Christian ecumenical 'Office on Interreligious Relations', the Roman Catholic 'Pontifical Council for Interreligious Dialogue' and the 'International Jewish Committee on Inter-Religious Consultations' or the 'Office for Interreligious Affairs of the Muslim World League'. Beyond this, increasingly inter-religious activities of individual believers or of religious groups are initiated. There is also some progress in the field of theological and doctrinal reflection about the respective religious basis for dialogue. Thus at the inter-religious meeting for peace in Assisi (1986), after a long period of a church-centred theology, Pope John Paul II emphasized in his address to the spiritual leaders of all religions:

> . . . the common path which humanity is called to tread . . . Either we learn to walk together in peace and harmony, or we drift apart and ruin ourselves and others. We hope that this pilgrimage to Assisi has taught us anew to be aware of the common origin and common destiny of humanity. Let us see in it an anticipation of what God would like the developing history of humanity to be: a fraternal journey in which we accompany one another towards the transcendent goal which He sets for us.[5]

In connection with theological considerations the practice of inter-religious dialogue and its various forms and expressions

---

[5] Gioia 1997, p. 350.

is sometimes reflected: there is the dialogue as the exchange between experts in the religious traditions or official representatives of these traditions; there is a sharing of respective spiritual experiences; there is the dialogue of life, in which believers of different religions bear witness in their daily lives to their own human and spiritual values and help each other to live according to those values; there is finally the inter-religious social acting in which, in connection with the global problematic, the religious partners aim at global peace, social justice, the realization of human rights and cultural values and the liberation of people.[6]

This inter-religious social dialogue is envisaged by many inter-religious organizations[7] which, according to the pluralism of religions and cultures in the world, are founded on the basis of at least several religious traditions. Some of them are traditional ones such as the International Fellowship of Reconciliation (IFOR). Some are new movements like the 'United Religions Initiative', which was founded in 1995 by Bishop Swing as an association that is conceived of as a multireligious parallel organization to the United Nations. With regard to the economical dimension of globalization the initiative of the so-called 'World Faiths Development Dialogue' (WFDD) is important, in which representatives of the World Bank and the world religions work together for overcoming worldwide poverty. Today, the largest international, inter-religious established movements are the International Association for Religious Freedom (1900), The World Congress of Faiths (1936), The Temple of Understanding (1960) and the World Conference of Religions for Peace (1970).

In 1993, at the occasion of the centenary of the first assembly of the World's Parliament of Religions in Chicago (1893), various inter-religious organizations and individuals attempted to unite all the inter-religious initiatives worldwide. They convened a wonderful religious festival for the 6,000 participants, with hundreds of programmes and performances but with little

---

[6] Cf. the Papal Encyclical 'Redemptoris Missio' No. 57, *ibid.*, p. 103.
[7] For the history of inter-religious organizations see Braybrooke 1980; Braybrooke 1992; Braybrooke 1998; Klaes 2000; Klaes 2002; Traer 1999.

religious representation and very few relevant structures for the future. In 1999, the initiative continued with the 'Parliament of the World's Religions' in Capetown (South Africa) and will take place again in Barcelona (Spain) in 2004. In 2000, 'The Millennium World Peace Summit of Religions and Spiritual Leaders', with almost 2,000 participants, was convened at the United Nations headquarters in New York to express its responsibility in face of the global challenges and its commitment to the work of the United Nations.

All these initiatives are too sporadic and there is a lack of continuity. Therefore, with the help of the Interfaith Centre in Oxford, representatives of 14 of the largest inter-religious associations in the world met together in Oxford in 2001 and in Budapest in 2002, to form a permanent network of international interfaith organizations.

The World Conference of Religions for Peace[8]

In this wider context of the globalization as a challenge for multi-religious co-operation, the World Conference of Religions for Peace (WCRP) was established as an international inter-religious association in order to contribute to the creation of a common, just and peaceful future. In 2002, its former name (World Conference on Religion and Peace) was changed by a decision of the International Governing Board. In accordance with the long- time European usage it is now called more appropriately World Conference of Religions for Peace, or in short: Religions for Peace.

In a flyer from 1993, WCRP introduces itself as:

. . . the world's largest multireligious coalition with consultative status with the UN's Economic and Social Council (ECOSOC). WCRP has over 50 national chapters worldwide and works at local, national and international levels in pursuit of peace and conflict management and resolution in more

---

[8] Cf. *Religions for Peace: A Newsletter*; *Religions for Peace: Secretary General's Update*; Jack 1993; Gebhardt 1994; Klaes 1996.

than one hundred countries. . . . WCRP is based upon respect for religious differences as well as the conviction that religious persons and groups can co-operate with great value on shared commitment for peace with justice. On local, national, regional and global levels, WCRP convenes meetings and assemblies to promote dialogue on the peace-promoting teachings of religions. This dialogue in turn, provides a basis for commitment to common actions in eight program areas.

These areas include:

1. Conflict Transformation and Reconciliation.
2. Disarmament and Security.
3. Economic and Social (Sustainable) Development.
4. Environmental Protection.
5. Human Rights and Responsibilities, especially the fight against racism and discrimination.
6. Peace Education.
7. Refugees and Displaced Persons.
8. Rights of Children, Youth and the Family.

Some of these programme areas are organized into so-called 'Standing Commissions'. They serve as programmatic instruments for the realization of WCRP's mission and operate permanently in between assemblies. Leaders and believers of the following religions regularly participate as members in WCRP: Baha'ism, Buddhism, Christianity, Confucianism, Daoism, Hinduism, Islam, Jainism, Judaism, Shintoism, Sikhism, Traditionalism of the indigenous cultures of Africa, the Americas, Asia, Australia and Oceania, and Zoroastrianism.

WCRP was founded in 1970 as a consolidation of separate movements in Japan, the United States and in India. In the face of the destructive nuclear armament and other threats which endangered the survival of humankind, Japanese Buddhists, American Christians and Jews, and Indian Hindus made the decision to convene an international gathering of religious leaders at Kyoto (Japan) in 1970: the first assembly of the 'World Conference on Religion and Peace' (as it was then called). World assemblies, acting as basic structures of the association, were subsequently held in Louvain, Belgium (1974); Princeton, USA (1979); Nairobi, Kenya (1984); Melbourne, Australia (1989); Riva del Garda and Rome, Italy (1994); and Amman, Jordan (1999).[9]

At the First World Assembly (1970) the newly elected president, the Roman Catholic Archbishop Angelo Fernandes, demanded as a main agenda of WCRP that religions of the world jointly co-operate for the realization of world peace. In doing so, WCRP is not primarily interested in the respective religions as such but in the future of this planet. In the light of unresolved problems of the survival of humankind, religions relativize their absolute claims and demands and devote themselves in full responsibility to the fostering of world peace in dialogue, in agreement and understanding with other religions. They are challenged to draw from the deepest and most vivifying of their respective traditions, sources and spiritualities, that which best advances justice and peace in the world. It is, therefore, *not* a direct intention to cultivate inter-religious dialogue as a possibility of a deeper mutual understanding, or of discovering elements of unity in diversity in the religions and of pondering about the problems of ultimate truth of one's own religion in comparison with the conviction of others. In practice, it makes inter-religious gatherings more easy if not the truth of the religions is at stake but the needs and wants of the human family. It alleviates the anxiety of being taken in by the other religions or of being inferior to the other religious traditions or of having to prove one's own superiority. The problem of the binding nature of one's own or somebody else's faith is ignored, missionary behaviour is kept out of the dialogue and syncretistic tendencies are strictly rejected. Nevertheless, the mutual understanding of the universal demands and beliefs of the various religious persuasions, with profound respect for their differences, is of significant importance for the practice of inter-religious co-operation as partners. This is expressed in the many multireligious services

---

[9] Cf. Jack (ed.) 1973; Jack (ed.) 1979; Jack (ed.) 1980; Taylor and Gebhardt (eds.) 1986.

which are held at all the occasions of national and international conferences and assemblies.

In its long history WCRP became a more and more recognized world movement which, as a Non-governmental Organization (NGO), is increasingly called upon to function as a multireligious resource and adviser for various commissions and conferences of the United Nations. Thus for example, at the request of the United Nations Children's Fund (UNICEF), WCRP convened an international inter-religious conference at Princeton University in 1990 as a result of which a declaration and the 'Plan of Action' were presented to the 71 heads of states who attended the 'World Summit for Children' in New York (September 1990). WCRP actively participated in the 'Earth Summit' in Rio, 1992 as well as in the 'United Nations International Conference on Population and Development' in Cairo 1994, and in the 'World Summit for Social Development' in Copenhagen (March 1994) by invitation of the chairman, Ambassador Juan Somavia. Subsequently, in 1998, WCRP together with the United Nations Development Program (UNDP) convened a conference in Tokyo (Japan).

Besides its global orientation, WCRP is a grass-root-level movement. It is represented by hundreds of local and national inter-religious groups in many countries of the world. Thus for instance in Germany larger cities host 12 local chapters. Meetings usually take place at the centres of the various religious communities. Personal contacts and friendships are encouraged. In order to get better acquainted, questions like the religious life in the family, religious teaching in kindergartens and schools, and community life in one's own religious institutions are discussed. Beyond this, co-operation with the city council is envisaged, expositions of world religions and multireligious conferences are planned, public demonstrations against racism, violence and war are supported, and multireligious prayer meetings are prepared. On the national level these groups and individual religious representatives form the national chapter with regular yearly meetings.

On the continental level, the Asians and the European members of WCRP created regional structures known as WCRP/

Europe and ACRP. There are European assemblies every other year; conferences have taken place in Gotland (Sweden), Brussels (Belgium), Budapest (Hungary) and Rovereto (Italy). The conferences concentrated on themes like racism and minority problems in Europe, the problem of economy and justice, and media in a multicultural world. In July 2003, the European assembly met in Graz (Austria) within the framework of 'Graz, cultural capital of Europe 2003' with the theme 'Shared Values for Common Living in European Cities'. On the international level, the world assemblies provide direction for the action programmes of WCRP and are the occasion for electing the new leadership of WCRP. In Amman (1999) religious participants gathered from 80 countries. It was the first time that such an inter-religious conference took place in an Arabic Muslim country.

Project-Centred Activities

The specific contribution of WCRP

WCRP has been always a project-oriented movement that has not only tried to use the inter-religious influence of its members for lobbying against rearmament and dangers of war and worked for more peaceful understanding among the peoples of the world, but in some utterly disastrous conflict situations it endeavoured to bring about a concrete change and relief, as for example in its work with refugees. The project for the so-called boat people[10] (1976–79) was initiated by American and Japanese WCRP members with the help of the well-known Vietnamese Buddhist monk Thich Nhat Hanh. Vietnamese refugees who fled in small boats over the sea to find asylum in some of the neighbouring states were picked up from the deep sea and were helped to find acceptance as temporary or permanent residents in these countries or in the USA, in Australia or in European countries. At the onset, the project succeeded in publicizing the plight of the boat people in inter-religious circles and beyond and in creating

---

[10] Cf. Jack 1993, pp. 277–92.

additional pressures in western countries to accept larger quotas of boat people. But on the other hand, this international inter-religious undertaking was not really successful. There was a lack of professional know-how and mistakes could have been prevented by closer collaboration with the UN High Commissioner for Refugees (UNHCR). Some years later, a project for the development of the people in Ethiopia and Somalia was initiated following the 1983 assembly of WCRP in Nairobi. Inter-religious activities were intended to support intercultural and inter-religious initiatives in these countries. Again, a lack of know-how led to the relatively poor result of a great amount of money collected worldwide being handed over to international relief organizations for their work in Eastern Africa.

Gradually WCRP realized that such international and inter-religious projects are mainly of a certain symbolic value: i.e., in the name of the world's religions, they point at urgent problems in the human family and emphasize that the victims of an increasingly globalized world will not be forgotten. The projects can in no way replace the work of international relief organizations and similar institutions. So what would be the specific kind of help that could be contributed by WCRP? In 1995, after long consultations among members of WCRP under the leadership of the new Secretary-General William Vendley, a paradigmatically new kind of project work began which has been given increasing importance in the field of inter-religious dialogue. WCRP tries to encourage the great religious traditions, with their leaders and organizations, to perform the needed inter-religious work themselves. The task of WCRP consists in initiating religious contacts, in providing possibilities of organizing the meetings, in offering a neutral platform for representatives of various religions to meet each other, in looking for financial resources, and in helping mediate between the religious partners. Let me record some examples.

Conflict resolution in former Yugoslavia

In 1996 members of WCRP contacted various religious leaders of Bosnia-Herzegovina[11] during the war situation. After extensive individual consultations with each of the principal religious leaders, the WCRP facilitated an ongoing dialogue among senior leaders of the Croatian Roman Catholic, the Serbian Orthodox Christian, the Bosniac Muslim and the Jewish communities. WCRP's objective was to promote the growth of mutual trust, provide an opportunity to clarify common moral commitments and initiate a process of establishing an organizational vehicle for inter-religious actions for peace and social reconstruction. After the ethnic massacres, the robbing and killing in which many common people of all traditions lost their lives, the co-operation among people of different ethnic and religious groups was extremely difficult. Religion was deeply involved in the war in Bosnia-Herzegovina. Weakened by nearly half a century of Communist rule, religious communities were vulnerable to political actors who hijacked religious symbols to divide the State. Hundreds of mosques, churches, graveyards, religious libraries and other spiritually significant sites were destroyed, along with whole communities of people. The conflict polarized the Muslims, the Roman Catholics and the Orthodox Christian communities, creating a history of suffering, fragmentation and mistrust that still remains. In this almost hopeless situation, WCRP helped the leaders of the respective communities in Bosnia to engage in a dialogue by enlisting the support of prominent international religious figures. These included Patriarch Aleksi, the head of the Russian Orthodox Church, Cardinal Etchegaray, President of the Pontifical Council for Justice and Peace, and Cardinal Arinze, the then President of the Pontifical Council for Interreligious Dialogue of the Vatican, and Middle Eastern Islamic leaders such as Kamel al-Sharif, Secretary-General of the International Islamic Council, and Prince El Hassan Bin Talal of

---

[11] WCRP International Council Bulletin, June 1997; Report of the Executive Committee of WCRP, 1998.

Jordan. In April 1997, after months of negotiations and amendments, the leaders of the four major religious communities published a common *Statement of Shared Moral Commitment*. It was widely publicized in the Bosnian media and received support in the international communities by personalities like KAFOR Ambassador Robert Frowick, head of Mission, Organization for Security and Cooperation in Europe (OSCE) – Mission to Bosnia and Herzegovina. The statement was signed by Dr Mustafa Ceric, the Reis Ulema (senior religious leader) of the Islamic community of Bosnia-Herzegovina, Metropolitan Nikolaj – in the name of and with the authorization of the Serbian Orthodox Patriarch Pavle (Belgrade), Cardinal Vinko Puljic, Roman-Catholic Archbishop of Sarajevo, and Mr Jakob Finci, President of the Jewish community of Bosnia-Herzegovina. In this statement the religious leaders appeal to all the believers, to all citizens of the country, especially to all the politicians for 'a durable peace based on truth, justice and common living'. They recognized that in spite of the religious differences, the

> religious and spiritual traditions hold many values in common and that these shared values can provide an authentic basis for mutual esteem, cooperation and free common living in Bosnia-Herzegovina . . . We jointly . . . condemn all violence against innocent persons and any form of abuse or violation of fundamental human rights. Specifically we condemn acts of hatred based on ethnicity or religious differences.

Finally, the religious leaders called for religious freedom and closed the statement with the golden rule as a criterion of common living:

> Let us treat others as we would wish them to treat us.

At the ceremony of the public signing of the document the religious leaders communicated their decision to establish a permanent mutual platform of the 'Interreligious Council of Bosnia-Herzegovina (IRC)' with the help of WCRP. The drafting of standing rules which had to be accepted by all the four communities in conformity with government regulations and the legal recognition of the council was achieved after two years of extensive lobbying and exchange. Furthermore, in October 2002, the Interreligious Council submitted the law on 'Freedom of Religion and Belief' to the Bosnian parliament.

The initiative of the Bosnian religious communities had its impact on the religious situation in the Kosovo conflict.[12] Leaders of the Serbian Orthodox, the Roman Catholic and the Islamic community met members of WCRP separately and asked the movement as an outside party to form a multireligious working group in Kosovo. With the support of religious leaders in Serbia, Bosnia-Herzegovina and Albania, WCRP convened a meeting of representatives from all three communities in March 1999. After the NATO military operation, a plan began to take shape under the leadership of the European Union and the World Bank to place the reconstruction of Kosovo in the context of the wider plan of reconstructing and developing all of south eastern Europe as the beginning of a new integrated Europe.

In this context WCRP designed an initiative to engage religious leaders from south eastern Europe in a process of co-operation to promote social reconstruction of common living in their societies. In November 1999, at the occasion of the seventh world assembly in Amman (Jordan), WCRP invited 40 Jewish, Orthodox Christian, Roman Catholics, Protestant and Muslim religious leaders from eleven south eastern European countries. After two-and-a-half days of heated discussions in a special forum they finally succeeded in identifying their common concerns and the ways of co-operation both within the respective states and throughout the region as a whole. In this context they argued about the future of Kosovo. In the joint 'Statement of Religious Leaders on Reconstruction and Development in South-Eastern Europe', they expressed their common responsibility for peace and committed themselves to promote dialogue and co-operation between themselves and prepared an action plan for the future role of religious communities in their societies. Later on, in private talks, participants of the forum emphasized

---

[12] Cf. Vendley 1999.

that such a multireligious and multi-ethnic conference had never taken place before. Not much later, in February 2000, religious leaders in Kosovo accepted an invitation from the inter-religious council of Bosnia-Herzegovina to Sarajevo. There, they agreed a 'Statement of Shared Moral Commitment', similar to the one issued by their colleagues in Bosnia, and directed it to all believers, to the political authorities in Kosovo, and to the foreign international representatives in the country. This paper was signed by Rexhep Boja, Mufti and President of the Islamic community, Artemije Radosavljevi, the Serbian Orthodox Bishop of Raska-Prizren, and Marko Sopi, the Roman Catholic Bishop of Prizren. Two months later a press statement was released, saying:

> We as the responsible religious leaders in Kosovo express our deepest gratitude for the visit of our brother religious leaders from Bosnia-Herzegovina to Kosovo on 11th to 13th April 2000. Appreciating their experiences, we have made the decision in Pristina today on the 13th of April to establish The Interreligious Council of Kosovo . . . Once again, we thank our distinguished guests from Bosnia-Herzegovina for their visit and their encouragement as well as the World Conference On Religion And Peace (WCRP) for its support and its continuous commitment to assist us in the process. We look forward to continuing with our close, brotherly relations and with God's help we will be able to work together to build a stronger future for all people in our blessed country.

I reported at some length about this kind of project in a situation of conflict and war, since it became a pattern of activities for WCRP in many similarly difficult situations, mainly in Africa.

Conflict resolution in Africa

In Sierra Leone the Interreligious Council of Sierra Leone was founded in the midst of the civil war. The council's efforts to facilitate communication during the 1999 peace talks led to its recognition by the international community as a legitimate party in the peace process. This culminated in an unprecedented invitation to participate in formal negotiations sponsored by the United Nations. Even in this extremely difficult situation, among other programmes, the council conducts weekly radio and TV discussions on reintegration and reconciliation led by prominent religious leaders (2002).

In 1999, amid similar conflict situations, the Interreligious Council of Liberia, WCRP was formed. During 2002, new WCRP Inter-religious Councils/Chapters were launched in Guinea, Mozambique and Cambodia, and in 2003 the creation of Inter-religious Councils continued in Botswana, Burundi, Ghana, Ivory Coast, Namibia, Swaziland and Zambia. Beyond this, a network of relations of the various Inter-religious Councils is encouraged. Thus representatives of the Inter-religious Councils of Sierra Leone, Liberia, Guinea and Ghana recently conducted a peace and solidarity mission to Côte d'Ivoire with the help and organization of WCRP. They jointly developed the 'Peace-Building Action Plan for the Forum of Religions Côte d'Ivoire' and pledged to meet regularly with each other and to engage in 'prayer, fasting and consultations, in order to reinforce inter-religious relations'.

In all these events, with the help of an employed so-called 'special representative for inter-religious co-operation in Africa' WCRP tries to co-ordinate the work of the councils, assists in programme development, facilitates the contacts to other international organizations and donors and especially to the international office of WCRP in New York.

All this sounds a bit schematic and almost bureaucratic. But one should not underestimate the experiences, challenges and the inspiring engagement of personalities who are involved in this still unusual and demanding multireligious undertaking. For example, on 8 January 2003, Brother David Kiazolu, the Secretary-General of the Inter-religious Council of Liberia, and Revd Christopher W. Toe, the Deputy Secretary-General, were arrested by the national police and charged with treason because of their peace initiative in the civil war. The Inter-religious Council and WCRP's International Secretariat in New York mobilized their protest with interventions to leaders including Liberian President Charles Taylor and Kofi Annan, Secretary-General of the UN. On 10 January 2003, Kiazolu and Toe were released and all charges dropped. It shows that the commitment to such inter-religious work can even endanger one's life and is certainly not just a 'free time hobby'. Another example: during the civil war in Sierra Leone the Roman Catholic Archbishop of Freetown, one of the presidents of the Inter-religious Council, was taken by rebel militia into the jungle. After many weeks of hardship and captivity he was released and related his story in a private talk. He ended by saying: 'The happiest and most moving moment for me was when after my return to my Catholic community I was told that in all the mosques the Muslims had prayed for the rescue of my life.'

Conflict resolution in the Middle East

WCRP is also involved in inter-religious peace-building activities in one of the most atrocious conflict areas, the Middle East. On 28 January 2002, under the leadership of George Carey, former Archbishop of Canterbury, and with the organizational support of WCRP, the 'First Alexandria Declaration of the Leaders of the Holy Land' was widely publicized. It was signed by many sheiks, rabbis and bishops of the three Abrahamic religions. Rabbi David Rosen, member of the Executive Committee of WCRP, called it 'a plan for inter-religious co-operation as an instrument to break the cycle of violence in the Holy Land'. In March 2002, WCRP was co-facilitator of the follow-up work for an inter-religious group of Palestinians and Israelis in Jerusalem which is strongly supported by both Israeli and Palestinian politicians.

Two days before the outbreak of the recent war in Iraq, the Secretary-General of WCRP held preliminary talks with Christian and Muslim leaders in Baghdad about the necessary co-operation in the time following the – then still possible – military conflict. After the war, from 27 to 28 May 2003, an international conference was convened in Amman, Jordan, 'to discuss the

crisis in Iraq, in view of the devastating and catastrophic consequences and repercussions resulting from the former regime,
the war and the occupation'.[13] WCRP hosted 21 religious leaders
of Iraq representing Shi'-ite, Sunni and various Christian communities together with international religious leaders, experts,
diplomats and members of humanitarian agencies. Through the
good offices of Prince El-Hassan bin Talal, the Iraqis had met
in Baghdad and from there travelled in a convoy of seven cars
along the dangerous route to Jordan. In their statement, among
other recommendations, the Iraqi religious leaders demanded
'that the permanent Iraqi government be built on the bases of
direct, free, democratic elections, a constitution and the rule of
law that protects equally all religious, ethnic and national group-
ings, while maintaining Iraq's sovereignty and territorial integrity'. And they recommended 'that WCRP be invited to work in
partnership with the Iraqi religious leaders regarding future conferences to be held in Baghdad and their formation of an Iraqi
multireligious council'. A Chaldean bishop told us that never
before had such an inter-religious meeting been convened in Iraq,
that the atmosphere was very friendly and they exchanged their
telephone numbers with one another. Here again the same pattern of worldwide co-operation with networks of Inter-religious
Councils is envisaged by WCRP.

Projects in aid of children

WCRP is not only involved in conflict resulution. There are other
areas of concern, for example the one for children, and here a
similar standard for inter-religious structures is applied. From
9 to 12 June 2002 WCRP convened the 'First African Religious
Leaders Assembly on Children and HIV/AIDS' in Nairobi,
Kenya. This unprecedented meeting brought together over 125
senior religious leaders, men and women from more then 25
countries including members of WCRP's Governing Board. It

---

[13] Joint Statement of the Representatives of Iraq's Religious Communities. Amman, 28 May 2003 (in Arabic and English).

was the first-ever Pan-African multireligious gathering to address
the impact of HIV/AIDS on African children and families. The
goal is the co-operation of the leaders of Muslims and the various Christian churches and some Hindu groups to help provide
joint support for the 12 million orphans whose parents died of
AIDS. Particular emphasis is given to overcoming social stigma,
mobilizing their own religious communities and encouraging
governments to create stronger policies and more resources.
As one of the results of the conference, the delegates decided to
form an African Religious Leaders Council under the auspices of
WCRP. A working group was constituted and prepared the first
Pan-African Council of Religious Leaders which addressed the
continent-wide challenges of vulnerable children, human rights
and poverty. The council meeting was held in Abuja, Nigeria,
in June 2003. WCRP President, Archbishop John Onayekam,
hosted the conference.

European integration

The last example of this model of inter-religious co-operation
concerns the very different and difficult situation of Europe which
has to become politically and economically, culturally and religiously integrated. In order to make its contribution towards this
goal the WCRP European Council of Religious Leaders (ECRL)
was established. This first multireligious structure of senior religious leaders was inaugurated in Oslo (Norway) from 11 to
12 November 2002. All the founding members are international
presidents of WCRP and include the Lutheran Bishop Gunnar
Stålsett of Oslo as the host, Roman Catholic Archbishop Cardinal Daneels of Brussels, Metropolitan Kirill of the Russian Orthodox Church, Grandrabbi René Sirat of Paris and Dr Mustafa
Ceric, the Grandmufti of Bosnia-Herzegovina. Jehangir Sarosh
(UK) became a member as the moderator of WCRP Europe, who
represents the national chapters of WCRP in Europe. In its final
statement, the 30-member council acknowledged the bloody
history of European conflicts but committed itself to working
to end conflicts and to promoting justice and peace for coexist-

ence among the diversity of peoples, religions and traditions in Europe.

Representativity and Responsibility

In all these activities of WCRP on the international level, the question of *representativity* is a very important aspect. Are – and if so how – the world religions represented through the participants in these processes and projects? In the beginning, members of WCRP were primarily religious individuals with a personal concern for peace. About 15 years ago the search for members became more explicitly concentrated on finding well-known leaders of religions or of religious institutions, in order to open up more possibilities of global influence and effective, publicly recognized co-operation. Thus at the seventh world assembly in Amman, Jordan (November 1999) leading personalities of the world religions were invited and were encouraged to participate in inter-religious peace work. Where possible, they were also elected into the enlarged Governing Board of WCRP. Prince El Hassan Bin Talal of Jordan became president and moderator of the Governing Board; the former Muslim WCRP President Abdurrahman Wahid of Indonesia came to the conference as President of the State of Indonesia; the former Anglican Archbishop of Canterbury, George Carey, and many other church leaders, among them four cardinals of the Roman Catholic Church, as Cardinal Keeler (Baltimore, USA) and Cardinal Daneels (Brussels, Belgium), were elected presidents or honorary presidents.

The reasons for the growing official interest in multireligious activities vary widely. Certainly there is a growing consciousness of globalization and how it affects the whole world. Therefore, the official inter-religious co-operation at the international level is no longer considered superfluous and 'offensive' as it was about 30 years ago. The example of famous personalities who dared to get involved in inter-religious dialogue was certainly inspiring.

Nevertheless, the view that inter-religious co-operation for the solution of global problems has to be mainly undertaken by official representatives of these religions, is by no means generally endorsed by all who are involved in inter-religious peace work. In WCRP there is both, an underlying tension between two different conceptions and the attempts to mediate between them. According to one conception, WCRP, as an inter-religious association, should be regarded as a global network of leading religious personalities who represent religious communities and who act as kinds of 'control centres' for contact with other peace-oriented organizations and pressure groups. Their function is to exercise their personal religious and political influence in their roles as well-known religious leaders and to provide WCRP with experts and colleagues for its various projects and responsibilities. Jointly they are qualified to speak out with moral authority so that their voice will hopefully be heard by and have its impact on the whole world. Institutionally, WCRP's headquarters consists of a very strong secretariat in New York which initiates the projects, organizes and mediates between the various personalities, institutions and worldwide organizations such as the UN. Finances are provided by foundations and governments, as for example by the Rockefeller and Ford Foundation and by governments like those of Norway, Finland or the Netherlands. Further financial support is provided through the United Nations, that is through UNDP, OHCHR or UNICEF. Also the various religious communities like the Buddhist Rissho Kosei-kai contribute to the wellbeing of WCRP by their financial support. According to the other conception, WCRP should be regarded primarily as an inter-religious grassroots movement which encourages more and more people of all religions and cultures to work wholeheartedly and jointly for a more peaceful and just world and to take action against any form of discrimination, intolerance, violence and environmental destruction. WCRP should aim at becoming a mass movement for peace comprising as many believers as possible from all the world's religions.

Of course, both these conceptions are not necessarily mutually exclusive and are compatible with each other. In the practice of a large international movement, however, these different visions are not always easily mediated. At the big assemblies, complaints sometimes surface from those supporting a grass-roots conception that occasionally there is a lack of transparency in the choice and election of those who represent the movement and its interests, and also in the decision-making processes of the committees. Further complaints concern failures in the area of communication, and sometimes it is questioned whether some of the well-known leaders of religions who became presidents of WCRP do fully represent the interests of the grassroots of WCRP. Understandably, as religious leaders they basically feel responsible for their own religious communities and participate in WCRP as far as it serves their ends and provides them with the facilities and possibilities of fulfilling their worldwide inter-religious interests. Their important function in WCRP therefore does not always imply a commitment to the movement itself. Consequently and quite often, it falls to the International Sec-retariat of WCRP to take responsibility for WCRP's planning, decision-making and inter-religious actions. Many representa-tives of WCRP have been well aware of such problems for a long time. Thus it is foreseen that representatives of these grassroots of WCRP will also be chosen to work in the international govern-ing structures together with the world's religious leaders. An important step was taken in 1994 when the standing rules were changed and the so-called 'International Council' which had been a kind of advisory board of experts became a committee in which the International Governing Board now meets with the senior officers of each national chapter in the world to 'share experiences, challenges and concerns within WCRP, especially among its different levels' of organization at local, national, regional, and international levels and to 'review the work of WCRP international . . .'.[14] Such a council meeting took place in connection with the EXPO 2000 in Hildesheim in Germany.

The problem of sharing responsibility among the movement as a whole is particularly clear concerning the role of women and youth. Within the structures of all the religious traditions of

---

[14] WCRP Standing Rules (10. 11. 1994) Art. IV, Section 1, B.

the world patriarchy is still deeply ingrained; normally only men not women play the decisive role in leading their communities. Even in the newly founded European 'Inter-religious Council' there are only 3 women among the 30 members. It took some time before WCRP became fully aware of this problem. During the 1984 assembly in Nairobi it was decided that a certain quota of women and young people had to be invited to participate in the assemblies and to be elected into the governing structures of WCRP. In 1994, at the sixth assembly of WCRP in Rome and Riva del Garda, about 30 per cent of the delegates were women. Many participants belonged to the younger generation under 35 years ('youth'). About 100 of them, coming from many different cultures and religions of the world, lived together for discussions, meditation and action during the five days leading up to the assembly. The women spent a full day before the conference preparing for the difficult task of making their voices heard on the conference concerning their specific interests. Similar meetings took place at the seventh assembly in Amman (1999). For many years now the programmes targeted for women have been given extra support. Recently Dr Azza Karam, a Muslim woman from Egypt, who works full time for WCRP to develop the WCRP women's programme, published a 'Global Directory of Religious Women's Organizations' to encourage the exchanging of experiences, ideas and information among groups of religiously committed women to assist them in their desire for multireligious collaboration.[15] In January 2003 a WCRP's 'African Women of Faith Network' was formed in Nairobi. Eighteen religious organizations have agreed to participate in the network. It is deeply committed to co-operating on the elimination of gender discrimination, marginalization, violence against women and girls, poverty, conflict and HIV/AIDS in Africa. Further interreligious conferences for grassroots religious leadership were launched, for example by the South African WCRP chapter on 'Interfaith Women Against Abuse' and a joint venture with

---

[15] Cf. WCRP Women's Program 2001.

UNICEF, entitled 'Religious Women, Children and Conflict' that was held in Cordoba, Spain, in March 2002.

In a multicultural and multireligious movement, the sharing of different cultural and religious views and ideas on peace, the participation in the flow of mutual communication, the involvement in the process of responsible decision-making are all achievements in themselves. In their own way they are the result of justice and peace being realized and a sign of an increasing transformation of consciousness. Often, the close co-operation leads to deep friendships across religions and cultures. This network of relationships is not always visible in the public but gives the inner strength and provides the new impetus necessary to developing common resolutions and activities.

Sometimes however these useful activities can also lead to 'activism' and to a neglect of sharing the various religious visions of a new, peaceful world. At international gatherings, one easily takes for granted that all are in agreement concerning the goals of overcoming injustice and violence in the world without taking seriously the pluralism of religious denominations, of their respective world visions and their understanding of peace and justice. This is fostered by a certain international usage of words like 'justice', 'peace', 'dignity of man', 'freedom', 'unity', 'creation', employing them without further differentiation in public statements in ways similar to their usage in official documents from the UN. At times this seems to suggest that the unspoken criterion of appropriateness is that these terms are understood in conformity with statements from leading organizations like the UN. But in some parts of the world this may be regarded as a kind of western 'cultural imperialism'. Or, these terms are used so generally that they become empty words and lose their power to express how religions work for peace, and no longer communicate that peace goes much beyond human efforts. In this sense, shortly before his death in 2000, the Roman Catholic Archbishop Angelo Fernandes of New Delhi, India, President Emeritus of WCRP, urged members of WCRP as a multireligious movement that 'the necessary search for social justice' coincides with 'applied spirituality . . . which is rooted in the respective experience of the divine'.[16] Rabbi David Rosen, Director of the Anti-Defamation League in Israel, and Co-President of WCRP, pointed out in a detailed address to the participants of the seventh assembly in Amman (1999):

> Behaving with global care and responsibility is not only the result of recognition of the Divine in our world, of the transcendent value of life and dignity of the other, but it is also the very expression of the Divine within ourselves. It is this sense of the Divine within us and within all others that can enable us to overcome our insular and isolating pain and alienation. The WCRP as an organization and this historic Assembly, serve as wonderful inspiration in this regard, for a practical programme of shared responsibility and care throughout our globe that will help to achieve what the Jewish mystical tradition calls 'repairing our world', bringing about what some of our traditions refer to as 'the Kingdom of Heaven on Earth'.[17]

Conclusion

To conclude, WCRP, as an inter-religious peace movement, has often been a contributory factor for reconciliation and mediation in many conflict situations, and today is recognized as an inter-religious partner by international associations like the UN. But in this success story, there is the permanent challenge to take seriously both the pluralism of religions and their respective religious ideas in fulfilling the tasks of creating a more peaceful world and the world-transcending dimension of peace work. The challenges and the commitment of WCRP can be summarized with the words of Prince El Hassan Bin Talal, Jordan, moderator of WCRP since 1999:

> Throughout history, religious differences have divided men and women from their neighbours and have served as justi-

---

[16] Fernandes 1999, p. 3, quoting from a document of the Third WCRP Assembly in Princeton 1979.
[17] WCRP 7th World Assembly, 2000, p. XIV.

fication for some of humankind's bloodiest conflicts. In the modern world, it has become clear, that people of all religions must bridge these differences and work together, to ensure our survival and realize the vision of peace which all faiths share.[18]

SELECT BIBLIOGRAPHY

Barney, G. O. (ed.), 1999, *Threshold 2000: Critical Issues and Spiritual Values for a Global Age*, Ada: CoNexus Press.

Braybrooke, M., 1980, *Inter-Faith Organizations 1893–1979: An Historical Directory*, New York: Edwin Mellen Press.

Braybrooke, M., 1992, *Pilgrimage of Hope: One Hundred Years of Global Interfaith Dialogue*, London: SCM Press.

Braybrooke, M., 1998, *Faith and Interfaith in a Global Age*, Oxford: CoNexus Press and Braybrooke Press.

Fernandes, A., 1999, Letters, in: *Dharma World – For Living Buddhism and Interfaith Dialogue* 26, 1999, September/October, 3.

Forward Studies Unit – European Commission, 1998, *Carrefours No. 8*, April 1998.

Gebhardt, G., 1994, *Zum Frieden bewegen. Friedenserziehung in interreligiösen Friedensbewegungen*, Hamburg: EBV Verlag.

Gioia, F. (ed.), 1997, *Interreligious Dialogue: The Official Teaching of the Catholic Church (1963–1995)*, Boston: Pauline Books.

Jack, H. (ed.), 1973, *Religion for Peace. Proceedings of the Kyoto Conference on Religion and Peace*, New Delhi, Bombay: Gandhi Peace Foundation.

Jack, H. (ed.), 1979, *World Religion/World Peace. Unabridged Proceedings of the Second World Conference on Religion and Peace (WCRP II). Louvain, Belgium, 28 August/3 September 1974*, New York: WCRP.

Jack, H. (ed.), 1980, *Religion in the Struggle for World Community, Unabridged Proceedings of the Third World Conference on Religion and Peace (WCRP III), Princeton, New Jersey, 29 August/ 7 September 1979*, New York: WCRP.

Jack, H., 1993, *WCRP: A History of the World Conference on Religion and Peace*, New York: WCRP.

Joint Statement of the Representatives of Iraq's Religious Communities, Amman, 28, May 2003 (in Arabic and English).

---

[18] World Conference on Religion and Peace 2001, p. 1.

Karam, A. (ed.), 2000, *A Woman's Place: Religious Women as Public Actors*, New York: Religions for Peace.

Klaes, N., 1996, Erfahrungen in der 'Weltkonferenz der Religionen für den Frieden' (WCRP), in: A. Peter (ed.): *Christlicher Glaube in multireligiöser Gesellschaft*, Immensee: Neue Zeitschrift für Missionswissenschaft, pp. 91–108.

Klaes, N., 2000, Globalisierung und interreligiöse Zusammenarbeit, in: K. Krämer and A. Paus (eds), *Die Weite des Mysteriums* (F. S. H. Bürkle), Freiburg: Herder Verlag, pp. 377–403.

Klaes, N., 2002, Die Herausforderung der Globalisierung und interreligiöse Zusammenarbeit, in: M. Heimbach-Steins (ed.), *Religion als gesellschaftliches Phänomen*, Münster: LIT Verlag, pp. 73–90.

Mosaic, WCRP-Women's Program, 2001, New York: WCRP, 2001ff.

Religions for Peace: A Newsletter, issued by WCRP (since 1974).

Religions for Peace: Secretary General's Update, WCRP (since 2000).

Report of the Executive Committee of WCRP, 1998, Bosnia Project Phase II. October 1998.

Taylor, J. and Gebhardt, G. (eds), 1986, *Religions for Human Dignity and World Peace. Unabridged Proceedings of the Fourth World Conference on Religion and Peace (WCRP IV), Nairobi, Kenya 23–31 August 1984*, Geneva: WCRP.

Traer, R., 1999, *Quest for Truth: Critical Reflections on Interfaith Cooperation*, Aurora: Davies Group Publishers.

Vendley, W., 1999, The Role of the WCRP in Peace for Kosovo, in: *Dharma World – For Living Buddhism and Interfaith Dialogue* 26, September/October, pp. 6–9.

WCRP 7th World Assembly, 2000, Assembly Summary, New York, 2000.

WCRP International Council Bulletin, June, 1997.

WCRP Women's Program, 2001, *Global Directory of Religious Women's Organizations*, New York.

WCRP-Standing Rules (10. 11. 1994) Art. IV, Section 1, B.

World Conference on Religion and Peace, 2001, New York.

Subject and Name Index